GENERAL REVELATION

HISTORICAL VIEWS AND CONTEMPORARY ISSUES

GENERAL REVELATION

HISTORICAL VIEWS AND CONTEMPORARY ISSUES

BRUCE A. DEMAREST

Foreword by Vernon C. Grounds

ZONDERVAN
PUBLISHING HOUSE
OF THE ZONDERVAN CORPORATION
GRAND RAPIDS, MICHIGAN 49506

GENERAL REVELATION: HISTORICAL VIEWS AND
CONTEMPORARY ISSUES
Copyright © 1982 by The Zondervan Corporation
Grand Rapids, Michigan

First printing, February 1982

Library of Congress Cataloging in Publication Data

Demarest, Bruce A.
  General revelation.

Bibliography: p.
  Includes indexes.
  1. Revelation. I. Title.
BT127.2.D4   231.7′4   81-16221
ISBN 0-310-44550-7   AACR2

Edited by John Danilson and Gerard Terpstra
Designed by Martha Bentley

Unless otherwise indicated, Scripture quotations are
from the Holy Bible, New International Version.
Copyright © 1978 by New York International Bible Society.

Lines from "The Second Coming" on page 11 are reprinted
with permission of Macmillan Publishing Co., Inc., from
COLLECTED POEMS of William Butler Yeats. Copyright ©
1924 by Macmillan Publishing Co., Inc., renewed 1952 by
Bertha Georgie Yeats. Permission for use in Britain, Canada,
and other Commonwealth countries has been granted by
A. P. Watt, Ltd., London.

Printed in the United States of America

CONTENTS

CONTENTS

FOREWORD

The *fin de siecle* mood of today is no historical novelty. With remarkably few exceptions—perhaps Rome's Augustan epoch or England's Victorian period—every age has tended to view itself as a time when an old order is undergoing disintegration. But as the twentieth century approaches its sundown, there is ample reason for feeling with William Butler Yeats that

> Things fall apart; the center cannot hold,
> Mere anarchy is loosed upon the world.

Whether or not a doom-and-gloom outlook is justified in the light of today's burgeoning problems, technology has been forcing all of us in the family of man to realize that we are indeed "members one of another." Technology is making humanity one in fact and in fate. By creating modes of communication and travel that virtually obliterate space and time, it is reducing our planet to, in Marshall McLuhan's phrase, a global village. Whatever happens anywhere has impact everywhere. Kansas, Kalamantan, and the Kremlin are no longer isolated from one another by distance. Today they are like passengers sitting side by side in the same imperiled spaceship.

More than that, technology has made mankind one in fate. It has provided the superpowers with the potential for writing *finis* to the human saga. So the end of the world is not the concern merely of those much-derided biblicists who are enamored of eschatology; it is now a grim possibility with which scientific and political realists must reckon. Once the dark humor of an anonymous poet could be dismissed with a wry smile:

> Let not the A-bomb be the final sequel
> In which all men are cremated equal.

But in the 1980s that sardonic couplet fails to elicit a smile. The poet speaks too obviously as a prophet—except that, given the progress (progress!) achieved since Hiroshima, the A-bomb is outmoded, a rather primitive means of mass destruction.

While technology has made humanity one in fact and fate, it has not yet made the world one in faith. Rival creeds and cults, to say nothing of secular ideologies such as communism that are dogmatic belief-systems, struggle to recruit adherents. And with the Westernization of the East now being reversed as Eastern influence floods into the West, that rivalry is by no means subsiding. Curiously, however, among religions a movement toward syncretistic unity is taking place at the same time. The powerful acids of relativism are eating away at traditional claims to infallible truth and exclusive salvific efficacy. A growing host of scholars support the contention of Arnold Toynbee that no one gospel, including the Christian message, is solely redemptive; instead there are many gospels, each a mixture of truth and falsity, each equally salvific, that lead stumblingly into the heart of the ultimate mystery of Being. We are told, therefore, that as strident dogmatism and intolerant exclusivism diminish, mankind may conceivably become one in faith. People will, it is hoped, embrace a benign universalism compounded of doctrinal pluralism and theological indifferentism. Christianity, in particular, will be compelled to undergo a radical reinterpretation, abandoning its stubborn insistence that the Lord it worships is *the* Way, *the* Truth, and *the* Life, apart from whom there can be no propitious relationship to Reality.

It is at this juncture in history and within this global context that Bruce Demarest has undertaken the herculean task of examining Christianity's epistemological foundations. Addressing himself to the issue that underlies all other issues—can we know God, assuming His existence, and how can we know that we know Him?—Dr. Demarest has produced an outstanding work of scholarship that places him in the front rank of evangelical theologians.

Several things about this book impress me. Impressive in my opinion is the range of its discussion. A glance at the chapter headings is enough to show that every important thinker and every significant school in the area of epistemology has been dealt with—from Augustine to Karl Rahner, from medieval Roman Catholics to contemporary South American liberationists, from French deism to the neo-Calvinism of Abraham Kuyper's disciples in the Netherlands. Thus Dr. Demarest has conducted an encyclopedia survey that provides the winnowed result of prodigious research.

Impressive also is the fairness, the objectivity, and the sympathy with which widely divergent viewpoints have been set forth. While in many instances discussion must of necessity be brief, it is never superficial. Here, then, is a model of high-level polemic and apologetic.

Impressive too is the strength of Dr. Demarest's position, which he expounds with skillful exegesis and cogent argument. That position, so ably articulated, will constitute a powerful challenge to the symcretistic tendencies of our day. Evangelicals will find in these pages a bulwark against the attacks of agnosticism and relativism.

Though I have sought to react without undue subjectivity to this praiseworthy essay on the crucial problem of epistemology, I am obviously proud to be Dr. Demarest's colleague.

Vernon Grounds
President Emeritus
Denver Conservative Baptist Seminary

PREFACE

One of the urgent issues confronting the Christian church in the late twentieth-century pluralistic world is the question of the sources of man's knowledge of God. Hosts of non-Christian ideologies and religions claim, on various grounds, to mediate a knowledge of God that leads to man's highest end. Modern naturalists, existentialists, and cultists join hands with Hindus, Buddhists, and Muslims in claiming that their systems lead to a knowledge of God and an experience with Him that transcend the world. The historic Christian claim that a redemptive knowledge of God is gained exclusively through the appropriation of Christ by faith is being severely challenged by alternative systems that claim to possess the truth. Liberal theologians, Eastern religionists, and primitive tribespeople, to varying degrees of sophistication, plead an enlightening experience of God on the basis of a universal divine self-disclosure, either in nature or in the depths of the individual soul. At the heart of the contemporary debate is the problem of general revelation. In the present study, we purpose to explore the character, scope, and utility of the several modalities of general revelation. Further, we seek to assess the extent to which general revelation mediates the knowledge of God. We also will try to explicate the relationship of that knowledge to the Christian assertion of a definitive revelation of God in Christ as recorded on the pages of inspired Scripture.

A glance at the table of contents will reveal that the problem of revelation and the knowability of God are undertaken from a historical point of view. The issues that cluster about the subject are traced through the main movements in the history of Christian thought. My special interest in the history of theology and its problems was kindled during doctoral studies at Manchester University and research at the University of Basel. My appetite for the problem of revelation and the knowability of God was whetted during a dozen years of overseas service, initially in my work as a missionary educator in Africa and subsequently during an itinerant ministry with the International Fellowship of Evangelical Students (IFES) in Europe, the Middle East, and Asia. I was impressed with the fundamental theological importance of the subject under consideration during frequent *in situ* encounters with post-Christian intellectuals, Buddhists, Hindus, Muslims, and indigenous religionists on four continents.

This study is presented with the hope that it may prove useful to college and seminary students pursuing the introductory course in theology. Students making their initial sojourn into the vast arena of theology may find the seedbed of the book—its overview of the history of theology—a useful learning exericse. Experience in theological education has shown that beginning students profit most from their studies when they are provided with a broad overview of the history of theology. Should the present work in some measure assist in the preparation of crosscultural servants who seek theological grounding for their ministries, I will be more than satisfied.

I wish to thank especially my colleague Dr. Gordon Lewis for reading the manuscript in its entirety and for offering valuable suggestions at many points. Appreciation is also extended to others who read individual chapters in their areas of expertise: professors Ed. L. Miller and John Gerstner and Viju Abraham of Bombay, India. In addition, I am much indebted to my students who stimulated and challenged my thinking on the subject during seminars at the Denver Conservative Baptist Seminary. Whatever deficiencies remain in the work must be charged to my account. Finally, without the patience and support of my wife, Elsie, and our three children, this project would not have been possible.

ABBREVIATIONS

BWTA   *Basic Writings of Saint Thomas Aquinas.* Edited by Anton C. Pegis. 2 vols. New York: Random, 1945.

CD   *Church Dogmatics.* Ed. G. W. Bromiley and T. F. Torrence. 13 vols. Edinburgh: T. & T. Clark, 1936−69

CR   *Corpus Reformatorum.* 59 vols. Brunsvigae: 1863−1900.

LCC   *Library of Christian Classics:* Vol. VI, *Augustine: Earlier Writings.* Translator J. H. S. Burleigh. Philadelphia: Westminster, 1953.

LW   *Luther's Works.* Edited by Jaroslav Pelikan and H. T. Lehman. 55 vols. St. Louis: Concordia, and Philadelphia: Fortress, 1955−76.

NIDNTT   *The New International Dictionary of New Testament Theology.* Edited by Colin Brown. 3 vols. Grand Rapids: Zondervan, 1975−78.

NPNF   *A Select Library of the Nicene and Post-Nicene Fathers of the Christian Church.* Edited by P. Schaff. First Series. 8 vols. Grand Rapids: Eerdmans, 1956.

RGG   *Die Religion in Geschichte und Gegenwart.* 6 vols. 3rd edition. Tübingen: J. C. B. Mohr (Paul Siebeck), 1957−62.

TCF   *On the Truth of the Catholic Faith.* Edited by Anton C. Pegis. 4 vols. Garden City, New York: Hanover, 1955−57.

TI   *Theological Investigations.* 14 vols. New York: Seabury, 1974−76.

WA   *D. Martin Luthers Werke. Kritische Gesamtausgabe.* Weimer, 1883−.

⓵ HOW IS GOD KNOWN?

The fundamental issue in Christian theology concerns the nature and validity of divine revelation. Before one proceeds to a consideration of specific doctrinal issues—be they the nature of man, the possibility of salvation, or the destiny of the human race—one must come to grips with certain preliminary questions that undergird the entire theological enterprise. These foundational concerns, which form a part of theological prolegomena, include man's sources of truth, the nature of divine revelation, and the relationship between revelation and reason. A. C. Headlam was right when he stated that "the primary question in theology must be, what is the source of our knowledge of God?"[1]

Revelation: General and Special   It is certain that nothing can be known of what Luther called the "hidden God" (*Deus absconditus*) save as the Deity stoops in kindness to disclose Himself. The fact of the divine transcendence (Job 11:7−8; 36:26), together with the reality of human sinfulness (1 Cor. 2:14; 2 Cor. 4:4), mandate that God must reveal Himself if He is to be known. Only God can make known God. In the twentieth century, no theological concern has been more fiercely debated and contested than the set of issues that cluster around the divine revelatory disclosure. John Baillie, a chief protagonist in the struggle, concedes that "If one were asked what was just at the present moment the most frequented hunting grounds of the theologians one would have to answer without hesitation that it was the doctrine of revelation."[2] In truth, the struggles concerning revelation have intensified in the decades since Baillie uttered that judgment. It is mandatory, then, that the church regard the problem of revelation as a first order of business on its current theological agenda.

Revelation not only is the starting point of theology, it is also the Achilles heel of the Christian religion. The history of the church and theology clearly indicates that the Christian system stands or falls with the concept of reve-

13

lation. When the church has had confidence in its sources for the knowledge of God, it has been a strong body and ministered effectively to the world. On the other hand, when the church has been unsure where truth is to be found, it has proved weak and useless to the culture in which it lives. But in addition to the vitality of the church, revelation—the fundamental problem of theology—is also a fundamental concern of Western civilization. As Brunner plainly points out, the stability of modern technological society is only as secure as the validity of its revelatory roots.[3] Hence the fortunes of the nations as well as the church turn on the issue of divine revelation.

The fundamental question in theology needs to be formulated more precisely. What specifically are the sources for man's knowledge of God? Alternatively, what is the nature of revelation data? Historically, Christian theology has differentiated between general and special revelation, both as to content and focus. General revelation, mediated through nature, conscience, and the providential ordering of history, traditionally has been understood as a universal witness to God's existence and character. Through the modalities of general revelation, man at large knows both that there is a God and in broad outline what He is like. But Scripture poses a more profound question: "Can you fathom the mysteries of God? Can you probe the limits of the Almighty?" (Job 11:7). Here Christian orthodoxy has insisted that answers to life's profoundest questions—the secret nature of God and His will for man—are provided by a supernatural revelatory disclosure to a special people. Through the modalities of God's mighty acts in history, the teachings and deeds of Jesus Christ, and the writing of the Bible, the divine salvific plan is unveiled to a particular people.

The controversy in the contemporary situation focuses on whether a distinction can legitimately be made with respect to the content and scope of revelation. Is a saving knowledge of God mediated to a particular people solely through reception of the written Word and encounter with the living Word, Jesus Christ? Or is the thinking human subject capable of discovering and apprehending the reality of God by the universal light of reason and conscience? Can knowledge of God be acquired by the rational workings of the mind and by the process of syllogistic reasoning? Can God's existence be satisfactorily established either by a priori arguments from first causes or by a posteriori arguments from observable effects? Alternatively, is a life-changing knowledge of God attainable from universally available ecstatic religious experience? Do people of all ethnic, cultural, and religious groups possess an immediate experiential encounter with the divine Presence? Does man as man immediately apprehend God in a moment of lived intuition in the depths of his being? Can we call those who make no particular evangelical profession "anonymous Christians" solely because they are unavoidably grasped by a Holy Mystery? Can we attribute to the benighted pagan "implicit faith" because he is enveloped by the reality of divine Presence? Must we with Christian tradition speak narrowly of a "special" salvation history, or might not God be known more broadly through a diversity of human and historical channels? These and a number of related questions compel a careful reconsideration of the character, scope, and content of general revelation. Hence in the present study, we wish to explore what about God can be universally known through the modalities of nature, reason, religious experience, and the flow of providential history. Can God through general revelation be known as Redeemer or only as Creator? Throughout history, theological liberalism by various means has inflated the value of general revelation, thereby reducing special revelation to but one aspect of God's universal providence. On the other hand, fundamentalism has tended to depreciate the value of general revelation, arguing that the only things worth knowing about God are supernaturally revealed in the Bible. Where in relation to these two poles should the biblical Christian place himself?

The Abuse of General Revelation: A Classic Example   A classic example of the claim that knowledge of God and His will is gained from general revelation is found in the ideology of Nazi Germany. Hitler's National Socialist propagandists appealed to the revelation of God in reason, conscience, and the orders of Creation as justification for the Nazi state theology or cultural religion. Biblical revelation in Old and New Testaments was regarded by the Third Reich as a "Jewish swindle" and thus was set aside in favor of the Nazi natural theology. The Göttingen theologians Friedrich Gogarten and Emanuel Hirsch, by postulating the primacy of conscience and the flow of history as the chief modalities of revelation, provided theoretical justification for the Nazi ideology, which later wreaked havoc in Europe and beyond. A majority within the state church (known as "German Christians") unwittingly or otherwise embraced the new national religion, founded not on the Word of God but on the divine will allegedly embedded in the natural order. Emerging from this fatal exchange came a semi-Christian natural religion (some would say a new paganism) in which the church became a servile instrument of Nazi policy. So it was in a speech to the *Landeskirche* (state church) that Dr. Hans Kerrl, Reich minister for Church Affairs, declared that "true Christianity is represented by the Party. The Fuehrer is the herald of a new revelation."[4]

The Confessing church, led by such staunch patriots as Niemöller and Bonhoeffer, mounted a powerful protest against the captivity of the *Landeskirche* to the new paganism. In the Barmen Declaration of 1934, the Confessing church insisted that Jesus Christ is the only Word of God that men should hear, trust, and obey. It firmly condemned the suggestion that any source other than supernatural revelation was normative for the church's proclamation. Natural theology could never be permitted to reduce Christianity to a religion of common sense. "We reject the false doctrine, as though the Church could and would have to acknowledge as a source of its proclamation, apart from and besides this one Word of God, still other events and powers, figures and truths, as God's revelation."[5] The tragic Nazi experiment thus provides one illustration of the truism that "the question of natural theology is not an abstruse theoretical consideration, but can be a matter of life or death for the church."[6]

The blurring of the lines between general and special revelation has been abetted by the resurgence of interest in the non-Christian religions,— an interest that has in turn been accelerated by the progressive convergence of world cultures. A leading vision of twentieth-century man undoubtedly is the progressive unification of the human race. By virtue of breathtaking technological advances in mass communications and intercontinental travel, peoples are no longer isolated from the experience of others half a world away. Increased immigration, urbanization, international political (UN) and ecclesiastical forums (WCC), and the world-wide exchange of ideas in education, science, and the arts have set in motion powerful centripetal forces promoting a new global consciousness. Scattered tribes and ethnic groups with diverse languages, customs, and religions are steadily moving in the direction of a new unity. Multiplicity and pluraformity are gradually giving way to a new convergence, which Marcuse styled a "one-dimension world." In this vein Whitson writes,

> Hardly any men are scattered out of contact with each other, the races are moving together, common languages are sought and therefore isolated traditions are cross-fertilizing one another, and all set in new cities and civilizations becoming so vast and hence moving so close to one another that the boundaries are becoming lost. And now we can see man's world from beyond it in space, and that world is clearly round with all parts leading to all others.[7]

A significant result of the contemporary formation of a global village is that one can no longer isolate himself from the beliefs and practices of peoples on the other side of the globe. Religions and ideologies once held to be remote and strange are now becoming familiar objects of knowledge.

Revelation and World Religions   In reality, the nineteenth-century scholarly study of world faiths (the science of comparative religions) today is giving way to widespread popular interest in the great living religions of the world. Many people in our day are asking questions about what Hinduism, Buddhism, and Islam teach. Record numbers of people are enrolled in university courses in Eastern religions, children from traditional homes study at the feet of Hindu gurus, and Christians practice Yoga and Transcendental Meditation. And in what must be viewed as a remarkable development, universities founded on the principles of Eastern philosophy are rapidly springing up on American soil.

To cite but two examples of mounting interest in non-Christian religions, we draw attention to the remarkable growth of Buddhism and Islam in American society. Whereas Buddhism is under pressure in Asia, its stock has risen greatly in North America. The task of numbering the adherents of Buddhism in America is rendered difficult by the great diversity of Buddhist sects and traditions that have taken root in American soil. But if we restrict ourselves to individuals, both immigrants and indigenous Americans, who have undergone some formal Buddhist ceremony of commitment, then there may be over half a million Buddhists in the United States.[8] The growing interest in Buddhism among American young people, together with accelerated immigration from Southeast Asia, is certain to cause that figure to rise appreciably in the near future. The visitor to the large urban centers of America is bound to be struck by the presence of Buddhist churches and temples, some of which by Western standards are extremely ornate. It is estimated that nearly 90 percent of all Buddhists in America are located on the West coast.

No less phenomenal is the spread of Islam in the United States. Compared with the some one million Muslims living in Britain, there are at present more than three million Muslims resident in the United States. Approximately two million of these are "indigenous Muslims," many of whom are converts to Islam from the black community. Moreover, there are approximately 750,000 university students from Muslim countries living in America, and there is a large number of Islamic Arab expatriots working in this country in connection with the oil boom. It is estimated that there are more than three hundred mosques and Islamic associations in America, with the Islamic Center of New York the most prominent. Given these statistics, it cannot be doubted that Islam has become a potent force in American life. Through such movements as the World Community of Islam, the religion of Mohammed is vigorously contending today for the soul of America. It boldly claims to possess the answers to evils such as alcoholism, promiscuity, the breakdown of the family, and racism that plague American life. In a real sense, Islam has become an American phenomenon.

The resurgence of Eastern religions and their growing impact on the West has led many people to conclude that Christianity is not the exclusive vehicle of divine revelation and thus not the absolute religion. The conviction is rapidly mounting in the modern world that there is no one scheme of truth that is universally binding on all races and cultures. No religion, many argue, dare be so arrogant and intolerant as to arrogate to itself supremacy and finality. In the contemporary world, claims advanced for the normativeness of any one religion are met with unrestrained hostility. Absolutism in religion is received with the same disdain as totalitarianism in politics. Radhakrishnan, who speaks from an Eastern point of view, insists, "It is not fair to God or man to assume that one people are the chosen of God, that their religion occupies a central place in the religious development of mankind, and that all others should borrow from them or suffer spiritual destitution."[9] From a European perspective, Arnold Toynbee maintains, "One ought . . . to try to purge our Christianity of the traditional Western belief that Christianity is unique."[10] And so many point out that Confucius enunciated the Golden Rule long before the birth of Christ and that Hinduism, Buddhism, and other Eastern faiths are much older than Christianity. The majority judgment of modern man is that the "Holy" is more or less adequately mediated in every world religion. By the light of universal general revelation, God is known and honored in all the great non-Christian systems. Thus the bottom line reads, "The religions of man are not the artistry of demonic beings or the corrupted projections of man's natural bent for philosophizing";[11] rather, they are reasonably valid routes to the knowledge of God.

The spirit of religious pluralism and relativism thus has burst into full flower in our day. No one religion is intrinsically false; all are essentially true. Just as there are many paths up the mountain and many spokes to the center of the wheel, so there are many ways to God. An Oxford-trained professor from West Africa expressed this modern viewpoint by posing the following question: "Although the member of a social group may wish to drink with others out of a great river, need he use only one sort of cup?" His point was that although there is one source of life, people nevertheless may partake of that source in a variety of ways. In the contemporary world, an ecumenical spirit pervades the religious scene. The world's faiths are being brought together in a pantheon of religions. Without being bound to the faith of one's fathers, modern man feels free to enter the pantheon and select from a number of possible religious options. In this spirit, Sun Myung Moon's Unification Theological Seminary lately has called for the convening of a Global Congress of World Religions. The stated objective of the proposed triennial Congress is to work toward the formation of a "U.N. of religions." A Unification spokesman describes what is envisaged in the projected modern pantheon of religions:

> What we're talking about is a lamb stew that has the peas and potatoes of Hinduism in it, and the lamb's meat of Islam, and the saffron of Buddhism, and the carrots of Christianity, and who knows what else floating around in what we hope will be a rich sauce. But the potatoes remain potatoes, the carrots are still carrots, and sometimes the lamb's meat is a bit tough to chew. There is a common sauce and rich gravy, where the stew's flavor is best tasted.[12]

It is inevitable that we should ask what these developments mean for the Christian missionary enterprise. If God has adequately disclosed Himself to every man in a universal general revelation, if the world's non-Christian religions mediate—albeit in diverse ways—a valid knowledge and experience of God, what justification is there for the continued existence of the Christian mission to other faiths? More and more voices are being raised, both within and outside of the church, calling for the end of Christian missionary activity. The Christian, so it is commonly argued, must dispel from his mind the notion that his business is to bring Christ to the non-Christian multitudes. In truth, the modern religious world takes a dim view of proselytism and conversion. The vision of the 1910 Edinburgh Missionary Conference, "the immediate conquest of the world," is viewed today as the height of imperialistic arrogance. Since God has reconciled the whole world to Himself in Christ, each person should remain within the purview of the religion and culture in which he was born. If the Christian mission has any business at all, it is limited to enriching the non-Christian's consciousness of the God who through the Logos is savingly operative in each of the world's faiths.

Identifying The Issues   A number of questions force themselves on the thoughtful observer. How does one correlate the revelation of Christ with the competing claims of other religions based on either general revelation or an alternative revelatory disclosure? What is the relationship between the knowledge of God affirmed by the Chrisitan faith and the natural knowledge of God claimed by non-Christian systems? To what extent does biblical faith agree with much anthropological research that the world's historic religions mediate a common experience of the Holy? In this regard, what should we conclude about the spiritual condition of the Hindu who casts flower petals in the Ganges River to ensure his passage to the next life? Or the Buddhist who prostrates himself before the golden statue of the Buddha? Or the Parsi who as an act of worship tends the sacred fire? Or the Muslim who makes a holy pilgrimage to Mecca? Or the African tribesman who practices juju in a remote rain forest? Does the missionary enterprise involve making explicit a knowledge that was implicit, or does it involve the proclamation of a message previously unknown? Moreover, what shall we say concerning the salvation of the great numbers of people to whom the gospel of Jesus Christ has never come? Can these "unreached" multitudes find God on the basis of universal general revelation? In the light of these and other considerations, we concur with Baillie's observation that "more and more the missionary problem is becoming a theological problem."[13]

In the chapters that follow our purpose will be to investigate the various sources by which man gains knowledge of God. In particular, we will seek to define the character and content of general revelation and to ask what can be known about God independently of a special revelatory disclosure. In the light of myriad attempts in the history of theology to learn how to understand these matters, we will address the issue of whether the existence and character of God can be firmly established by rational argumentation. Although no detailed exposition of the tenets of the non-Christian religions will be offered (a task beyond the scope of the present work), the worth of the world's historic religions as a means of attaining the knowledge of God and salvation will be assessed. Finally, we intend to discuss the place of Christ in man's quest for God and the relationship of Christianity to other religions of the world. In an age of religious pluralism, in what sense can the Christian faith be regarded as unique? Does Christianity alone mediate a certain word from God about man's eternal destiny, or do all religions incorporate a valid message from above? Indeed, the themes of general revelation, the knowability of God, and the validity of the world's religions introduce a nest of thorny theological problems that will require careful and patient exploration.

Our approach to the subject is primarily historical and exegetical. Problems will be explored by tracing the leading strands of the discussion through the main movements in the history of Christian thought. This tack was chosen in the conviction that theology is best understood against the background of its cultural and historical context. Our conclusions concerning the nature and scope of general revelation and its relationship to world religions will be drawn primarily from an inductive study of the relevant Old and New Testament texts and secondarily with an eye to the history of the doctrine in the church.

Revelation In History: An Overview   The following represents a broad overview of the detailed study to follow. Postulating the existence of an "analogy of being" between God and man, classical Thomistic theology maintained that unaided reason, by reflecting on the *sensibilia* of the created order, is capable of informing man both *that* God is and *what* God is like. Indeed, following Aristotle, medieval Catholicism formulated in various ways a series of philosophical arguments in order to establish not only God's existence but also His greatness, goodness, and universal providence. The pinnacle of this development was Thomas Aquinas's famous Five Ways that sought a formal demonstration of God for pagan Greeks. But since the path of philosophical inquiry can be trodden by only a few learned souls, God granted a second source of knowledge, including insight into His saving purposes, through Holy Scripture, Jesus Christ, and the church. Thus scholastic Catholicism taught that the knowledge of God gained by reason was supplemented by rational knowledge provided by revelation. In the Thomistic scheme, faith completes understanding.

The Protestant Reformers countered the Aristotelian-Thomistic philosophical quest for God by asserting that the Word of God, living and written, is the only serviceable route to heaven. True, conscience, nature, and providential history mediate to the rational soul a fundamental knowledge of God's existence and character. But stressing the debilitating effects of sin, the Reformers argued that fallen reason is incapable of making its way savingly to the living God of the Bible. Luther and Calvin minimized the sinner's power of rational discovery and paid little attention to the construction of a natural or philosophical theology. They believed that God is savingly known only when Christ is honored in the heart. The Reformation divines thus called for a balanced relation between faith and reason.

At the hands of Enlightenment rationalism in eighteenth-century Europe, reason, which classically served as the servant of revelation, was ascribed with virtual omnicompetence. Unaided reason, working on the data of the space-time world, so laid bare the hidden things of God as to make revelation redundant. Rationalistic theologians thus invested the *lumen naturale* with the potentiality of special divine revelation. The whole of theology became natural theology, and religion a garment that man spins out of his own human resources. In the nineteenth century, the romantic movement in theology protested the dry intellectualism of the rationalistic school. According to the romantic theologians, knowledge of God was sought not in the conclusions reached by bare reason but in the direct experience of God in the depths of the soul. Assuming a Kantian epistemology, the school of Schleiermacher postulated that through the noncognitive faculty of feeling, or imagination, the human soul is brought into immediate contact with the Spirit of the universe. Once again, revealed theology was supplanted by natural theology, only in the case of romanticism the victor was a natural theology of mystical religious experience. Then around the turn of the twentieth century, the comparative religions movement built on the subjectivist theology of the romantics and the Ritschlians to assert that the reality of God wells up within the experience of every man. God is apprehended not through a supernatural Word from above but through a mystical experience within. Since all men stand in an immediate knowing relation to God, every religion is endowed with relative validity; no one religion legitimately can advance the claim of absoluteness or finality. The general approach of theology in the Enlightenment era thus may be described as reason without faith.

In the second decade of the twentieth century, Karl Barth, a redirected liberal, shattered the man-centered schemes of theology proudly promulgated by generations of humanists. Rebutting the claim that God is an inescapable datum of human experience, Barth insisted that man, the hopeless sinner, is incapable of discovering God by his own resources. In truth, the tables must be turned completely around. Man does not apprehend God; rather, the radically transcendent and sovereign God lays hold of man in a shattering experience of spiritual crisis. Since there is no possible point of contact (*Anknüpfungspunkt*) between the infinite Creator and the finite creature, general revelation is an illusion. In Barth's mind, every ingenious scheme of natural theology is obliterated by the radical Word of divine address. Hence in the Barthian and existentialist schemes, faith operates without reason. Contemporary evangelical confessionalists such as Berkhouwer and presuppositionalists in the tradition of Van Til, while granting the reality of a universal general revelation, end up with Barth in asserting that man can know nothing about God save by supernatural special revelation.

Recent Protestant neoliberalism, reluctant to speak of God as a personal being analogous to the human being, tends to conceive of God impersonally and philosophically as the ground and power of being. In the spirit of romanticism, cognitive knowledge of God is supplanted by immediate mystical awareness of the Absolute in the depths of the soul. Modern man finds no need to embark on the tortuous path of attempting to prove God philosophically, for the unconditional is perceived by every person in moments of lived insight and intuition. Revelation, in fact, is no longer viewed as a rational communication from God to man, but as man groping to find the significance of his deepest experiences. Protestant neoliberalism thus propounds a radical natural theology of mystical awareness in which there is no need for a supernatural propositional revelation.

On the Roman Catholic side, the classic Thomistic scheme of natural and supernatural knowledge of God is rapidly collapsing in favor of the Protestant neoliberal emphasis on man's existential encounter with God in the human psyche. Revelation, defined as man's noncognitive awareness of transcendent reality, is an ever-present datum in human experience. Consequently, all people—non-Christians and atheists included—implicitly *know* God, even if many explicitly deny His existence. Post-Vatican II Catholicism has taken the revolutionary step of claiming that all who take their existence seriously are "anonymous Christians" and are mystically united to Christ. In the new-shape Catholicism, all people of good will enjoy an authentic experience with God. Consequently, the entire world exists in a saved condition.

The contemporary spirit of nationalism that pervades the social, political, and economic life of the Third World is not without its impact on the theological reflections of the developing nations. Although the indigenization or contextualization of theology today assumes many forms, the powerful conviction exists among the younger countries that Western expressions of Christianity must be replaced by traditions native to the local situation. Thus in Africa spokesmen insist that a faith meaningful to the people of that continent must somehow be adapted to the time-honored beliefs and practices of African traditional religion. On the other hand, given the fact that the dominant mood in Latin America is political and economic liberation, Latin theologians and church leaders vigorously insist that a theology truly relevant to the poor and oppressed masses of that part of the world must be shaped by Marxist ideology and practice. In a similar vein, Asian Christian theologians, surrounded by a vast sea of humanity who follow the religions of Hinduism, Buddhism, Confucianism, et al., claim that a theology that speaks to the needs of the Asian man or woman must incorporate emphases from the ancient religions of the East. Thus in Africa, Latin America, and Asia subtle syncretistic forces are at work creating indigenous deities that frequently bear little resemblance to the living and personal God of the Bible.

Persuaded of the correctness of the a priori scheme of Augustine, we propose the following hypothesis concerning the relationship of revelation, knowledge of God, and world religions. Man, made in the image of God and enabled by common grace, effably intuits (in the first moment of mental and moral self-consciousness) eternal changeless principles, including the existence, character, and moral demands of God. Thus equipped with a rudimentary intuited knowledge of God, man adduces further knowledge of God's character and purposes by rational reflection on the data of nature and history. From the light of general revelation, then, all people know God as Creator, Preserver, and Judge of the world. But controlled by a darkened heart and stubborn will, natural man refuses to cultivate the elemental knowledge of God afforded by general revelation. Instead, he tramples underfoot the knowledge of God as Creator and worships false gods of his own manufacture. Hence the knowledge mediated by general revelation does not save; rather, it serves only to condemn. Nevertheless, God in grace revealed to wayward sinners His saving purposes through mighty acts in history and supremely through the life, teachings, and deeds of His Son, Jesus Christ. God's special revelation to mankind was amply attested by signs of miracles and fulfilled prophecy. The body of historical knowledge about Christ preserved in inspired Scripture provides the rational basis for the sinner's Spirit-guided decision of faith. Faith is not a matter of a subjective leap; rather, it involves both a whole soul trust and a resting of the mind in the sufficiency of the evidences. In response to assent to scriptural truths about God and personal commitment to Christ, the believer is granted ineffable intuition of God's saving wisdom. The knowledge of God as Redeemer, or the knowledge that issues in the salvation of the soul, is mediated, not indiscriminately through any religious system, but solely through the Christian gospel, which concerns "the mystery that has been kept hidden for ages and generations, but is now disclosed to the saints" (Col. 1:26).

Having now come to the point where the issues have been raised and the problem stated, we turn to the development of the themes of general revelation, the knowability of God, and world religions in their historical context.

CLASSICAL CATHOLIC POSITIONS: LAYING THE FOUNDATIONS

Just as every structurally sound building rests on a solid foundation, so the theological enterprise must be supported by viable philosophical and theological underpinnings. In the early centuries of the church's history, theologians strove to consolidate the bases on which generations of later Christian thinkers would build. To a large measure the fortunes of the church down through history would be shaped by the theological reflections of a select number of creative and influential thinkers. The character and integrity of Christendom today owes much to doctrinal approaches worked out in the church many hundreds of years ago.

Two theological thinkers whose impact on the Christian church has been incalculable are Aurelius Augustine and Thomas Aquinas. As one looks back across the pages of time, Augustine stands out as the towering figure in the first 750 years of Christian history, and Aquinas emerges as the leading personality in the second 750 years of the church's life. The former justly has been acclaimed the father of Western Christianity. The power of Augustinianism is seen in the fact that most of Augustine's thought survived the split that rent Western Christendom in the sixteenth century. Aquinas, on the other hand, is universally acclaimed the principal authority in the Roman Catholic Church. St. Thomas was proclaimed in 1567 the *doctor ecclesiae,* and in 1800 Pope Leo XIII declared the Angelic Doctor the "patron of all Catholic schools." With his emphasis on the ascent of the soul to God, Augustine is the Christian Platonist *par excellence.* On the other hand, with his speculative, philosophical approach to sacred knowledge, Aquinas is the great Christian Aristotelian. Augustine and St. Thomas, together with Anselm of Canterbury (the great medieval philosophical theologian), made momentous contributions to the issue of revelation and the knowability of God. Because their approaches to our subject continue to weigh heavily in the contemporary discussion, a closer examination of the positions of these three seminal thinkers will now be undertaken.

Augustine and Christian Platonism   Augustine of Hippo (354–430), the illustrious Manichaean convert to Christianity, was the principal theologian of the Latin church. In his view of the sacraments and church authority, Augustine may be regarded as the father of Roman Catholicism, but in his evangelical doctrines of man, sin, and grace, he was the forerunner of the Protestant Reformation. As a churchman, theologian, and apologist, Augustine was the noble successor of the apostle Paul and the precursor of Luther and Calvin. Augustine's influence on the Western church has been incomparable for more than a millennium and a half. The genius of his thought is seen in the fact that both the pope and Reformation Christians acknowledge him among their theologians.

Neoplatonic philosophy, championed by Plotinus (d. 270) and Porphyry (d. 305), exercised considerable influence on Augustine's religious thought. The latter's emphasis on self-transcending contemplation of truth, the primacy of cognitive intuition over sense perception, and the direct union of the soul with God as all significant Platonic themes. Augustine acknowledged in Greek philosophy the presence of considerable truth, since God has made a universal disclosure of His glory in general revelation. But of all the Gentile philosophers, Plato attained the highest level of truth. Said Augustine, "It is evident that none came nearer to us than the Platonists."[1] Moreover, "their gold and silver [were] dug out of the mines of God's providence which are everywhere scattered abroad."[2]

Through the pursuit of reason, the Platonists constructed a comprehensive natural theology. They believed that the invisible things of God are known through the things that are made. Plato and his school reasoned that God is the cause of all existence, the ultimate good, the ground of understanding and knowledge, the end to which life is to be regulated, and the bountiful bestower of blessedness.[3] Augustine relates in his *Confessions* that the books of the Neoplatonists that he read prior to his conversion to Christianity affirmed the existence of the infinite God and His Word, the creation of the world, and the inner presence of the divine light. "Their juster thoughts concerning the one God who made heaven and earth, have made them illustrious among philosophers."[4] Although they gained a knowledge of many eternal truths through general revelation,[5] the Neoplatonists nevertheless had no knowledge of God's saving purposes. They failed to recognize that particular grace of God displayed to humanity in Jesus of Nazareth. They acknowledged the validity of John 1:1, but they were ignorant of the truth of John 1:14. The Platonists missed altogether the incarnation of the Son of God, the efficacy of His suffering on the cross, and His triumphant resurrection and ascension.[6] Thus, lacking a biblically informed faith, the Platonists fell into overt idolatry, corruption, and a menagerie of errors.[7] Augustine was persuaded that Christianity's special revelation represents the fulfillment and perfection of what was lacking in the Platonic tradition. Augustine held out little hope for the salvation of the heathen apart from the gospel of God's grace.

Augustine's thought is rendered more difficult by the voluminous and unsystematic character of his writings. Unlike Thomas Aquinas, Augustine wrote no systematic *Summa*. Neverthless, the bishop's fundamental commitments relative to the knowledge of God are sufficiently clear. First, Augustine differentiated between truths that are eternal and changeless and those that are temporal and changing. In both the eternal and temporal realms, some truths are immediately perceived by the knower, whereas others are mediated through signs requiring faith. The goal of eternal truths is contemplation, but the proper end of temporal truths is action. Moreover, Augustine made a fundamental distinction between "understanding" (*intellectus*) and "reason" (*ratio*) and also between "wisdom" (*sapientia*) and "knowledge" (*scientia*). Through understanding or intellectual cognizance (*intellectus*), man intuits directly or through signs eternal changeless principles of mathematics, logic, ethics, and truths of God that the bishop designated as wisdom (*sapientia*). On the other hand, through the faculty of reason or rational cognizance (*ratio*), man gains a knowledge (*scientia*) of changing things. The legitimate object of man's quest in the changeless, eternal realm is *sapientia*, whereas in the changing, temporal realm it is *scientia*.[8] In Augustine's aprioristic scheme, intuitive understanding logically precedes discursive reason, and wisdom precedes knowledge.

Before proceeding further, a brief sortie is necessary into Augustine's understanding of sin's effect on the human intellect and will. The bishop insisted that natural man's cognitive powers have been crippled by the effects of sin.[9] In matters pertaining to the eternal realm, the sinner is unable to intuit eternal, changeless truths, whereas in the temporal realm man's knowledge of changing things is distorted. The mind of natural man has been darkened and weakened by original sin. As Augustine argues, "Every man is born mentally blind."[10] In addition, the will is not free but is bound by the power of reigning sin.[11] Only what is loved and embraced by the will is known. But the fact is that the unregenerate will is perverse and corrupt. Fallen man's proclivity to self-love and pride compels him to turn aside from God. With Paul, Augustine insists that autonomous man holds down or suppresses God's presentation of Himself to the soul.[12] God must heal, perfect, and free the will to make it willing to respond positively to Him.[13] It is only when faith is established and sinful pride is routed that the intellect is enabled and the will freed to receive wisdom. Plainly, Augustine upheld a total moral depravity affecting every part of man's nature.

But Augustine further postulated the reality of common grace, although he did not use the term as such. A general illumination from God overcomes man's depravity in relation to eternal things. Through the benefits of God's common grace, the powers of the intellect and will are partially restored. As a result, man made in the image of God is enabled to intuit eternal, changeless principles of mathematics, logic, ethics, and truths about God. Man qua man, enabled by common grace, is empowered to acquire and contemplate wisdom (*sapientia*). Hence Augustine's prayer uttered shortly after his conversion was "Oh that they could behold the internal Eternal."[14] But God's common grace also enables natural man to evaluate accurately the data from the changing, temporal realm.[15] Reason, or rational cognizance (*ratio*), thus leads to historical knowledge about Jesus of Nazareth (*scientia*), and this knowledge functions as the objective foundation for faith. In Augustine's changing, temporal realm knowledge (*scientia*) attests the validity of Scripture and the divine origin of Jesus Christ. Thus he could say, "Reasoning does not create truth but discovers it."[16] In short, at the historical level knowledge (*scientia*) precedes faith (*fides*). Said Augustine, "Thinking is prior to believing."[17] Faith is not blind but rests on knowledge of the object to be believed and on the reason one is to believe. Augustine's balanced treatment of faith and reason in the temporal realm avoids, on the one hand, the blind fideism of Tertullian,[18] and, on the other, the autonomy of reason posited by skeptics and rationalists.

But what can be said of Augustine's estimate of the nature and validity of general revelation? From the signs of data displayed in nature, providence, and history, common grace enables all people to intuit cognitively eternal truths concerning God's existence, character, and moral demands.[19] Although by general revelation God is not redemptively known, He is nevertheless known as supreme Creator and moral Judge, even by Platonists and other unbelievers.[20] Thus through external signs general revelation provides the basis for man's recognition of the God who has acted and spoken in special revelation. Sinful man, however, rebels against the knowledge of God mediated by general revelation. Rather than loving the elemental truth about God and cleaving to it, natural man volitionally opposes it. Consequently, general revelation fails to lead to the knowledge of God that saves. Nevertheless, it does serve as the basis of man's universal accountability before the Judge of the universe. And further, God's universal disclosure in Creation, man, and history serves as an indispensible prolegomenon to God's fuller redemptive revelation in Scripture and in Christ.

In his writings Augustine mentions nearly all the classical proofs for God's existence. He cites, for example, the historical argument that focuses on the universal religious consensus: "Except for a few whose human nature is too depraved, the whole human race acknowledges that God is the author of this world."[21] He also appeals to cosmological data that point to the fact that the universe, earth, man, and beast were not self-created but were made by a higher power.[22] The entire complex of cosmic phenomena unites to praise God's name.[23] In its beauty and beneficence, the created order makes no sense apart from the prior reality of God.[24] Appealing to teleological data, Augustine further acknowledges that the design, order, and harmony everywhere displayed befits the existence of a divine Architect of intelligence and wisdom.[25] "Noble philosophers looked and knew the Maker from His handiwork."[26]

But even more significant than the foregoing arguments is Augustine's a priori line of reasoning from timeless and eternal truths.[27] Augustine's epistemological argument is developed as follows: The human mind perceives immutable truths that cannot be doubted, for example, that three plus four equals seven. Such truths have not been created by any finite mind, for all other minds acknowledge their validity. Unless there be an infinite, unchangeable being behind such truths, they are in fact inexplicable. The timeless and unchangeable mind that grounds universal truths, Augustine argued, is God. All men know God's mind insofar as by common grace they know any changeless truths or principles at all.

The aforementioned arguments were not intended by Augustine to prove formally the existence and character of God, as later scholastic theologians sought to do. Augustine did not deal with the data of the external world by means of inductive inference, concluding that God is, as in the case of Aquinas. Rather, Augustine intended to show that finite man rebels against the truth of common grace if he fails to acknowledge the reality of an infinite and eternal God who undergirds the whole of life. The theistic postulate offers the most coherent and consistent explanation of the myriad data displayed in the natural and historical realms.

Augustine's solution to the problem of the knowability of God is faith in (assent to) the knowledge (*scientia*) of the incarnate Christ disclosed in Holy Scripture.[28] Many redemptive truths, such as the triune nature of the Godhead and the Father's love for sinners, lie beyond the power of the human intellect to fathom. That is, the immediate intuition of wisdom via the assistance of common grace fails to lead sinners to the city of God. Said Augustine, "We were too weak by unaided reason to find out the truth, and for this cause needed the authority of holy writings."[29] Through a supernatural working of the Holy Spirit, God set forth saving wisdom on the pages of the Old and New Testaments. The Spirit-inspired testimony to Christ is attested by the signs of miracles and fulfilled prophecy. In response to a faith assent to Christ's incarnation, death, and resurrection, the sinner is cleansed of sin and justified before the bar of God's justice. Augustine is insistent that saving wisdom (*sapientia*) is not possible without faith, understood both as intellectual assent to truths mediated in Scripture and personal commitment to Christ. It is in this sense that Augustine writes of the priority of faith: "If you will not believe, you will not understand" (*nisi credideritis, non intelligetis*).[30] Again, "If you cannot understand, believe in order to understand" (*si non potes intelligere, crede ut intelligas*).[31] Since faith in Christ opens the eyes to the truth and beauty of God, Augustine could say, "Contemplation is the recompense of faith."[32] In sum, then, God is redemptively known neither by induction from the data of the finite external world, nor by reflection on the internal data of experience. Augustine's distinctive Christian philosophy is succinctly stated thus: "Faith is in some way the starting point of knowledge."[33] In order to attain the certainty of saving knowledge of God, Augustine issues this plea: "Believe steadfastly in God, and in so far as you can, entrust yourself wholly to him."[34] Thus we have seen in Augustine that investigation into the historical phenomena of

Jesus of Nazareth provides the objective basis for faith, which in turn provides effable intuition of God's saving wisdom. The attainment of man's highest end—the city of God—is due to the special grace of God operative in the sinner's heart.[35]

Augustine thus held that via the enablement of common grace all men effably intuit eternal changeless principles, including the existence and character of God. Moreover, the indicia of both the created order and the historical continuum constitute occasions by which further truths about God are mediated to the human mind. The religious a priori and general revelation together ensure that preliminary wisdom (*sapientia*), defined as knowledge of God's existence, character, and moral demands, becomes an actual possession of man made in the image of God and enabled by common grace. In Augustine's scheme God must be in the head before He is in the heart. But Augustine is adamant in his insistence that this partial and preliminary wisdom falls short of the knowledge of God and His purposes necessary for salvation. Hence God entered history in the person of the Savior, and through the Holy Spirit inspired the inerrant record of Jesus' teaching, works, and claims. Discursive reason (*ratio*), working on history's changing data recorded in Scripture, yields a fund of knowledge (*scientia*) concerning God's purposes in Jesus Christ. When moved in the heart by the Holy Spirit, the sinner responds in faith to the truths about God revealed in His Word and commits his life to the person of Christ. In response to man's assent to the doctrinal content concerning the Savior and commitment to the living person of Jesus Christ, God grants saving wisdom (*sapientia*) and citizenship in the city of God. Augustine thus postulates the dual reality of general and special revelation and the utility of each in leading natural man to wisdom. The bishop's scheme of knowledge, furthermore, does justice to the complex relationship of faith and reason. Reason precedes faith in that it provides man with a corpus of knowledge upon which to make an informed and meaningful decision concerning Christ. Yet faith in

AUGUSTINE ON HUMAN COGNIZANCE

Reality	Capacity	Content	Immediate	Mediate	End
God's changeless (1) principles (2) plans for history	Intellect (*intellectus*)	Wisdom (*sapientia*)	Effable intuition (seeing)	Faith in (assent to) (1) inspired writings (2) incarnate Christ attested by signs of (1) miracles (2) fulfilled prophecy	Meditation
History's changing (1) persons (2) events	Reason (*ratio*)	Knowledge (*scientia*)	Sense perception	Faith in (assent to) historical data critically assessed	Action

Christ opens to the new believer unimaginable vistas of knowledge of the Creator and Redeemer God. Eternal truths formerly taken on faith now become for the believer a matter of spiritual sight. As Augustine puts it, "Faith is understanding's step; and understanding faith's attainment."[36]

Anselm and Christian Scholasticism   Anselm (c. 1033−1109), archbishop of Canterbury and author of the famous essay on the Incarnation *Cur Deus Homo* (*Why God Became Man*), is regarded by many as "the second Augustine." One discovers in Anselm the typical late medieval emphasis on reason's power to attain a comprehensive knowledge of God by metaphysical reflection. Anselm's starting point and primary source was Augustine, the most highly esteemed of all the church fathers. Yet Anselm subtly departed from Augustine by attempting a more extensive philosophical explication of theism than Augustine seven centuries earlier had been prepared to undertake. Anselm thus represents a transitional link between the faith perspective of Augustine and the rationalism of the later Scholastic tradition championed by Aquinas (d. 1274) and Duns Scotus (d. 1308).

Following Augustine and in opposition to rationalists of his day, Anselm affirmed unaided reason's inability to attain to saving wisdom. Two obstacles hinder man's quest for the understanding that leads to eternal bliss: human finitude (the doctrine of Creation) and human sinfulness (the doctrine of the Fall).[37] Uninformed by special revelation, natural man fails to comprehend the demands of God's justice and righteousness. In the tradition of Augustine, Anselm postulated the primacy of faith for the saving knowledge of God. Hence he declared in a now-famous statement, "I do not seek to understand in order to believe, but I believe in order to understand. For I believe even this: that I shall not understand unless I believe."[38] Anselm's foundational commitment thus is clear: special revelation assented to by faith issues forth in salvation.

Yet in opposition to the fideism of certain early-church theologians, Anselm argued that reasons must be adduced in support of the Christian faith. "The rational mind itself," he insists, "is most able to advance toward finding the Supreme Being."[39] In the case of the Christian, rational demonstration heightens faith's understanding of the gospel. And in the case of the infidel, speculative argumentation serves to convince those who have no faith. Anselm thus set out to prove to the fool the validity of Christianity, so as to facilitate his journey to faith.[40] Even though the Fall has crippled human nature, still "the corrupting influence of sin is not such that it can prevent the natural man's reason from assenting to the 'necessities' of the Christian faith once these have been presented to him."[41] From this epistemological base Anselm attempted to prove not only God's existence and attributes, but also the Trinity, the immortality of the soul, the necessity of salvation through the incarnation of Christ, and so on. Grounding Anselm's speculative case for theism is the presupposition of a universal general revelation. God via general revelation confronts the sinner with His holy character and demands. The light of God is disclosed to the sinner internally through the innate God-idea and man's moral constitution and externally through nature. Given the reality of a universal general disclosure of the Creator, Anselm develops in remarkable detail the leading tenets of the Christian system short of any appeal to the data of special revelation.

Anselm's *Monologion* was written shortly before (1076) his more celebrated *Proslogion* (1078). Concerning these two essays, Anselm commented, "I wrote [them] especially in order to show that what we hold by faith regarding the divine nature and its persons—excluding the topic of incarnation—can be proven by compelling reasons apart from appeal to the authority of Scripture."[42] In his *Monologion, Proslogion*, and the later essay *Cur Deus Homo* (1094–97), Anselm set out to demonstrate philosophically a wide range of theistic truths.

In chapters 2 through 4 of the *Proslogion* Anselm develops what at the time of Kant came to be known as the ontological argument. This proof purports to establish the existence of Deity based on the innate God-idea supplied by the Logos. All men acknowledge "something than which nothing greater can be thought" (*id quo majus cogitari nequit*).[43] Anselm argues that it is greater to exist both in the understanding and outside the understanding than in the understanding alone. Hence if God existed only in our thoughts, we could think of something greater and more perfect, namely, the same being existing in reality as well as in the mind. Anselm thus concludes that the very thought of God as a perfect Being necessitates His real existence. Since Anselm's formulation of the proof in the eleventh century, a barrage of criticism has been mounted against the ontological argument. Guanilon, a monk contemporary to Anselm, argued that a mere mental conception does not guarantee the reality, for one could conceive of the most perfect island or a most perfect unicorn which, in fact, has no counterpart in the real world. Later, Thomas Aquinas rejected the proof on the grounds that it involved an invalid leap from the sphere of logic to the sphere of ontology. A host of other thinkers have challenged the claim that whatever exists in the mind necessarily possesses objective reality outside the mind. Thus it seems preferable to conclude that at best Anselm established only the bare God-idea and not the reality of the living and active God of the Bible.[44]

But not content to deal merely with the fact of God's existence, Anselm moved on to consider the unfathomable riches of God's nature. Developing further his argument from Platonic realism, Anselm argues that God is life, light, wisdom, goodness, truth, and justice. He attempts, in addition, to establish by rational reflection other divine attributes such as God's immensity, omnipotence, and eternity. Moreover, pressing further the ontological argument, Anselm concludes not only that God is supreme simplicity and unity but also that He is triune, consisting of Father, Son, and Holy Spirit. And finally, from the innate God-idea, Anselm speculates that God extends mercy to the elect and heaps punishment on the reprobate. It is transparent, then, that from a single a priori argument Anselm speculatively developed an extensive rational theology. Ostensibly working independently of special revelation, he formulated detailed assertions from the innate God-idea that far exceed the warrant of Scripture. It is difficult to avoid the conclusion that Anselm's theology underlay his speculative philosophy. Or as Henry argues, Anselm's prior faith commitments gained by special revelation have subtly infiltrated his speculative argumentation in the ontological proof.[45]

Turning to the *Monologion*, or *Soliloquy*, Anselm constructed a threefold proof for the existence and character of God that is broadly cosmological. In the preface to that meditation, Anselm writes that "nothing in Scripture should be urged on the authority of Scripture itself, but that whatever the conclusion of independent investigation should declare to be true, should . . . with common proofs and with a simple argument, be briefly enforced by the cogency of reason."[46] Anselm invited his readers to evaluate life's experiences and to order them on an ascending scale of goodness, perfection, etc. Unless one is prepared to settle for an infinite series, then one good, one perfection, must occupy the highest place. Thus in chapter 1 of the *Monologion* Anselm argues that the existence of goodness points to a single supreme Good; namely, God as the only adequate cause. In chapter 2 he reasons that the existence of perfection likewise points to the existence of a supreme Perfection, who is none other than the God of the Bible. In chapters 3 and 4 Anselm insists that the totality of all entities and actions demands a causation supremely great, which is the God of theism. Thus Anselm concludes via a process of speculative reasoning that God is supreme being, justice, wisdom, truth, goodness, greatness, beauty, incorruptibility, immutability, blessedness, eternity, power, and unity.[47] Such a God must necessarily subsist without beginning and without end. Moreover, Anselm reasons that God of His own will created the contingent universe *ex nihilo*.[48] And finally, by philosophical argumentation Anselm purports to establish conjecturally the consubstantiality and coeternity of the three persons of the Trinity.[49] The begetting of Word and Spirit from the unity of God and the creative operations of the three persons are adduced by further philosophical speculation. Quite apart from special revelation, the unbeliever should be prepared to concede all these truths of the Christian faith. So Anselm argues that the foregoing tenets should be "clear to the rational man."[50]

In sum, Anselm is biblical and Augustinian in his assertion of the corruption of human nature by the Fall and in his insistence on the necessity of faith for salvation. Philosophically, Anselm is a rationalist who believes that man can acquire knowledge of God independently of sense-experience. Both his *Monologion* and his *Proslogion* constitute arguments drawn from the realm of rational thought. But in his speculative attempt to prove the triunity of God, creation *ex nihilo*, the doctrines of election and reprobation, etc., Anselm demanded more of the innate God-idea and general revelation than they are capable of delivering. As noted, Anselm loaded his philosophical arguments for theism with the conclusions of special revelation. In fact, anticipating Aquinas, Anselm believed that God could be approached from two directions: by the way of ascent (reason) and by the way of descent (revelation). Anselm, however, differs from Aquinas in that whereas the latter began with the facts of the external world, Anselm began with the idea of God in the mind. Anselm thus took the a priori route of intuition and thought, whereas Aquinas traveled the a posteriori route afforded by experience. On balance, Anselm's case for theism displays a significant scholasticizing tendency fittingly described as rationalistic or "philosophical-speculative."[51] In this regard, Anselm not unjustly may be regarded as the father of orthodox scholasticism.

Aquinas and Christian Aristotelianism

Our attention now turns to Thomas Aquinas (1225–1274), the renowned Italian Dominican philosopher and theologian. The Angelic Doctor's profuse writings include a commentary on Peter Lombard's then popular *Four Books of Sentences* and expositions of nearly all the works of Aristotle. On the theological side, Thomas wrote exegetical commentaries on the Gospels, Epistles, and portions of the Old Testament, in addition to the two renowned *Summae*. The *Summa Contra Gentiles* (1259–1264), a major medieval essay on natural theology, was directed apologetically to Muslim and pagan protagonists. The unfinished *Summa Theologica* (1265–1272), Thomas's undisputed *opus magnum*, propounds an intricate system of philosophical theology in response to the question, How is God known?

As Augustine and Anselm were indebted to Platonic realism, so Thomas worked within the framework of Aristotelian philosophy. Aristotle's hierarchical vision of reality differentiated sharply between terrestrial and celestial realms. The lower order of nature and the higher supernatural order were bridged by the human mind. In the Aristotelian scheme, the intellect is the key that opens the door to the knowledge of God. By rational induction from temporal effects, Aristotle concluded the existence, intelligence, and providential care of the Prime Mover or Absolute Perfection, without uniting these characteristics in a single personal being. The Aristotelian tradition optimistically affirmed the ability of the human intellect to ascend to divine truth.

Thomas' dependence on Aristotle relative to the knowability of God shows itself in several significant ways. One similarity is Thomas's fundamental distinction between nature and grace, or between reason and faith. Thomas commonly spoke of "the twofold truth of divine things."[52] By this Thomas meant that superimposed on Aristotle's realm of nature explored by reason is the higher reality of grace apprehended by faith. Two distinct kinds of knowledge are thus open to man—namely, a knowledge that is revealed and a knowledge that is natural.

II. CLASSICAL CATHOLIC POSITIONS: LAYING THE FOUNDATIONS

> There is a twofold mode of truth in what we profess about God. Some truths about God exceed all the ability of human reason. Such is the truth that God is triune. But there are some truths which the natural reason also is able to reach. Such are that God exists, that He is one, and the like.[53]

The former mode of knowing involves the way of rational ascent, the latter the way of revelational descent.

In the Thomistic scheme, rational induction from the sense world without any appeal to revelation data leads to a certain knowledge of God and the divine order. Within specified bounds, the way of rational ascent and the way of revelational descent are two independent routes to apprehension of divine truth. In reality, Thomas's epistemological scheme was one with his vision of the apologetic task. When one communicates the faith to Gentiles, appeal to biblical authority is of little value. "We must," Thomas argues, "have recourse to the natural reason, to which all men are forced to give their assent."[54]

A second theoretical element in Thomas's system that is crucial to the problem of God's knowability is the concept of analogy of being (*analogia entis*). Aristotle held that all knowledge presupposes an essential likeness between knower and that which is known. From the postulate of a real similarity between created and uncreated being, knowledge of contingent effects leads to knowledge of the divine Reality. Thomas, with Aristotle, acknowledged the existence of an infinite distance between Creator and created entities. But the finite creature can know in part the infinite Creator by virtue of the analogy that exists between God and all created things. In the case of humanity, the analogy rests on man created in the *imago Dei*. God is not totally other than man, nor identical with man's being. God's existence is analogous to man's existence. Even in his fallen condition, man's being involves being like God. For example, if man possesses a measure of goodness or truth, it may be inferred that God is supreme goodness and truth. Moreover, lower forms of life and the inanimate world bear in themselves the *vestigia Dei* (traces of God). Hence by an examination of created effects, employing the principle of the analogy of being, man is able to gain some knowledge of God's uncreated nature. Thus Thomas writes, "It is not necessary that God considered in Himself be naturally known to man, but only a likeness of God. It remains, therefore, that man is to reach the knowledge of God through reasoning by way of the likeness of God found in His effects."[55]

Furthermore, it is clear that Thomas's inflated emphasis on reason betrays a depreciation of the effects of the Fall on the human cognitive powers. Whereas man lost his ethical likeness to God in his reckless quest for autonomy, his natural likeness to God remained untarnished by the Fall. Hence Thomas, unlike Augustine, saw no need for a general illumination of reason as it evaluates the data of the cosmic order. Burtt thus concludes correctly that in Thomas "human reason is metaphysically competent . . . to attain absolute truth concerning God's existence and attributes."[56] Given Thomas's vision of an untarnished *imago*, a self-sufficient natural theology is for Christian and non-Christian alike a fruitful possibility.

A closer examination of Thomas's twofold source for the knowledge of God is mandated. First, we consider the Thomistic tenet that natural or rational knowledge is universally accessible to all men, be they Christians or non-Christians. Rejecting Anselm's intuitive ontological argument, Thomas proceeded along Aristotelian lines to argue that rational induction from sensible experience leads to the knowledge of God's existence and the infinity of His perfections. Crucial to his argument is the assumption that the existence and nature of a cause may be deduced from its effects. "Because they [sensible things] are His effects and depend on their cause, we can be led from them so far as to know of God, *whether He exists*, and to know of Him what must necessarily belong to Him, as the first cause of all things."[57] Thomas, then, is persuaded that the empirical data of nature, interpreted by the principle of cause and effect, lead to demonstrable proof of God's existence and character. Since the knowledge of God is not innate or self-evident (as in Augustine and Anselm), His existence and character must be established by formal a posteriori proofs based on effects.[58] Hence Thomas affirms in the *Summa Theologica*, "The existence of God can be proved in five ways."[59] The first three of Thomas's renowned Five Ways are variants of the cosmological argument, the fourth is an axiological argument, and the fifth is a form of the teleological argument. Virtually the entirety of Thomas's argumentation in the Five Ways was adopted from the formulations of Aristotle more than a millennium and a half earlier.

Thomas's first Way argues from movement to the existence of a Prime Unmoved Mover. Empirical observation readily discloses that objects in the world are in motion. Objects that move pass from a state of potency to actuality. But nothing can go from potency to actuality unless it is moved by another. Regressing a finite number of steps in the causal chain leads back to the ultimate source of all movement, the first Unmoved Mover, which everyone understands to be God.

Thomas's second Way argues from causation to the existence of a First Cause. The sense world discloses what Thomas called "an order of efficient causes."[60] There is no empirical evidence to support the possibility that a thing can be its own efficient cause. The causal chain cannot extend back to infinity, since without a first efficient causation succeeding causes would also be nonexistent. Hence there must be a First Cause of all potential efficiency in the world, and all acknowledge this to be God.

The third Way argues from contingent beings to an absolutely Necessary Being. All that we observe in the world are contingent entities. The very existence of such implies that their reality is predicated on another being. If there were nothing but contingent beings, then at one time or another there would be nothing in existence, but this is clearly absurd. Thus at some point short of infinity, one must postulate the existence of a being that has received its existence from no other and is the cause of all other beings. The name of that absolutely Necessary Being is God.

The axiological argument contained in the fourth Way reasons from degrees of perfection to a being of Absolute Perfection. Thomas argues that among beings there are found gradations of goodness, truth, nobility, and the like. But degrees of perfection are meaningful only in the light of a superlative perfection. Hence there exists "something which is truest, something best, something noblest, and, consequently, something which is uttermost being."[61] This supremely perfect source of all gradations of perfection Aquinas calls God.

The final and teleological Way reasons from the wise governance of the world to the existence of a Divine Designer. Subhuman entities such as natural bodies, lacking intelligence, nevertheless display an order, harmony, and purpose in their workings. The manner in which they function for the maximal result is a matter of design rather than fortuitous chance. Entities lacking intelligence are incapable of consistently achieving the optimal end unless they are directed by a being of great knowledge and wisdom. An arrow, for example, cannot hit the target unless it is shot by an archer possessed of knowledge and skill. The intelligent Designer and Governor of the world Thomas defined as God.

Having thus established God's existence by causal demonstration from effects displayed in the natural world, Thomas proceeded philosophically to elucidate the infinity of God's perfections. Knowledge of God's character is gained by a twofold mode of reasoning: by the process of negation and by the method of analogy.[62] Thus in the remainder of the first book of *Summa Contra Gentiles*, Thomas argues that the Unmoved Mover, First Cause, and Divine Designer is infinite, eternal, incorporeal, immaterial, and immutable.[63] Moreover, reason establishes that the God who is one is living, good, free, intelligent, truthful, loving, and blessed. Thus by rational induction from observable effects in the temporal world and by utilization of the principles of negation and analogy, Thomas constructed a formidable natural theology independent of propositional revelation. From this brief overview, it is clear that Thomas's a posteriori approach differs markedly from the a priori method of Augustine, who postulated both an immediate "seeing" and a mediated "seeing" by faith. The latter held that by common grace man cognitively intuits from the occasions provided by general revelation more limited conclusions concerning the existence and character of God. Augustine failed to share Thomas's optimism regarding the shaping of an extensive natural theology by philosophical argumentation.

Whether or not Thomas's proofs provide an irrefragable demonstration of God's existence and perfections has long been a matter of debate. Our evaluation of the validity of Thomas's arguments necessarily must be brief.[64] As already noted, Thomas set out to prove God's existence before establishing the infinity of His perfections. But how could one prove to the satisfaction of pagan Gentiles the existence of a being whose qualities and characteristics, according to Thomas, are as yet unknown? With respect to the proposition "God exists," can one establish with certainty the validity of the predicate when one is ignorant of the subject? Since there is no such thing as pure being without specific defining attributes, Thomas's arguments hold out less promise than Augustine's mediate-immediate scheme of cognitive intuition.

Second, many judge that Thomas's Prime Unmoved Mover, First Cause, Necessary Being, et al., is more an abstract philosophical principle than the living and communicating God of Abraham, Isaac, and Jacob. That is, one is not compellingly persuaded of the validity of the conclusion Thomas drew to each argument: "And this (Unmoved Mover, First Cause, etc.) everyone understands to be God." Brunner insists that "the 'God' of the proofs for the existence of God is not the Living God of faith, but an intellectual abstraction."[65] Even a Roman Catholic scholar as friendly as Frederick Copleston, S.J., judges that Thomas was unduly hasty in identifying the philosophical principles of the Five Ways with the warmly personal God in whom Christians trust and to whom they pray. Thus he writes, "It is not so obvious that the necessary being must be the personal Being whom we call God."[66] Carnell argues that the infinite personal God of the Bible cannot be demonstrated from finite empirical data in the a posteriori manner Thomas employed. Hence Carnell concludes that Thomas's pure empiricism has proved, "not the Christian God, but the God of Aristotle."[67] We agree, moreover, with Kroner that apart from the religious a priori Thomas's proofs fail to lead to the one infinite and personal God of biblical faith.

> They are not conclusive, unless we know a priori that the infinite and unconditional or absolute for which the understanding is seeking is identical with that being which the religious name of God signifies. Without such a priori knowledge only the existence of a being such as the One of Parmenides or some other philosophic Absolute is established by the arguments of Thomas Aquinas.[68]

Third, the force of Kant's criticism continues to cast doubt on the validity of Thomas's arguments as air-tight, logical demonstrations of theism. Kant called into question the empiricist procedure of reasoning back from phenomenal effects to metaphysically real things-in-themselves as antecedent causes. Can it be said that the law of causality operates flawlessly across the interface of physics and metaphysics? Many doubt its capability to do so. It is thus problematic whether the causal law may be interpreted beyond the visible space-time world to the invisible, transcendent realm of spirit, God, and immortality. Gordon Lewis is justifiably dubious of this fundamental Thomistic tenet: "On strict empirical bases the causal principle cannot be applied beyond the observable realm. No verifiable evidence could possibly be produced to support that application of the law."[69]

Moreover, Thomas's proofs for God's existence display a certain amount of circularity. To illustrate, in the first proof in support of a Prime Unmoved

Mover, Thomas argues that a series of things set in motion by other moving things cannot be extended back to infinity. The reason why an infinite regression of the mover-moved relationship could not occur is that "then there would be no first mover."[70] But the introduction of this factor in support of the argument is precisely the conclusion Thomas sought to establish.

What shall we conclude concerning the validity of the Thomistic proofs? We could say with Gordon Clark that as formal demonstrations the theistic proofs are invalid, on the grounds that the arguments are circular and that they conclude with impersonal principles rather than a single transcendent personal Agent.[71] Protestants generally agree that Thomas's attempt to establish the existence of God and the infinity of His perfections falls short of rigorous logical demonstration. Nevertheless, whereas the Thomistic arguments in actual fact fail to prove the case, they are not entirely wanting in value. The proofs appeal to sufficient data or evidence to form a significant cumulative argument for the reasonableness of belief in the God of the Bible. They challenge the skeptic to account for the very existence of the universe, for order and design in the cosmos, and for the ultimate source of values and morality. Thus the evidence to which the arguments appeal may be regarded as pointers or suggestions that lead the inquirer in the direction of theism rather than atheism, pantheism, or polytheism. As Pascal astutely observed, "There is enough light for those who desire only to see, and enough darkness for those of a contrary disposition."[72] The Thomistic arguments, if not logically demonstrative, at least perform the salutary service of pointing the unbeliever to God and to further light.

But the question arises, What was Thomas's understanding of what post-Reformation Protestantism referred to as general revelation? When Thomas strove for knowledge of God by the way of ascent—namely, when he sought to establish God's existence and perfections by rational induction from the data of the sensible world—did Thomas explicitly or implicitly ground his argumentation in a divine revelatory disclosure in nature and man? To be sure, Thomas never specifically spoke of natural or general revelation as such, primarily because he worked within the framework of Aristotelian philosophy. Thomas's categories were reason and faith, nature and grace, natural theology and revealed (sacred) theology.

But it is sufficiently clear that when Thomas referred to "the natural light of reason" he consistently regarded nature as illumined by the infusion of gratuitous light from God. In the *Summa Theologica* Thomas writes, "The knowledge which we have by natural reason contains two things: images derived from the sensible objects; and the natural intelligible light, enabling us to abstract intelligible conceptions from them."[73] Thomas, then, was not unaware of natural or general revelation. In accepting data from the space-time world, one, in fact, receives revelation from God. Just as faith rests on special revelation in Scripture, so rational explication of causes in the sensible world rests in God's general disclosure in nature and man. Although the conclusions Thomas drew from nature were more extensive than those of Augustine or the Protestant Reformers, nevertheless his position (expressed in Calvin's terms) briefly works out as follows. Just as faith apprehends salvation truth, so reason apprehends creation truth. Although Thomas held to the reality of general revelation, one wishes that he had made more explicit revelation's informing of nature in order that his rather stark antithesis between nature and grace might have been softened.

Thomas, however, is most explicit in teaching that the knowledge of God gained by causal induction from nature is incomplete. There are significant truths about God and His ways that cannot be inferred from the natural world. Thus Thomas writes, "Our intellect cannot be led by sense so far as to see the essence of God; because the sensible effects of God do not equal the power of God as their cause. Hence from the knowledge of sensible things the whole power of God cannot be known."[74] Insofar as Thomas set firm limits on what may be known of God by human ratiocination, he is more biblical than earlier medieval theologians such as Anselm and Abelard, who built up a considerable corpus of theology by philosophical speculation alone.

As regards human salvation, Thomas insists on the inadequacy of the way of rational ascent. Causal induction from the data of nature cannot demonstrate such saving truths as predestination, original sin, the Trinity, the incarnation of the Word, atonement, the resurrection of the body, and eternal life. Needed for salvation are an instruction and knowledge that transcend the powers of reason. Those salvific truths that philosophy never could attain God has supernaturally revealed in the Christian Scriptures. So Thomas writes,

> It was necessary for the salvation of man that certain truths which exceed human reason should be made known to him by divine revelation. . . . In order that the salvation of man might be brought about more fitly and more surely, it was necessary that they should be taught divine truths by divine revelation.[75]

Plainly, then, according to Thomas, the higher knowledge that pertains to salvation must be given by God Himself.

In the Thomistic scheme, revelation spills over into the province of reason so that also those who are incapable of pursuing the path of reason might possess the knowledge of God. Thus Thomas judges that many unlettered people are unable to follow the intricacies of the philosophical arguments. Others beset with the practical demands of daily life have little leisure time for speculative thinking. Some by nature are too indolent to engage in metaphysical reasoning. And finally, history teaches that philosophical speculation all too often becomes contaminated with errors. Given these limitations, Thomas concludes, "If the only way open to us for the knowledge of God were solely that of reason, the human race would remain in the blackest shadows of ignorance. For then the knowledge of God, which especially renders man perfect and good, would come to be possessed only by a few."[76] For Thomas, then, the matter is firmly settled. "We have a more perfect knowledge of God by grace than by natural reason."[77]

It should now be clear that Thomas postulated a distinction between two kinds of knowing and also between two kinds of knowledge thereby attained. The natural light of reason affords the first mode of knowing, which we have identified as the process of rational induction via cause and effect from the data of the natural world. The second mode of knowing involves faith reception of the divine disclosure in Scripture, which transcends reason's ability to apprehend God. Reason, the first mode of knowing, establishes a philosophical science that includes the knowledge of God's existence and perfections. Supernatural revelation, the second mode of knowing, constitutes sacred science or that knowledge of God's essential nature, including the specific Christian or salvific doctrines of the Trinity, Incarnation, and Atonement.[78]

Thomas was firm in his insistence that since God is the author of both natural and revealed theology, it is impossible that the two should prove contradictory. "Grace does not destroy nature, but perfects it."[79] Reason, in fact, is enlisted in the service of faith as its minister. Knowledge of God causally inferred from nature provides the empirical base for the fuller revealed knowledge of God and His saving purposes. In the Thomistic scheme, then, reason functions as a preamble to faith. As Thomas put it, "Faith presupposes natural knowledge, just as grace does nature."[80] From the fundamental knowledge of God's existence and perfections acquired by rational induction from temporal effects, "revealed theology gets a flying start."[81]

Thomas Aquinas must be commended for stressing the rationality of the Christian faith. Throughout his extensive writings the message comes through that rational examination of the data of the space-time world constitutes the necessary preamble to faith. Thomas firmly linked the Christian faith with the world of human experience. He stressed the indisputable connection between the divine Reality "out there" and empirical data "down here." Moreover, Thomas unequivocally affirmed the correlate truth that faith is needed to complete reason. Salvation is wholly predicated on the faith-reception of God's supernatural disclosure in Scripture. He fully embraced the evangelical assertion that in order to attain eternal bliss one must transcend philosophy and lay hold of salvific truths contained in "sacred doctrine."

Our chief criticism of Thomas is that he broke with the Platonic-Augustinian intuitive approach and promoted the Aristotelian method that seeks knowledge of ultimate Reality on the basis of a purely empirical analysis of natural phenomena. Thomas mistakenly held that the idea of God's existence is not properly an innate idea, but is at best confused and vague.[82] By denying man's possession of first principles, including intuitive apprehension of the Creator, Thomas in his quest to demonstrate the existence and infinite perfections of God was crippled from the start. Whereas the apostle Paul teaches in Romans 1:19–21 that God is *known* from His created effects, Aquinas made the much more ambitious claim that the existence and infinite perfections of God can be demonstrably *proved*. Paul, Augustine, and the later Protestant Reformers taught that man approaches the data of general revelation armed with the religious a priori, on the basis of which limited conclusions about God's character and moral demands are inferred.

Moreover, Carnell has convincingly shown that the Thomistic appeal to the analogy of being (*analogia entis*) fails to lead the creature to knowledge of the Creator as alleged.[83] Apart from the religious a priori, the analogy of being between God and man proves to be an unserviceable instrument. It could also be added, by way of critique, that Thomas's speculative or philosophical approach to God lacks immediacy and warmth. His rational quest for truths about God has a certain coldness and detachment about it when compared with the more direct revelational approach of Luther, Calvin, and later Protestant orthodoxy.

In his insistence that truths about God can be attained by the empirical route of rational ascent, Thomas undoubtedly opened the door to later humanistic efforts to postulate the primacy of unaided ratiocination in matters divine. The Thomistic bifurcation between nature and grace and between philosophy and theology proves to be excessively rigorous. The biblical model mandates a greater interpenetration of nature and grace than Thomas has allowed. Although Francis Schaeffer's paradigm of "nature eating up grace" is certainly true of Enlightenment humanism and later liberal theology, it is unjustly applied to the Angelic Doctor himself. As noted above, Thomas painstakingly delineated the upper limits of reason's competency.

Thomas, along with other medieval theologians, failed to account sufficiently for the debilitating effects of the Fall on man's cognitive faculty. Sin has left the *imago Dei* untarnished; only the *donum superadditum* (the superadded gift of grace) is lost. Hence for Thomas, an unrefracted and extensive natural theology lies within the capability of natural man. Postulating the capacity of man as man to discover God for himself, Thomas unrealistically assumed that philosophy would not in practice contradict faith. Thomas's inflated estimate of the power of natural reasons runs counter to the biblical realism of Paul and other New Testament writers.

On the matter of the knowability of God the way forward would, in fact, require a return to the principles enunciated centuries earlier by Augustine of Hippo. To the Reformation rediscovery of these crucial insights we now turn.

RETURN TO FUNDAMENTALS: III THE REFORMATIONAL RESPONSE

No figure highlights more dramatically the shift from philosophical speculation to faith reception of divine revelation than Martin Luther (1483–1546), the Augustinian monk turned Reformer. Located at the terminus of late medieval throught, Luther launched the Reformation movement in Germany and Scandanavia with the landmark principles of *sola fide, sola gratia,* and *sola Scriptura.*

The measure of Luther's greatness is reflected in the fact that more books have been written about him than about any other figure in history, save Jesus.[1] Luther studied philosophy at the University of Erfurt and, after entering the Augustinian order, was appointed in 1508 to a lectureship at the University of Wittenberg. After earning the doctor of philosophy degree in 1512, Luther was awarded a professorial post a year later in the same university. During his studies at Erfurt, Luther was brought under the influence of Ockhamist nominalism, which was prevalent in the universities at the time. The Ockhamists strongly criticized Aristotle's metaphysics and upheld the impossibility of establishing on philosophical grounds the existence and character of God. They held that only the concrete data that could be observed, analyzed, and tested was real. Although Luther later abandoned Ockhamist principles, this early exposure to the empirical nominalist tradition confirmed him in the conviction that reason was incapable of apprehending God.

Thus the intellectual climate in which Luther was trained pointed away from the Aristotelian-Thomistic system. Luther himself regarded the marriage of Christian theology to the philosophy of Aristotle, with the resultant exaltation of reason, as an illegitimate and destructive enterprise. Said he, "There is more wisdom in a verse of the Psalms than in all the metaphysics an Aristotle could write."[2] Or as Luther stated in the fiftieth thesis of the "Disputation Against Scholastic Theology," "Compared with the study of theology, the whole of Aristotle is as darkness is to light."[3]

Through the late medieval nominalism of his teachers, Luther found his way to Augustine, and through Augustine, he found his way to the Bible. Between 1509 and 1511, Luther read a number of Augustine's major essays, including *The Confessions, City of God, On True Religion,* and *On Christian Doctrine.* Following his spiritual conversion, Luther committed himself not only to Augustine's interpretation of the Scriptures but also to many features of his theological system. From 1516 onward, clear evidences of Augustinianism surfaced in Luther's writings. Signs of his Augustinian orientation emerge in a letter written to a friend, John Lang, a lecturer at Erfurt. Wrote Luther:

> Our theology and St. Augustine are progressing well, and with God's help rule at our University. Aristotle is gradually falling from his throne, and his final doom is only a matter of time. It is amazing how the lectures on the *Sentences* are disdained. Indeed no one can expect to have any students if he does not want to teach this theology, that is, lecture on the Bible or on St. Augustine.[4]

As one turns to Luther's writings, he confronts a volume of material that is little short of overwhelming. In addition, one is struck by the heterogeneous character of the literature. Seldom does Luther treat a given subject in systematic fashion. One theme that is thoroughly foundational in Luther is his teaching on the two kingdoms. Luther's two-kingdom doctrine is similar to Augustine's doctrine of the two cities—viz., the city of God and the city of the devil. The whole of the Reformer's thought builds on the fundamental dualism between the earthly and the heavenly kingdoms. "The first kingdom," argues the Reformer, "is a kingdom of the devil."[5] A fundamental falsification of the kingdom of God, the earthly kingdom is the realm of human autonomy, darkness, disobedience and wrath. The heavenly kingdom, in sharp contrast, is the domain of the free and sovereign God. The latter is the realm of truth, righteousness, peace, love, and every other virtue. The disparate character of the earthly and heavenly kingdoms prompts Luther to postulate the existence of a chasm between man's natural groping for God and God's supernatural disclosure to man. The sinful creature's quest for the Creator is a futile venture. When sinful inhabitants of the earthly kingdom attempt to apprehend by natural means the divine Majesty who dwells in the heavenly kingdom, they "exert themselves to ascend to heaven without ladders."[6] Knowledge of God originates from the kingdom of heaven, not from the kingdom of earth. Luther underscores the fact that all knowledge of God, be it natural or supernatural, *in toto* is God-given.

Luther's General Knowledge of God   In his Galatians commentary, Luther lays down the all-important prinicple that there is a twofold knowledge of God—general (*generalis*) and particular or proper (*propria*). Concerning the former, Luther explains that "all men have the general knowledge, namely that God is, that He has created heaven and earth, that He is just, that He punishes the wicked, etc."[7] On the other hand, particular or saving knowledge comes only through faith in Christ and the gospel. The Reformer used several striking antitheses to underscore the chasm that there is between these two kinds of knowledge. The contrast between general and particular forms of knowing is described as a difference between "legal knowledge" and "evangelical knowledge." Underlying the latter pair of terms is Luther's famed distinction between law and grace and the deadly enmity that exists between these two proposed routes to God. Legal knowledge is a knowledge of God sought on the basis of human works and achievements. This knowledge is legal because it chiefly informs man of his obligations to a just God. As we will observe, Luther placed all philosophical quests for God in the category of legal knowledge. Evangelical knowledge, on the other hand, is a knowledge that proceeds from the gospel and from grace. This knowledge is evangelical because it informs man of the saving work that God has freely accomplished on his behalf. Evangelical knowledge is a gift of God that leads to eternal life.

Luther contends that legal knowledge, such as is sought by philosophers, is "left-handed" knowledge. This kind of theoretical knowledge is incomplete; it speaks in a vague tongue. In short, it cannot save. Evangelical knowledge, on the other hand, gained from God's self-disclosure in Scripture and Christ, is "right-handed" knowledge.[8] It alone affords an authentic knowledge of God's purpose and will. "The proper way to acquire knowledge of God," Luther insists, "is the right-handed one."[9] But the two kinds of knowing are further described as "superficial" (*von aussen*) knowledge and "inside" (*von innen*) knowledge of God.[10] Only the knowledge revealed from heaven and set forth in the Evangel penetrates to the innermost depths of God's being and purpose.

Luther's primary thesis is that all people possess a general knowledge of the Creator-God. Following the aprioristic system of Augustine, Luther held that the general knowledge of God, which consists of conceptual notions of the divine Being, is immediately "seen" by the minds of all men. All people, therefore, "have had the truth of God."[11] The fact that God exists and that He possesses certain characteristics is untaught and universal. Moreover, this a priori conviction cannot be eradicated from man's breast. "This light and understanding is in the hearts of all men and can be neither suppressed nor put out."[12] This immediate form of knowledge is grounded in God's special creation and preservation of man in His own image. Since a remnant of the *imago Dei* remains intact subsequent to the Fall, man is capable of intuiting the reality of God from the data both external world of nature and of his own internal world.[13]

Luther argues that the existence of idolatry is proof of the fact that all people possess an intuitive knowledge of God. The fact that pagan religions venerate various gods proves that people everywhere possess an intuitive knowledge of a supreme Being—a knowledge that cannot be erased. "How," Luther asks, "could they call an image or any other created thing God, or how could they believe that it resembled Him if they did not know at all what God is and what pertains to Him?"[14] In support of his position, Luther in his commentary on Jonah 1:5 appeals to the response of the pagan mariners in the turbulent storm at sea. If the seafarers had been ignorant of the existence of a supreme Being capable of assistance in extremity, they would not have cried out to God nor urged Jonah to do the same. Luther concludes the matter by arguing that "such a light and such a perception is innate in the hearts of all people; and this light cannot be subdued or extinguished."[15]

General knowledge of God is mediated by a further a priori factor, namely, the divine law that is inscribed on men's hearts. The moral law is so indelibly written in the human constitution that the heathen, both learned and unlearned, recognize God through conscience's compelling witness to right and wrong. As a result, Luther can say the following about the heathen who have not been blessed with the Word of God: "They are all acquainted with the law of nature. The Gentiles are all aware that murder, adultery, theft, cursing, lying, deceit, and blasphemy are all wrong. They are not so stupid that they do not know very well that there is a God who punishes such vices."[16] Notwithstanding the denial of atheists, all people actually know God in a general way. Those who explicitly reject the existence of God implicitly acknowledge His reality when they speak of moral obligation, duty, or right and wrong.

But Luther adds that man gains a knowledge of God through certain a posteriori factors; namely, through the things that God has made. The fact that general knowledge is not saving knowledge does not mean that man acquires no knowledge at all from the cosmos. To the contrary, in his exposition of Romans 1, the Reformer insists that God is known in certain respects from the works of His hands. In a comment on Genesis 1:2, Luther writes, "God . . . does not manifest Himself except through His works and the Word. . . . Whatever else belongs essentially to the Divinity cannot be grasped and understood."[17] Thus Luther argues that from the created order and the divine operation in history, natural man concludes not only that God created and sustains the space-time universe, but also that He is "invisible, immortal, powerful, wise, just, and gracious to those who call upon Him."[18] There is no mistaking the apostle's teaching: All people possess a valid natural knowledge of God by virtue of the divine self-disclosure in man's universe. "People, if they would only use their understanding beyond what their senses show them, could easily recognize God."[19] The very fact that the entire world is held accountable before God is explicable only on the supposition that a rudimentary knowledge of God is the possession of all people. Luther, however, nowhere defines the precise manner in which the general knowledge of God is acquired from the space-time order. Given, as we shall see, Luther's polemic against scholastic philosophical quests for God, we should perhaps limit ourselves to the conclusion that ideas about God are formed in man's mind as he confronts the reality of God in nature and history.[20] For Luther, God in the soul is of greater potency than the light of God in nature.

But sufficiently clear is the universal light of God that people would be saved if they responded to it with a positive heart.[21] Yet tragically sinners have turned their backs on this general knowledge of the Creator-God and have blindly worshiped figments of their own imagination. In the darkness of their minds and the stubbornness of their wills, fallen man perverts this elemental knowledge of God into unspeakable idolatry. In the day of judgment, no one can object that adequate opportunity had not been given to know God and His moral demands. Nothing but man's stubborn refusal to have God stands in the way of life. Thus whereas Luther's general knowledge is not gospel knowledge, it nevertheless involves an adequate elemental knowledge of the divine Reality.

Notwithstanding Luther's clear affirmation that a general knowledge of God is attainable from His works, the Reformer had many harsh things to say about proud reason and philosophical speculation. Luther, in fact, differentiated between three kinds of reason. *Natural* reason, ruling in its appointed domain, the earthly kingdom, is a serviceable gift from God. Man's possession of reason differentiates him from the beasts. Natural reason performs valid mundane tasks that facilitate the orderly conduct of temporal affairs. It competently manages households, builds cities, and governs in civil matters. Likewise, *regenerate* reason in a faithful, Spirit-filled person "is a fair and glorious instrument,"[22] particularly as it interprets the data of divine revelation. God expects Christians to use their sanctified minds in the service of the heavenly kingdom.

On the other hand, Luther describes *arrogant* reason, which attempts to usurp the function of faith in the heavenly kingdom, as "blind and poor,"[23] as "Frau Hulda"—the personification of subtle cunning—and as the "arch-prostitute and Devil's bride."[24] The Reformer countered medieval Scholasticism's high view of human nature with the assertion that through Edenic disobedience man's faculties became so corrupted with satanic venom that he no longer can see God as God. Thus Luther could say of man's condition: "All our faculties today are leprous, indeed dull and utterly dead."[25] In matters pertaining to the heavenly kingdom, unregenerate reason dwells in irrevocable darkness. It is so blind that even when it discerns God's existence, it knows nothing of His will toward us. On the one hand, Luther's severe statements decrying natural reason should be regarded as characteristic overstatements uttered in the heat of his polemic against Rome. For as we have seen, man legitimately employs his cognitive faculty in drawing conclusions about God from created effects. In the second place, by such statements Luther warns that when reason tries to supplant faith in matters evangelical, it leads to man's usurpation of the place of God. Luther has no quarrel with reason as such; but he does protest man's proud and arrogant misuse of this God-given gift.

In addition, Luther waxes adamant that philosophical speculation fails to rise to evangelical knowledge of the living God. The God behind nature and history, the God who decrees all that comes to pass, is the transcendently hidden God (*Deus absconditus*). The human mind cannot adequately comprehend the divine majesty. Philosophers engage in speculative disputations that produce a kind of knowledge. But that which lies at the end of their quest is a primal Power, primal Substance, or primal Spirit. The propositions of the philosophers have nothing to do with the loving God who meets man at the level of his fear, guilt, and rebellion. The philosophic schemes of the Neoplatonists are too abstract, too theoretical, and too impersonal to satisfy human needs. Luther boldly likened Plato's metaphysical thinking to a disinterested cow's staring at a new gate.[26] He spoke disparagingly of medieval cosmological and teleological speculation as "sickly" and "weak."[27] Speculative philosophy only facilitates the cause of human egocentricity. From these brief remarks it should be clear that Luther allowed no opening for a speculative natural theology independent of divine revelation. As he put it, "You must disabuse your mind completely of all speculation and investigation into the majesty of God."[28] Valid knowledge of God is given only by God Himself. Again, "Spurn all speculation about the divine Majesty; for whoever investigates the majesty of God will be consumed by His glory. I know from experience what I am talking about. After all did not God say to Moses, 'Man shall not see me and live'? (Exod. 33:20)."[29] If the true focus of theology deals with the issues of guilt, grace, and redemption, all attempts to create a speculative natural theology, or a "theology of glory," must be judged a failure. There is no possible way that man can ascend to heaven and directly investigate the majesty of God.

From this disgression on reason and philosophical speculation, we return to Luther's twofold scheme of knowledge. General or natural knowledge of God, as we have noted, involves a rudimentary understanding of His existence and character. But in the mind of the Reformer general knowledge suffers at least two significant defects. First, reason acknowledges that the powerful, all-knowing God is capable of rendering aid; but it provides no assurance that God is actually disposed to render such assistance to *me* personally. "Reason believes in God's might and is aware of it, but it is uncertain whether God is willing to employ this on our behalf."[30] Given the existence of evil and suffering in the world, natural reason left to itself continually questions God's intention to help. In the second place, revelation's natural light affords a knowledge that is abstract and impersonal, rather than immediate, practical, and experiential. "Reason . . . knows that there is a God, but it does not know who or which is the true God."[31] Luther goes on to say that reason plays blindman's buff with God. It reaches out to grasp God but misses Him, seizing instead a dream fabricated by the devil. Thus Luther insists, "There is a vast difference between knowing that there is a God and knowing who or what God is. Nature knows the former—it is inscribed in everybody's heart; the latter is taught only by the Holy Spirit."[32]

In short, the general knowledge of God amounts to "sniffing the existence of God without tasting it."[33] It knows that a supreme, powerful, and wise Being exists, but it is ignorant of His will.

Luther's Particular Knowledge of God   Luther, therefore, turns from the general, propaedeutic knowledge of God to that particular knowledge granted by the Word and the Spirit. Proper, or redemptive, knowledge is that which is mediated through Christ, the supreme revelation of God. The transcendent and majestic God comes to man humanly in the flesh of His own Son. "I avoid all speculations about the Divine Majesty and take my stand in the humanity of Christ."[34] For Luther, Christ crucified is the beginning of true knowledge. Only the suffering Savior discloses God's gracious intentions toward us. "It is no good to recognize God in his glory and majesty unless [one] recognize him in the humility and shame of the cross."[35] Hence the philosopher's "theology of glory" must give way to the Bible's "theology of the cross." The Cross marks the end of all speculation about the invisible nature of God. Plainly, then, in Luther's biblical vision, a saving and reconciling knowledge of God is gained only by dependence on Christ. "Life resides exclusively in the grace and truth of the dear Son of God, our Lord Jesus Christ, and only he who remains in Him Knows God."[36] God displayed in Christ is the central and all-controlling theme of Luther, the evangelical churchman and theologian.

Through the light of the soul and of nature, people may learn of God's existence and character; but only through Christ is God known as Savior. Articles of gospel truth such as the Trinity, Incarnation, and Atonement lie beyond the reach of reason's natural light. Reason may lead to monotheism, but only the faith reception of Christ will lead a person to a Trinitarian faith.

> What mortal has ever discovered or fathomed the truth that the three persons in the eternal divine essence are one God; that the second person, the Son of God, was obliged to become man, born of a virgin; and that no way of life could be opened for us, save through his crucifixion? Such truths never would have been heard . . . learned and believed, had not God Himself revealed it.[37]

As night is different from day, so is the general light of nature and conscience different from the wisdom of the Cross. Moreover, according to Luther, particular knowledge of God in Jesus Christ does not supplement general knowledge; rather, the knowledge of God in Christ is the very beginning of true knowledge.

Plainly, Luther has set forth a rigorously Christocentric theology that upholds the exclusiveness of Jesus Christ for salvation. "Any saving knowledge of God . . . can come only by taking hold of Christ, who, by the will of the Father, has given Himself unto death for our sins."[38] Where Christ is not honored in the heart, God is not redemptively known. For Luther, then, Jesus Christ is everything. "Outside of Christ there is no basis on which we can pray, hope, be religious, or live."[39] Emphatically and categorically

Luther reiterates that "there is no salvation or knowledge of God outside of Christ."[40]

Luther was a keen student of world religions, with special interest in Islam. But there is not a shadow of doubt in Luther's mind that Christianity is the only valid religion. The world's non-Christian religions represent distortions of the one true faith and thus properly are an abomination to God. "To seek God outside Jesus is [the work of] the Devil."[41] In their rejection of the gospel, "All the religions of all the nations . . . are absolutely nothing."[42] In a comment on Galatians 1:4, Luther describes the doctrine of salvation through Christ as "gunshot and artillery" with which "the papacy and all the religions of the heathen" must be destroyed.[43] Christ and the gospel pronounce the death of all human religion.

Under the rubric of general and particular knowledge of God, Luther articulated a fundamentally sound system of religious knowledge. His adoption of the Augustinian a priori as the starting point of knowledge of God is valid. Luther's distinction between "legal" and "evangelical" knowledge leaves no room for doubting that the preliminary knowledge of God gained by intuition, the implanted law, Creation, and history are not sufficient for the saving of the soul. His firm conviction that the highest form of knowledge is something personally appropriated and experienced was a necessary corrective to the more abstract approaches of medieval philosophy.

But in his reaction against the Thomistic nature-grace schema, whereby grace perfects nature, Luther failed to explicate adequately the propaedeutic function of the general knowledge of God. That is, he did not sufficiently unfold the positive service general revelation provides by laying the foundation for God's saving Word of address in the gospel. His handling of the matter, however, may be viewed as a deliberate emphasis of one side of the truth in order to demolish the unbridled optimism of philosophical contemporaries who insisted that man could come to God savingly on his own.

Moreover, from the point of view of a complete philosophy, one might wish that Luther had stated more clearly his theory of knowledge as it relates to how God is perceived from His created effects. But Paul primarily focuses on the results, while not explicitly delineating the precise means by which knowledge of God is gained from general revelation. The fact is that Luther's reaction against the philosophical speculation of Neoplatonists and medieval scholastics prompted him to stress the warmly personal and redemptive knowledge of God displayed in Christ and to pay less attention to the preliminary knowledge afforded by the natural order. An understanding of the polemical situation in which Luther found himself thus clarifies the somewhat one-sided development of the Reformer.

Calvin on Knowledge of God as Creator

The towering figure of Reformation theology is John Calvin (1509–64), the French theologian and Genevan reformer. As a humanist scholar, Calvin studied law and literature, but following his conversion about 1530 he renounced all secular pursuits and devoted himself entirely to the service of God. Calvin's chief contributions to theological science are enshrined in his biblical commentaries and in his life's work, the *Institutes of the Christian Religion*. As a systematic exposition of Christian doctrine, the latter work remains the classic formulation of Reformed theology. Melanchthon identified Paul as "the apostle," Thomas Aquinas as "the philosopher," and John Calvin as "the theologian." Many would agree that Calvin stands out as the premier theologian in the history of the church. The main outlines of Calvin's theology were drawn from the aprioristic scheme of Augustine, while considerable agreement also exists between the Genevan Reformer and his older contemporary Martin Luther on the subject of revelation and the knowability of God.

Toward the beginning of the *Institutes*, Calvin makes the point that all knowledge of God is revealed. Everything that man knows about God, the world, and his own self flows from the eternal Fount of knowledge. As Calvin writes, "Not a particle of light, or wisdom, or justice, or power, or rectitude, or genuine truth, will anywhere be found, which does not flow from him, and of which he is not the cause."[44]

Calvin then proceeds to argue that people possess two kinds of religious knowledge—a knowledge of God as Creator and a knowledge of God as Redeemer. God may be known as Creator by general and special revelation, whereas He is known as Redeemer only via special revelation. God, in fact, gives general revelation for two purposes: (1) that people everywhere might worship Him and (2) that all might be provided with the hope of eternal life.[45] Calvin continues by saying that God as Creator is universally known through two categories of general revelation, one of which is internal and the other external. Internal knowledge of God, in Calvin's view, is that knowledge with which man created in the *imago Dei* is naturally endowed. Independent of sense data from the external world and the cause-effect relation in nature, the creature rationally intuits the reality of the divine Being. Related to God on the basis of the divine *imago* and enabled by common grace, man the creature possesses an immediate effable apprehension of God the Creator.

This intuitional knowledge of God is inextricably linked with the knowledge of ourselves. As Calvin writes in the opening paragraph of the *Institutes*, "Our wisdom . . . consists almost entirely of two parts: the knowledge of God and of ourselves."[46] Man created in the image of God cannot reflect on his own existence without being led to a contemplation of God upon whom his life is dependent. Calvin's point is that consciousness of the human self involves consciousness of God. Thus Calvin writes, "No man can survey himself without forthwith turning his thoughts toward the God in whom he lives and moves; because it is perfectly obvious, that the endowments which we possess cannot possibly be from ourselves; nay, that our very being is nothing else than subsistence in God alone."[47] Since man is created in the *imago Dei* and is sustained by God in the rationality of his soul, knowledge of human finitude prompts remembrance of God's infinite perfections. For example, consciousness of one's unhappiness reminds us of the divine felicity. Likewise, consciousness of personal ignorance, weakness, and corruption promotes the memory of the divine wisdom, strength, and righteousness. "We are accordingly urged by our own evil things to consider the good things of God."[48] Knowledge of oneself shaped in the image of God thus leads to a cognitive understanding of the reality and character of God.

Calvin attributes the instinctive knowledge engraved in the human heart to the universally diffused light of the Logos. Here the reformer follows Augustine's theory of a divine general illumination of mankind by the Word. In his commentary on John 1:9, Calvin refers to the universal divine illumination by which man created in the *imago Dei* is brought into immediate knowing relation to the living God. "Men, above all other living beings, have the singular superiority of having been endowed with reason and intelligence, and that they have engraved in their conscience the ability to discriminate between right and wrong. There is no one therefore who is without some intuition of the eternal light."[49]

Calvin further defines this constitutional knowledge afforded by the divine light as the "sense of divinity," or "sense of Deity." He argues, "That there exists in the human mind, and indeed by natural instinct, some sense of Deity, we hold to be beyond dispute."[50] The direct, cognitive consciousness of the Creator-God is not gained by ratiocination but is an intuition possessed by man as man. It constitutes an insight or an immediate apprehension that arises from an impulse implanted in man's heart at the time of Creation. "All men of sound judgment will therefore hold, that a sense of Deity is indelibly engraven on the human heart. And ... this belief is naturally engendered in all, and thoroughly fixed as it were in our bones."[51] Although dimmed by sin, this rational intuition of Deity can never be completely eradicated.[52]

That mankind is universally endowed with a sense of Deity is confirmed by the global reality of what Calvin called the "seed of religion" or "religious propensity."[53] Throughout the entire world, one finds a servile fear of the Almighty, a troubled conscience, the worship of a God (or gods), and the practice of various religious rites. The existence of pagan religion and idolatry affords clear evidence that God has graciously sown the seed of religion in people's hearts.[54] Because man is universally endowed with a sense of Deity, "there is no nation so barbarous, no race so brutish, as not to be imbued with the conviction that there is a God. Even those who, in other respects, seem to differ least from the lower animals constantly retain some sense of religion."[55]

The light that illumines man in the fallen condition includes, in addition, the universal endowment of conscience. Calvin describes conscience as the inner witness to the moral law of God inscribed ages ago on the two tables of stone.[56] Conscience bears silent testimony to the ethical character of God, distinguishes between good and evil, and reminds man of his duty to God. When people fail to worship and honor God in keeping with their inner sense of Deity, "the worm of conscience, keener than burning steel, gnaws them within."[57] Thus given the instinctive sense of divinity and the endowment of conscience, no one can justly plead ignorance. All people know that there is a righteous God of truth and that He requires honor, worship, and moral obedience.[58] The point needs to be underscored that Calvin posits the whole scope of internal knowledge—i.e., the sense of divinity and conscience—under the heading of universal general revelation. The Reformer thus sides with the apostle Paul that all men in elementary fashion actually know God within.

To the universal internal revelation detailed above, God has added an external revelation in nature, the frame of man, and providence. Calvin thus argues that God is known not only intuitively through the sense of Deity and the conscience but also inferentially through His works in the space-time world.

Calvin describes the heavens and the earth, the first modality of external general revelation, as a mirror in which the invisible God is reflected,[59] and as a beautiful and glorious theater in which His handiwork is openly displayed.[60] The celestial bodies in the precision and regularity of their courses are lucid preachers of the glory of God.[61] The heavens form an open book in which all may read of the divine Reality.[62] Hence Calvin can say that God was pleased "to manifest his perfections in the whole structure of the universe, and daily place himself in our view, that we cannot open our eyes without being compelled to behold him."[63] Moreover, "even wicked men are forced, by the mere view of the earth and sky, to rise to the Creator."[64] But what specifically is known of God from the majestic cosmic display? Not merely God's existence, but also as the apostle teaches, God's "invisible qualities—his eternal power and divine nature." Reaffirming his thesis of the indivisibility of the divine existence and essence, Calvin adds that "the divinity cannot exist except accompanied with all the attributes of God, since they are all included under that idea."[65] Although the divine essence is incomprehensible, God's existence and a wide range of divine perfections—including His eternity, power, wisdom, righteousness, goodness, mercy, truth, justice, and judgment are displayed in the universe.[66] Hence he who has eyes to behold the beauty and majesty of the created order can in no wise feign ignorance of God. Man thus knows God from the works of Creation.

But Calvin insists that God reveals Himself through a second external modality namely, through "the structure of the human frame."[67] If the first modality is cosmological in character, the second is broadly teleological. Man made in the divine *imago*, and thus possessing a formal likeness to God, is a microcosm (miniature world) of the divine Reality. In the human body and its interconnected members—particularly in its utility and beauty—the power, wisdom, and goodness of God are reflected. People thus "have in their own persons a factory where innumerable operations of God are carried on, and a magazine stored with treasures of inestimable value."[68] Persons, therefore, find God a hundred times over in their bodies as well as in their souls. "All men acknowledge that the human body bears on its face such proofs of ingenious contrivance as are sufficient to proclaim the admirable wisdom of its Maker."[69] So clear and numerous are these evidences of the Godhead from the structure of man that one need go no farther than himself to discover God.

But if further light were needed, God's perfections are clearly displayed through His providential workings in the world. In his commentary on Acts 14, Calvin argues that the watering of the earth with rain, the heat and light provided by the sun, and the fructification of the soil are compelling evidences for the existence of the Deity who wisely and mercifully governs all things.[70] God graciously sustains, cherishes, and superintends all that He has made. In particular, a pattern of moral discrimination emerges in the divine providential working in the world. God so arranges the course of fortuitous events that the righteous become the special objects of His favor and the wicked the objects of His severity. In Calvin's theodicy, innocence is avenged and crimes are punished.[71] The righteous are marvelously protected and comforted by a loving hand. Hence Calvin argues, "He takes care of the whole human race, but is especially vigilant in governing the church, which he favors with a closer inspection."[72] Thus through the wise and beneficent governance of the world, the power, goodness, and justice of God are plainly manifested to all men.

In sum, we see that in Calvin's scheme of general revelation a divine external disclosure in nature, man, and providence is added to the internal disclosure through the sense of divinity and conscience. Through general illumination, the knowledge content afforded by the latter is intuited, whereas the former is rationally inferred. Warfield seems to agree with this summation, claiming that Calvin holds to "the postulation of an innate knowledge of God in man, quickened and developed by a very rich manifestation of God in nature and providence."[73] From the several modalities of general revelation, Calvin maintains that man in truth acquires a rudimentary knowledge of God as Creator, Preserver, and Governor of the universe. It is difficult, then, to refute the fact that Calvin has built a solid case in support of the position that natural man universally knows God in a valid, albeit rudimentary, way.

But Calvin continues that the knowledge of God as Creator afforded by general revelation does not result in piety and true religion, for in man the sinner it is crippled by weakness and corrupted by insolence. The fact that redemptive knowledge is not attained from nature, conscience, or history is not a fault of God, who has initiated a valid self-disclosure, or of the revelation, which is sufficiently clear, but of man who is dull and perverse. Between the countless bright lamps exhibited in the Creation and the soul of man stands the stark reality of the Fall. As Calvin insists, "In regard to true knowledge of him, all are so degenerate, that in no part of the world can genuine godliness be found."[74]

General revelation fails to accomplish its purpose of producing worship of God and true piety, first, because the sinful man is afflicted with disability due to sin's corruption of his cognitive faculties. Calvin repeatedly emphasizes the human mind's inability to know God savingly by virtue of the sin factor. Because the fallen mind is clouded by sin, the sinner is not capable of rising to that pure and clear knowledge of God which saves.[75] With respect to evangelical knowledge, Calvin boldly insists that even the most brilliant sinners are "blinder than moles."[76] Calvin adds, "So great is our stupidity, so dull are we in regard to these bright manifestations, that we derive no benefit from them."[77] Contemplating redemptive knowledge rather than rudimentary knowledge of God's existence and character, Calvin writes, "In vain for us, therefore, does the Creation exhibit so many bright lamps lighted up to show forth the glory of its Author. Though they beam upon us from every quarter, they are altogether insufficient of themselves to lead us on the *right path*" (italics added).[78] In the same vein, Calvin in his Ephesians commentary remarks, "With respect to the kingdom of God and all that relates to the spiritual life, the light of human reason differs little from darkness; for, before it has pointed out the road, it is extinguished; and its power of perception is little else than blindness."[79] Since the fallen mind is incapable of gaining from general revelation the full knowledge that God intended, a more complete and objective revelation is mandated. Thus Calvin adds, "If we aspire in earnest to a genuine contemplation of God, we must go, I say, to the Word, where the character of God, drawn from his works, is described accurately and to the life."[80]

In the second place, general revelation fails to produce true piety because of the insolence that flows from the sinner's corrupted heart. Fallen man's blindness, Calvin argues, is invariably accompanied by vain pride, stubbornness, and evil intentions. Instead of cultivating the seed of the knowledge of God and allowing it to bear the fruit of godliness, sinful man rebels against it and tramples it underfoot. Calvin thus writes, "We see many, after they have become hardened in a daring course of sin, madly banishing all remembrance of God, though spontaneously suggested to them from within, by natural sense."[81] Again referring to sinful humanity, Calvin asserts, "No sooner do we, from a survey of the world, obtain some slight knowledge of Deity, than we pass by the true God, and set up in his stead the dream and phantom of our own brain, drawing away the praise of justice, wisdom, and goodness from the fountain head, and transferring it to some other quarter."[82]

For Calvin, the condition of the soul—intellect, sensibility, and will—is determinative of the suppression and corruption of the natural knowledge of God. Had man remained in his original unfallen condition, he would not have failed to know God savingly from His works. But with the entry of sin, man's affections are now ranged against God, and his attitude is one of determined hostility to Him. Fallen man refuses to allow God to rule over him and thus insolently banishes every thought of God from his mind. But man's rejection of the rudimentary knowledge of God afforded by general revelation manifests itself in horrendous degradation and corruption. Sinful man turns his back on the living God of heaven and in the delusion of his mind fashions lifeless idols of wood and stone. "Like water gushing forth from a large and copious spring, immense crowds of gods have issued from the human mind, every man giving himself full license, and devising some peculiar form of divinity, to meet his own views."[83] But the dark and depraved end to which man has sunk ought not blind us to the fact that in Calvin's mind the sinner, in fact, possesses a knowledge of God as Creator, albeit a knowledge that is partial and distorted. From internal and external sources, natural mans knows that there is a God and that He bears certain defining characteristics. As Henry observes, "Calvin assuredly holds that, entirely apart from the biblical revelation, man still has genuine, limited albeit privately distorted knowledge of God."[84]

By refusing to cultivate the knowledge of God as Creator, man has become judicially guilty before the bar of divine justice.[85] In distorting the divine self-disclosure and substituting monstrous fictions for the true and living God, the sinner is left in a position of responsibility before the Judge of the universe. Ignorance of the supreme Being cannot be pleaded. Excuses of inadequate light cannot be proferred. Soberly Calvin concludes, "Man must bear the guilt of corrupting the seed of divine knowledge so wondrously deposited in his mind, and preventing it from bearing good and genuine fruit."[86]

Calvin on Knowledge of God as Redeemer   Since nature within man and nature without has failed to produce an evangelical knowledge of God, a new help in the form of special grace was mandated. Thus the Reformer argues that not ineffectually God "added the light of his Word in order that he might make himself known unto salvation."[87] Only God's special revelation in Scripture leads to "right and sound doctrine" and to "true religion."[88] Scripture, in Calvin's scheme, serves a twofold function. First, the written Word facilitates a fuller knowledge of God by clarifying the data of general revelation. Nature in its cursed condition occasionally miscommunicates information. The propositional revelation of Scripture provides the necessary clarification of nature's testimony, which is garbled at its source. Moreover, at the subjective level Scripture clears away the mist of those confused notions of God that lay embedded in the sinner's sluggish mind. "Scripture, gathering together the impressions of Deity, which till then, lay confused in their minds, dissipates the darkness and shows us the true God clearly."[89] Through this dual clarifying work of Scripture, God is known more clearly and fully as the Creator and Architect of the universe.

But Scripture performs a second essential work, namely, supplementing the limited knowledge content of general revelation. Calvin insists that from nature we can know the hands and feet of God but not His heart.[90] The Word of God discloses to us those otherwise unknowable parameters of the divine plan that pertain to salvation—including the Trinity, Incarnation, Atonement, and Resurrection. For this reason Calvin could write, "If true religion is to beam upon us, our principle must be, that it is necessary to begin with heavenly teaching, and that it is impossible for any man to attain even the minutest portion of right and sound doctrine without being a disciple of Scripture."[91] In Calvin's mind, Scripture was given that God might be known not only as Creator but also as Redeemer: "To the first knowledge was afterwards added the more intimate knowledge which alone quickens dead souls, and by which God is known, not only as the Creator of the world, and the sole author and disposer of all events, but also as a Redeemer, in the person of the Mediator."[92]

In dealing with knowledge of God as Redeemer, Calvin attaches great importance to the supernatural illumination of the Holy Spirit. The Spirit enables the sinner to grasp the meaning of special revelation and provides subjective assurance of the truth. Through the Spirit's internal testimony to the truth of the Word, the knowledge of God for salvation is mediated to the soul.[93] Moreover, Calvin adds, "The special grace of Holy Spirit illumination of the Word God bestows on his elect only, whom he separates from the rest of mankind."[94] In sum, "The only true faith is that which the Spirit of God seals on our hearts."[95] The objective Word of divine revelation and the subjective operation of Holy Spirit illumination work together to mediate to man the saving knowledge of God.

Calvin's distinction between knowledge of God as Creator and knowledge of God as Redeemer may be viewed from another angle. Evangelical knowledge, or knowledge of God as Redeemer, is not the naked conviction that a supreme Being exists and that He bears certain defining characteristics. To be sure, for the Reformer *what* God is cannot be separated from the fact *that* God is.[96] But the knowledge Calvin talks about is the perception that "God our Maker supports us by his power, rules us by his providence, fosters us by his goodness, and visits us with all kinds of blessings."[97] In short, it is a knowledge that bears fruit in true religion or piety. In Calvin's own words, "the knowledge of God which we are invited to cultivate is not that which, resting with empty speculations, only flutters in the brain, but a knowledge which will prove substantial and fruitful wherever it is duly perceived, and rooted in the heart."[98] Calvin's knowledge, in fact, is *notitia*—that warmly personal religious knowledge that culminates in worship. According to Dowey, "It is a material and existential concept describing an actual, vital knowing relationship of the human mind with God."[99] Evangelical knowledge, far from being disinterested knowledge, involves reverence, trust, and submission to the authority of the reconciling God.

But the ultimate object of God's special disclosure to the sinful race is Jesus Christ. The Son, who was sent from the Father on an errand of saving mercy, intelligently communicates the fullest knowledge of God and His redemptive purposes. Calvin unmistakably limits saving knowledge of God to those who have put their trust in Christ, the wisdom of God. In this sense, he insists that "there is no having knowledge of God without Christ."[100] "Whoever aspires to know God, and does not begin with Christ, must wander, as it were, in a labyrinth."[101] God is savingly found nowhere except in His self-disclosure through the Son. Thus "God himself would remain far off, concealed from us, were we not illumined by the brightness of Christ."[102] Calvin is most explicit that Christ is the only way whereby mankind comes to God on an intimate basis.

Predictably, Calvin was highly critical of all non-Christian systems. The polytheistic indigenous religions have arisen from man's depraved corruption of God's universal general revelation. The idols of the primitive peoples represent the substitution of "monstrous fictions for the one living and true God."[103] The world's historic religions, which claim knowledge of God while rejecting Christ, wallow in the delusion of their numerous errors. Said Calvin of the non-Christian religions:

> Not holding the head, that is, Christ, their knowledge of God was evanescent; and hence they at length fell away to gross and foul superstitions, betraying their ignorance, just as the Turks in the present day, who, though proclaiming, with full throat, that the Creator of heaven and earth is their God, yet by their rejection of Christ, substitute an idol in his place.[104]

The Samaritan religion, which Calvin judges the closest non-Christian system to true piety, nevertheless was "deluded by vain errors."[105] In his commentary on Acts 17, Calvin spared few words in denouncing heathendom and unbelief. The non-Christian systems "wander and err in darkness like blind men" (v. 22), "they apprehend vain shadows and ghosts instead of God" (v. 24), they follow "wicked and perverse rites" (v. 16), and their adherents are "altogether blockish and brutish" (v. 16). Calvin contemplates the whole of non-Christian religion as bewitched and seduced by the devil. Muslims, Jews, and papists claim to know God, but they are ignorant of the truth that saves.[106]

The Debate Over Calvin Reexamined

Calvin, as we have noted, subscribes to the a priori scheme of Augustine, which postulates that from the first moment of mental and moral self-consciousness man created in the image of God effably intuits the reality of God. Moreover, he argues that from the revelation embedded in Creation and providence further truths about God's existence and character are rationally inferred. Thus Calvin has argued correctly that on the basis of general revelation, which is both internal and external to himself, man universally knows God as Creator, Preserver, and Judge. But Calvin rightly adds that by virtue of the sinner's cognitive inability and moral hostility to God, such elemental knowledge does not develop into the full flower of piety and true religion. Sinful man, in the deceitfulness of his heart and the stubbornness of his will, tramples the remembrance of God underfoot and asserts his own ultimacy. Consequently, general revelation fails to mediate a knowledge of God that saves the soul. To secure this highest good, God provided further light in the form of an objective supernatural revelation in Scripture and a supernatural illumination of the Holy Spirit. As an evangelical theologian committed to the primacy of Scripture, Calvin rightfully insisted that apart from Jesus Christ no one attains a saving relationship with the Lord of heaven.

Whereas few competent authorities dispute Calvin's teaching that salvation is mediated only through Christ and the message of Scripture, not a few dispute the claim that Calvin taught an actual knowledge of God on the basis of general revelation. Neoorthodox theologians, such as Barth, Bonhoeffer, and Dowey, as well as those who are orthodox, such as Berkouwer, Clark, and Van Til, claim Calvin never taught that fallen man gains actual knowledge of God from general revelation. In one way or another, the above argue that in the case of sinful man knowledge of God mediated by general revelation is unreal or untrue. The Fall vitiates the possibility of natural knowledge of God in sinful man. One cannot, indeed, deny that Calvin made several (perhaps even many) statements on the subject of natural theology that were more negative than those advanced, say, by Thomas Aquinas. The apparent inconsistency between Calvin's claim that all men know God as Creator from general revelation and occasional pessimistic statements on the subject is greatly relieved by a careful examination of the facts. Statements by Calvin that allegedly deny natural man's acquisition of valid knowledge of God from general revelation fit in three main categories.

First, certain statements of Calvin were intended to oppose the conjectural speculation of scholastic natural theology. Thus Calvin argued that knowledge of God is not achieved by the fruitless and "frigid speculations of the philosophers and scholastic theologians."[107] The way of rational ascent, as opposed to the way of revelational descent, offers no certain route to God. All human knowing must be predicated on the prior reality of supernatural revelation. Only as man is enveloped by the divine self-disclosure is he capable of apprehending truth. Moreover, following Luther, Calvin opposed the confident empiricism of the Thomistic tradition, which failed to give a large place to a rational knowledge of God in human self-consciousness (the religious a priori). Calvin wanted no part of a proud natural theology that could be made to rival revealed theology and the gospel.

Second, many of Calvin's negative statements merely uphold reason's inability to effect *evangelical* or *saving* knowledge of God. Thus understood, he rightly refutes the saving utility of general revelation in the unredeemed. In this vein Calvin writes, "The human mind, through its weakness, was altogether unable to come to God."[108] Similarly, regarding sinners, Calvin writes, "By that guidance of their reason they do not come to God, and do not even approach to him; so that all their understanding is nothing else than mere vanity."[109] With a view to a saving relation, he comments, "It is undoubted that we with our senses and powers of understanding will never reach a true knowledge of God."[110] The burden of the preceding statements is more explicitly expressed in the following assertion: "The human mind, which thus errs in inquiring after God, is dull and blind in heavenly mysteries."[111] Calvin so stresses the debilitating effects of sin that one might be tempted to infer that he taught that natural man actually possesses no knowledge of God. But in most of these cases Calvin spoke of the impossibility of the sinner's gaining *saving* knowledge of God through his own fallen resources.

In the third place, Calvin occasionally made certain rhetorical outbursts in the heat of argument with his opponents that were never intended to serve as statements of doctrinal commitment. We might place in this category his inflated assertion that "the brightest manifestations of divine glory [in nature] finds not one genuine spectator amoung a hundred!"[112] Speaking of the hidden wisdom of God (1 Cor. 2:7), Calvin exclaims, "How great is the blindness of the human mind, which in the midst of light discerns nothing!"[113] In the same context he adds, "This world is like a theater, in which the Lord presents to us a clear manifestation of his glory, and yet, notwithstanding that we have such a spectacle placed before our eyes, we are stone blind!"[114] Surely Calvin did not believe that man created in the image of God and enabled by common grace is so blind as to preclude the possibility of any knowledge at all.

In sum, then, we conclude that Calvin taught (against Barth) that God has given a valid revelation of Himself in nature. Likewise, he taught (against numerous neoorthodox and orthodox authorities) that sinful man gains from general revelation a genuine, albeit partial and distorted, knowledge of God as Creator. If Calvin asserts that natural man gains from a survey of the world only "some slight knowledge of Deity,"[115] a knowledge that is no more than "a small flame,"[116] we interpret him as declaring that when compared with the Christian's full-orbed knowledge of God as Redeemer, the sinner's natural knowledge is indeed modest. For Calvin, partial knowledge of God is nevertheless *knowledge* of God. The fact that Calvin depicted special revelation in Scripture as a lens that enlarges the revelation in nature suggests that the primitive revelation, although dim, was nevertheless real and the resultant knowledge acquired true. However, the burden of Calvin's teaching is that when natural man acquired natural knowledge of God, he immediately moved to suppress that knowledge. Instead of cultivating the fundamental knowledge of God given in His works and humbly looking to God for additional light, man in the deceitfulness of his heart trampled the remembrance of God underfoot and asserted his own autonomy. Moreover, Calvin rightly recognizes that it is precisely on the basis of possession of natural knowledge of God as Creator that all people are accounted guilty before the throne of divine justice. Notwithstanding man's perverted response to general revelation, Calvin would be one of the first to protest the elimination of the natural knowledge of God from the church's theology.

GODLY WISDOM:
IV THE PURITAN CONTRIBUTION

Puritanism was a radical reform movement in sixteenth- and seventeenth-century England whose influence spilled over into eighteenth-century American religious life. The distinguished catalog of Puritans in the Old and New Worlds includes such figures as John Jewell (1522–1571), Cambridge tutor and Chaplain to Prince Charles; William Perkins (1558–1602), Fellow of Christ's College, Cambridge, and renowned preacher; Thomas Goodwin (1600–1679), Head of Magdalen College, Oxford, and later Congregationalist minister in London; Samuel Rutherford (1600–1661), Scottish scholar and delegate to the Westminister Assembly; Thomas Manton (1620–1677), minister of St. Paul's Church, London, and tireless preacher; John Owen (1616–1683), learned Congregationalist theologian, Chaplain to Cromwell, and head of Oxford University; Richard Baxter (1615–1691), Anglican pupil of Owen and minister of Kidderminister; Stephen Charnock (1628–1680), Chaplain and Fellow at Oxford; John Bunyon (1628–1688), Baptist author of *Pilgrim's Progress*; Samuel Willard (1640–1707), teacher at Old South Church, Boston, and acting President of Harvard College; Jonathan Edwards (1703–1758), powerful preacher and President of Princeton University; and Samuel Hopkins (1721–1803), pupil of Edwards and pastor in Massachusetts and Rhode Island.

In the main, the Puritans were articulate and forceful preachers whose ministry was shaped by a strong theological orientation. Frequently, the Puritan preacher held the office of teaching minister or "doctor," in which capacity he delivered learned lectures on biblical and theological themes. The Puritan teacher and preacher was a man of great intellectual power and burning zeal for God. His life was an exemplary synthesis of orthodox doctrine and practical divinty, of cool rationality and warm-hearted piety. The Puritans' dual emphasis on sound doctrine and practical godliness earned them the reputation of being "theologians of the Christian life."[1] Far from being abstract scholars, they stressed "practical exegesis"—the application of Scripture to Christian faith and living. The Puritans' writings are often weighty and learned, but always practical. In truth, the Puritans knew nothing of the separation of heart and head practiced in some sectors of contemporary conservative religion. True godliness was cultivated by the marriage of doctrinal truth and spiritual grace.

The Puritans were diligent and careful scholars, often endowed with immense erudition. Generally they were trained in Hebrew and Greek and were at home in the world of medieval philosophy, especially metaphysics and dialectics. They read the church fathers (e.g., Aquinas, Scotus, and Ockham) and often the writings of French, German, and Dutch divines. In addition, the Puritans were men of God with an unusual measure of dedication and single-mindedness of purpose. Richard Baxter once gave the following word of advice concerning marriage to his students: "So great are the matters of our studies and labours, requiring our total and most serious thoughts, that I earnestly advise all that can to live single."[2]

Although Puritanism included Anglicans, Presbyterians, Congregationalists, and Baptists, and thus displayed differences of polity, the movement otherwise was united in its main doctrinal emphases. The Puritans treasured the Bible as the Word of God and affirmed its absolute authority in all matters of doctrine and life. They were committed with few exceptions to the Augustinian-Reformed system of theology. They were profoundly conscious of the glory and majesty of God and the corruption and moral inability of fallen man. The Puritan preacher vigorously stressed the necessity of personal regeneration, justification, and sanctification by the Holy Spirit. They generally held to the triumph of the gospel on earth and the certain return of Christ to consummate the the present age. In outlook, the Puritans were serious-minded and methodical. Richard Rogers, a senior statesman of English Puritanism, was once accosted by a cautious "gentleman" who said to him, "Mr. Rogers, I like you and your company very well, only you are too precise." "O sir," replied Rogers, "I serve a precise God."[3] This simple incident reflects something of the spirit and genius of the Puritan movement.

On the issue of general revelation and the knowability of God, the Puritans largely were of one mind. We will see that they highly esteemed general revelation as a clear witness to the reality of God. They gave careful attention to the rational explication of natural evidences in response to the objections of atheists and other opponents of biblical theism. Nevertheless, in the tradition of Augustine, Luther, and Calvin they asserted the spiritual blindness and moral incapacity of the unregenerate sinner. Hence the redemptive initiative must come from the God of all grace. Saving knowledge is acquired not by adherence to religious traditions, nor by any philosophical quest, but by the faith reception of the Word made flesh as disclosed on the pages of Holy Scripture.

Following the Reformers, the Puritans set forth a broad twofold scheme whereby the knowledge of God is attained. On the one hand, they postulated a natural knowledge of God and on the other, a revealed knowledge, or knowledge arising from the book of nature and from the book of the Law. On closer inspection, Puritan theology could be said to advance a threefold source for the knowledge of God; namely, the natural light within, rational reflection on the data of the created order, and truth secured by faith reception of special revelation. Briefly, let us examine Puritan interaction with each of these three sources of religious knowledge.

Knowledge of God Innate   Almost without exception, the Puritans spoke of the inbred principles of natural light, the first workings of the mind, or the first dictates of reason, which produce an indelible sense of God's existence, character, and authority. Charnock, for example, could say of pagan peoples that "the notion of a deity was as inward and settled in them as their own souls, and indeed runs in the blood of mankind."[4] That is, the human mind, grounded in God, ascends to ultimate truths through the assistance of the Logos, which Thomas Goodwin described as a seminal light or candle in the soul.[5] This "self-evidencing power, acting itself in the minds of all men endued with natural light and reason,"[6] was viewed by the Puritans as the first apprehension of higher realities that nature affords without express reasonings. The impressions of Deity naturally engraved on the human heart correspond to the power of instinct in the lower creatures. As Hopkins observes, "Though there be reasoning in the case, it is so short and easy, that it strikes the mind at once, and it is hardly conscious of any reasoning upon it, and of the medium by which the evidence comes to mind."[7] Thus Charnock notes, "Every plant, every atom, as well as every star, at the first meeting whispers this in our ears, I have a Creator, I am witness to a Deity."[8] This process to which the Puritans refer corresponds to the power of effable intuition affirmed by Augustine and the Reformers. This intuitional knowing, implanted in the soul independent of the discursive workings of the mind, suggests that God exists, that He is eternal, and that He is infinitely powerful, good, and righteous. The Puritans locate their support for this prereflective intuition of God in Romans 1:19, where Paul writes, "What may be known about God is plain to them," and in verse 32, "They know God's righteous decree."

Some Puritans identified this innate knowledge as a vestige of primitive revelation granted to Adam in Paradise. This primordial communication, which transcended what Adam's unassisted faculties might have attained from the created order, was transmitted down through the race by religious instruction and customs. Although thoughtlessly and wantonly corrupted, the truth content of this primordial disclosure remains partially intact. In this way, the general acknowledgment of God among the nations is attributed to remnants of knowledge passed down the human line by our first parents. Charnock, for example, interprets man's natural knowledge of God as "a relic of knowledge after the fall of Adam, like fire under ashes, which sparkles as soon as ever the heap of ashes is open; a notion sealed up in the soul of every man."[9] In a similar vein, Jonathan Edwards insisted that the knowledge of divine truths evidenced by Plato and other wise philosophers stemmed from a primitive revelation transmitted from mouth to mouth. Argues Edwards, "That some of the ancient philosphers and wise heathens had so good notions of God as they had, seems to be much more owing to tradition, which originated from divine revelation, than from their own invention."[10] On balance, we can safely conclude that elemental notions about God and certain religious practices, such as the sacrifice of animals to appease the Deity, undoubtedly were handed down the human line in the form of tradition. But with the majority of the Puritans, we may also affirm the reality of an immediate intuitive knowledge of God, His character, and His holy demands, which is held in common by the entire human family.

Following Augustine and the Reformers, the Puritans believed that men everywhere possess a conscience, which further attests the reality of God. All people are endowed with a sense of right and wrong and the conviction that the good is to be pursued and evil avoided. Thomas Goodwin expressed this conviction in the following words:

> The Lord, seeing man's nature to be wholly corrupted, hath put a viceroy of his (viz., conscience) into their hearts, to rule and curb their spirits, which conscience he hath put into the very heathen; which principle is not only appointed merely as an overseer, or a witness against them, to take notice of the evil of their actions, but also it hath some stroke and power in men to restrain and curb them from many sins, and to make them do many things agreeable to the law.[11]

The sinner is naturally aware that there is a judgment of God and that transgression is punishable with death. The reality of the universally acknowledged moral law is best accounted for by the existence of the God of the Bible. As Charnock put it, "As there is a *rule* in us, there must be a *judge*, whether our actions be according to the rule."[12] The inner comfort that accompanies good actions and the torment that follows evil deeds are sufficient to convince every right-minded atheist of the existence of an omniscient, holy God who avenges evil.

The Puritans agreed with Calvin that the universal phenomenon of religion provides further confirmation of the existence of a higher Power. Man, an incorrigible *animal religiosum,* is born with a restless instinct to practice one religion or another. In every age since the beginning of the world man has worshiped a supreme Being. Although geographically dispersed and culturally diversified, people have observed a similar regimen of sacrifices, rites, offerings, vows, and prayers. Man's universal observance of religion points to the existence of a Deity who created the world, who confers daily benefits, and who is to be worshiped.

The Value of Theistic Evidences

But in addition to the natural light within, the Puritans postulated that rational reflection on the data of Creation and providence provides further important clues to God's existence and character. As the mind exercises its discursive faculty on the data of the space-time universe, it forges a compelling case for theism. Here the strong Puritan emphasis on the rationality and verifiability of the Christian faith comes into view. In arguing that God has provided a clear witness to Himself in the works of Creation, the Puritans appealed to such texts as Psalms 8:3; 19:1–4; and Romans 1:20. From a reading of these Scriptures, Jonathan Edwards asserted that "the works of God are but a kind of voice or language of God to instruct intelligent beings in things pertaining to himself."[13] Similarly, John Preston of Cambridge insisted that "there is enough in the very creation of the world to declare him [God] unto us."[14] Samuel Hopkins, moreover, said, "The more we attend to the creation, and examine the great works, the sun, moon, and stars, or this globe on which we live, and the various ranks of creatures which come under our notice, the more clear and striking will be the evidence of . . . the power, wisdom, and goodness of the Creator."[15] The only Bible the heathen possesses is God's sensible demonstration of Himself through His stupendous works. The Puritans frequently referred to the created order as a looking-glass that reflects the image of the Creator, as a set of organ pipes through which the voice God is trumpeted abroad, and as a great volume in which the reality of God is read off.

By the discursive power of the mind, whereby one thing is inferred from another, conclusions about the reality of God are drawn to various degrees of certainty according to the strength of the evidence. Thus from the evident magnitude, precision, and beauty of the universe, rational men rightly ought to conclude both *that* God is and *what* God is. The data of Creation cogently point not only to God's existence but also to His unity, eternity, power, wisdom, goodness, and holiness. Moreover, from a careful analysis of the cosmos, the reasonable conclusion ought to be drawn that God is to be served and that He rewards good and punishes evil.

Man is also invited to reflect on the patently providential ordering of human affairs cited by Paul the apostle in Acts 14:15–17 and 17:24–28. The potentially destructive forces of nature directed to the human good and the just judgments meted out in the flow of history strongly suggest that the world is guided by a wise hand. The furnishing of man with bounteous provisions bears testimony to the fact that God is, that He does good, and that He rules the world. John Owen therefore asserts, "We must rationally consider the works of God, both of creation and providence, or we cannot learn by them what God intends to reveal of himself."[16] From the light of Creation and providence, man rightfully ought to conclude that the universe owes its existence to the divine Workman, that man's highest good is to love God, and that man stands condemned for violating the natural law written on the heart. Without any doubt, "God calls unto men for the exercise of their reason about these things, reproaching them with stupidity and brutishness where they are wanting therein."[17]

The Puritan emphasis on the rationality of the Christian faith is reflected in the willingness of many to argue the case for theism on philosophical and metaphysical (rather than revelational) grounds. For example, Richard Baxter wrote in 1667 a quarto volume of six hundred pages that bore the title *The Reasons of the Christian Religion*. In 1672 he prepared a smaller volume entitled *More Reasons for the Christian Religion and No Reasons Against It.* In drawing out all that could be adduced by an appeal to evidences, the Puritans were under no illusion that they were advancing deductive proofs for God's existence. Rather, the inductive evidence to which they appealed served to support the reasonableness of God, morality, and the future life. The Puritans were convinced that firm evidences render the Christian claims more credible. Charnock, for example, refers to the Puritan case for God as a set of "probable arguments."[18] Taken in context, many of the Puritans' arguments were constructive attempts to highlight the fallacies of the reductionist allegations of the Deists and naturalists in English society. The Puritan divines believed that there was sufficient force in the arguments to convince their opponents of the probable validity of theism.

Jonathan Edwards and other Puritans sought to build a viable case for Christianity by an appeal to the argument from motion. There must be an adequate reason why a given body is in a state of motion rather than in a state of rest. Neither the absence of a moving force nor an infinite regression of finite causes adequately explains the phenomenon of bodies in motion. Edwards restates the problem and suggests a solution: "Why doth this move and that rest; why doth this body move with just such a degree of velocity; why doth [*sic*] the planets move West to East and not East to West? Something must be the reason of it."[19] The hypothesis of the God of the Bible, Edwards concludes, offers the most coherent explanation for the universal phenomenon of bodies in motion.

In arguing the case for God's existence, the Puritans repeatedly appealed to the argument from causation. All will acknowledge as a self-evident truth that no effect came to be without a cause. The world in all its richness and diversity cannot be accounted for in terms of itself alone. The heavenly bodies, man, beasts, fish, and vegetation are not self-created entities. Reasoning backward in time, one arrives at an invisible first cause adequate for the production of all observable effects. Who, for example, would deny that an intricate timepiece was fashioned by a watchmaker, or a beautiful statue by an artist, or an elegant piece of furniture by a skilled craftsman? And as the creativity of the artist is stamped on all his works, so is the wisdom of the Creator engraved on all His works. Charnock formulated the argument most succinctly: "As the cause is known by the effects, so the wisdom of the cause is known by the elegancy of the works."[20] Richard Baxter concurs that there must be a first cause or Creator of all entities in the space-time world. If one postulates only secondary agents of causation, namely caused causes, one is logically led back to an uncaused first cause of all effects. Baxter thus concludes, "There is certainly a first, uncaused, independent cause of men and all things else besides that cause."[21] The first cause, the maker and preserver of all things, is precisely the Creator-God of biblical theism. Indeed, on the basis of the preceding argument, Baxter contends, "Every atheist that is not mad, must confess that there is an Eternal Being, that had no beginning or cause."[22]

A further Puritan argument for the reasonableness of Christian belief in God is the argument from degrees of perfection. The majesty, constancy, and beauty of the heavens presupposes the existence of a being of greater majesty, constancy, and beauty. Similarly, the wisdom, goodness, and power of man is explicable only in the light of a being of higher wisdom, goodness, and power. Whatever possesses the sum of all excellencies in absolute perfection is that which we call God.

Frequently, the Puritan writers adduced arguments for the reality of God based on the order, harmony, and design of the visible universe. So numerous are these indications in nature, the Puritans argued, that if fully explored, they would fill volumes. Hopkins, Charnock, and Edwards observe how intelligently the cosmos has been designed for the maintenance of life. The distance of the earth from the sun, the inclination of the sun's rays to the earth, the composition of the air we breathe, and the sea that provides water for earth's rivers and streams collectively point to an all-powerful and beneficent wisdom.

Similarly, man in the complexity, intricacy, and interdependence of his parts is a product not of chance but of special creation by a God of infinite intelligence and goodness. In considerable detail the Puritans examined the structure and function of the human heart, brain, eye, ear, stomach, and arteries, concluding that nothing short of an infinite intelligence could have fitted such complexity into a harmonious whole. Likewise the soul, that glorious faculty of reason, volition, and memory, is inexplicable save for the existence of a transcendent Mind that fashioned it. Hopkins typically concludes, "If we attend only to our own bodies, we shall find them so admirably contrived, and so curiously formed, and though of so many parts, each one is suited to the rest, and all so contrived as to form one harmonious system of animal life, without any defect or anything superfluous."[23]

Lower forms of life as well attest the wisdom, power, and goodness of the Creator. Camels have a large water-storage capacity for survival in desert conditions; sheep are provided with wool for warmth in cold climates. For defense, some animals are fitted with tusks, others with sharp quills, still others with speedy legs by which to flee danger. Woodpeckers, beavers, cougars, and countless other creatures are specially adapted to their own set of circumstances.

The harmonious interrelationship between man, beast, and plant life points in the direction of a world wisely ordered. Man turns to plants and animals for food, and those animals that serve as food for man depend on vegetation for sustenance. All three need the sun for light and heat, and the heavens for rain. John Preston argued that the balance between man, beast, and plant life is as much a matter of providential design as is the organization of the twenty-six letters of the alphabet into a powerfully moving poem.

If, as appears to be the case, the world is disposed to an intelligent end, then there must exist an infinitely intelligent designing Agent. The atheist or infidel who turns his back on the collective force of the foregoing arguments is nothing short of "a grand fool."[24]

Thus it should be clear that the Puritans were staunch evidentialists rather than doctrinaire fideists. Nature within man and nature outside of man conspire together to display the reality of God. And in support of this thesis, the Puritan theologians made a strong appeal to truths discoverable through the light of reason, open to inspection by all people, and justifiable on philosophical grounds. Thinking in terms of an inductive case for theism that is valid to a high degree of probability, John Owen concluded, "By arguments taken from the works of God, both of creation and providence, the apostle proves the being and the properties of God."[25] In the main, the Puritans concurred that through the innate light of nature and rational conclusions adduced from the space-time world, the heathen possess a knowledge of God. After all, the Puritans reasoned, did not Paul teach that through general revelation the nations had *to gnōston* (Rom. 1:19), i.e., knowledge of the true and living God, the Maker and Governor of all things.

A cursory examination of the arguments the Puritans used to support theism will confirm the fact that they had carefully read Thomas Aquinas and other medieval theologians. While concluding that Thomas's a posteriori reasoning lacked the force of demonstrative proofs, the Puritans nevertheless maintained that the classical arguments possess a certain validity and cogency. They pointed in the direction of theism rather than in the direction of pantheism or atheism. Although they were the direct heirs of Calvin's theology, the Puritans spoke more freely of the positive truth content of general revelation than Calvin did. The fact that Calvin taught that natural man could derive from general revelation no more than "some slight knowledge of Deity" may be attributed, as we have noted, to his reaction against the excessive optimism of medieval natural theologies.

General Revelation Sinfully Suppressed

But beyond affirming the validity of general revelation, the Puritans stressed the practical inefficacy of the universal light in fallen and depraved man. Sin has so corrupted the *imago Dei* that the human mind is grossly darkened and the heart severely alienated against the source of its life. That unregenerate man cannot read the message of nature clearly is a common Puritan theme. Frequently, we hear the Puritans lamenting the "stupid insensibility," "brutish blindness," and "appalling ignorance" of the sinful mind. In this vein Jonathan Edwards comments,

> God gave man understanding for this end, that he might know him and heavenly things . . . but man has debased himself, and has lost his glory in this respect. He has become as ignorant of the excellency of God as the very beasts. His understanding is full of darkness; his mind is blind, is altogether blind to spiritual things. Men are ignorant of God, and ignorant of Christ, ignorant of the way of

salvation, ignorant of their own happiness, blind in the midst of the brightest and clearest light, ignorant under all manner of instructions.[26]

From the inbred notions of Deity and the judgments of discursive intelligence, God was authentically known. But sinners became "so vain and foolish as to draw convictions directly contrary to the first principles of natural light and the unavoidable notions which they had of the eternal being of God."[27] Indeed, the natural darkness of the mind will not be dispelled until the light of faith arises.

Moreover, fallen man's stubborn will and rebellious heart alienates him further from the truth content mediated by general revelation. Far more crucial to the Puritans than the rational workings of the mind were the moral sentiments of the heart. Thus even when right judgments about God are formed by the mind, the anti-God biases that lurk in the soul cause such elemental knowledge to vanish as mist. Natural man is totally incorrigible in his enmity against God. The sinner is as much an enemy of God as the wolf is an enemy to the lamb. Samuel Hopkins unites these two fatal weaknesses in fallen man—the incapacity of the mind and the enmity of the will—with the following observation:

> Mankind are so "alienated from the life of God, through the ignorance that is in them, because of the blindness of their hearts," and so disposed by their depravity and wickedness to sink down into brutish ignorance and stupidity with regard to everything invisible, that if they were not first told that there is a God, they would most probably grow up without believing, or ever thinking of this truth.[28]

The practical consequences of God's universal self-disclosure in man, nature, and providence are most clearly summed up by Jonathan Edwards:

> Man has faculties given him whereby he is well capable of inferring the being of the Creator from the creatures. The invisible things of God are very plainly and clearly to be seen by the things that are made; and the perfections of the divine Being, his eternal power and Godhead, are very manifest in the works of his hands. And yet grossly absurd notions concerning the Godhead have prevailed in the world. Instead of acknowledging and worshipping the true God, they have fallen off to the worship of idols. Instead of acknowledging the one only true God, they have made a multitude of deities. Instead of worshipping a God, who is an almighty, infinite, all-wise and holy Spirit, they have worshipped the hosts of heaven, the sun, moon, and stars; and the works of their own hands, images of gold and silver, brass and iron, wood and stone.[29]

Clearly, those who have no other guide but the light of nature are left to wander in perpetual uncertainty, darkness, and unbelief. More pointedly, the general light of reason provides no knowledge of sin's forgiveness and of reconciliation with God. As John Owen firmly insisted, "It is a great and rare thing to have forgiveness in God discovered unto a sinful soul."[30] General revelation, in sum teaches no redemptive truths. But if general revelation in the Puritan scheme provides insufficient light for the salvation of the soul, it does nevertheless serve at least two practical ends. In the first place, general revelation leaves the unrepentant sinner without excuse. Objectively, the divine self-disclosure in Creation, history, and conscience is sufficiently clear that God should be known as Creator, Ruler, and Judge. Thomas Manton observed that "nature in some measure told them what was well or ill done, pleasing or displeasing to God. The law of nature taught them their duty, and the course of God's providence, that God was placable, and so invited them to repentance (Rom. 2:4)."[31] But man, through the depraved and vicious habits of his mind, spurned the clear light from above and chose rather the worship of idols. Hence "the wicked will be turned into hell," not because they did not hear the gospel, but because they rejected the natural knowledge of God and failed to cast themselves on His mercy. Once again, the words of Manton pertain: The wicked "shall not be judged for not believing in Christ, but for not knowing God."[32]

General revelation, secondly, serves as a necessary prolegomenon to the divine special revelation. The evidence of Creation, history, and conscience establish a necessary point of contact between the sinner and the gospel. In Puritan thought, general revelation relates to special revelation as the foundation of a building to the superstructure. When God addresses man with His saving message in the living and written Word, man recognizes Him as God on the grounds of His preliminary universal disclosure. Human acceptance of the free gift of salvation is most reasonably made on the basis of prior knowledge of the one who extends the invitation.[33] In the words of Charnock, "Faith presupposes natural knowledge, as grace supposes nature."[34] General revelation thus plays an indispensable propaedeutic role in the divine scheme of redemption.

The Saving Utility of Special Revelation

Above and beyond both the knowledge of God that is innate and that which is rationally adduced from the created order, the Puritans postulated that God is savingly known by the faith reception of His special self-disclosure in Holy Scripture. The later Puritans polemicized against contemporary naturalists who argued that man attains eternal felicity simply by following the sufficient light of nature and reason. The Puritans insisted that although God's existence and character have been made known to people of all ages, the righteousness of God in the gospel is disclosed solely in the objectively given "thus saith the Lord." Whereas nature teaches many truths about God's character and demands, it leaves the sinner ignorant of the heart of God, of Christian divinity, and of redemptive truths. General revelation elicits the anxious interrogation, "What shall I do to be saved?" It prompts the question and poses the difficulty, but it cannot provide the solution. Only the Word of God, preserved in the Old and New Testaments, teaches "how God will be served, how they shall be rewarded or punished, or how they shall escape punishment."[35] Samuel Hopkins put it plainly; "They who enjoy this book have more clear evidence of the being of God, as well as unspeakably greater advantages to know his true character; and consequently are far more inexcusable than the heathen, if they do not believe."[36]

The Puritans were united in the affirmation that without faith in biblical revelation man would be hopelessly and eternally doomed. The Word of God alone provides the higher knowledge of saving truths that the sinner so desperately requires. In the words of Samuel Willard, "The mystery of the Trinity of persons in the unity of the Godhead; of the two natures infinitely disproportional in themselves, united in the person of Christ; and of the union of a believer in Christ in regeneration, are depths which the line of our understanding is not able to fathom."[37] With the sobriety and severity characteristic of the Puritan movement, Edwards made the following remark concerning the light of Holy Scripture:

> It is the only remedy which God has provided for the miserable, brutish blindness of mankind, a remedy without which this fallen world would have sunk down for ever in brutal barbarism without any remedy. It is the only means that the true God has made successful in his providence, to give the nations of the world the knowledge of himself; and to bring them off from the worship of false gods.[38]

It was incomprehensible to the Puritans that God's forgiveness and favor could be achieved in any other way than through the testimony of His Holy Word. Man without the revelation of God's heart in Scripture is a man without knowledge and without hope.

But the knowledge of God afforded by Scripture is the knowledge of God in Christ. Manton expressed it in this way: "The Scriptures are the picture of Christ, and Christ is the image of the Father."[39] The Puritans turned to the record of the person, life, and work of Christ to discover the heartbeat of God. "In Christ's person and kingdom the majesty of God is known; in the divine power of his operations, the strength of God; in the excellency of his benefits, the love of God."[40] As Manton again put it, "Come to Christ; you are in need of salvation, and there is no other way."[41]

The Puritans underscored the warmly practical character of the knowledge of God gained by the faith reception of Christ. Indeed, they drew a distinction between speculative understanding ("barely knowing knowledge") and practical understanding ("working and affecting knowledge").[42] The former affords some kind of judgment about divine truths; the latter stirs the heart to acts of pure devotion. Philosophical speculation yields only frigid and lifeless ideas about God and religion. But to trust, love, and obey Christ is to know God from the heart in all spiritual wisdom and understanding. Only this internalized knowledge of God in Christ is genuine saving knowledge. Thomas Manton underscored this point by insisting,

> It is not a naked sight of his essence that will save a man: I must know him for a practical end, to choose him, and carry myself to him as an all sufficient portion:

71

I must honor him as the giver of all things: revere and worship him as the just governor of the world; and worship him in a way suitable to the infiniteness, perfection, and simplicity of his nature. A man is not saved by holding a right opinion of God.[43]

Puritanism and Non-Christian Religion

In view of the foregoing discussion, the Puritan estimate of the validity of the non-Christian religions holds few surprises. They all, without exception, roundly rejected the claim that through natural insight or reasoning the heathen come to know God redemptively. In fact, they argued that not a single person in the pagan world has lived up to the light afforded by general revelation. No one will gainsay that some pagans display certain moral virtues. Nevertheless, "the greater part of the inhabitants of the world are to this day gross, barbarous heathens, who have not the knowledge of the true God, but worship *idols* and *devils*, with all manner of absurd and foolish rites and ceremonies."[44] Islam, Hinduism, and other non-Christian systems are false religions fabricated by carnal minds.

Simply stated, there is no salvation except through Jesus Christ. "No knowledge of God is sufficient to eternal life but the knowledge of God and Christ."[45] The claim that devout Muslims, Jews, and pagans attain salvation through the practice of their religious rites flies in the face of the clear teaching of the Word of God.[46] If such claim be true, then Christ died in vain, and the philosophy of Aristotle and Seneca would be as much the power of God for salvation as the gospel of the grace of God. Edwards typically observed that the nations have dwelled "in the midnight darkness of heathenism for above three thousand years; and not one people have delivered themselves, who have not had the light of the Gospel."[47]

The Puritans were justly intolerant of the naturalist assertion that all religions are of equal value. William Law once made the following remark of a critic who placed the religions of the world on the same plane: "He might have shown himself a friend to truth and sobriety, by asserting that all arguments are equally conclusive, all tempers equally virtuous, all designs equally honest, and all histories and fables equally supported by evidence of fact."[48] Manton issued a potent warning against any who were tempted to cherish inflated opinions of the non-Christian religions: "We must take care lest, by going about to make them Christians, we make ourselves heathens."[49]

In sum, we discover in the Puritan tradition a commendable emphasis on the rationality and verifiability of the theistic position. The data of general revelation are regarded as a necessary and important feature of God's self-disclosure to man. The knowledge content afforded by nature, conscience, and history is neither depreciated, as in fideism, nor exaggerated, as in rationalistic theology. The Puritan theologians struck what we regard to be an authentic biblical balance in their explication of the character, content, and scope of general revelation and its relationship to God's special revelation in the written and living Word. While positing the reality of general revelation and a rudimentary knowledge of God, they had a realistic understanding of natural man's consistently negative response to the light of God displayed in the Creation. Although a bit extreme in their language, they properly viewed the non-Christian religions as distortions of God's universal general revelation. The Puritans, moreover, must be applauded for courageously upholding the finality of Christ and the uniqueness of the Christian faith as the only redemptive way to God. Given these biblical emphases, one readily understands why a lively renaissance of Puritan theology and spirituality is taking place in our day.

HARROWING HEAVEN:
V THE ENLIGHTENMENT CHALLENGE

We have seen that the historic Augustinian-Reformed position, while not positing a complete natural theology, nevertheless upheld the validity and limited utility of general revelation. The knowledge of God gained through the divine self-disclosure is both subjective and objective. By common grace, the existence, character, and moral demands of God are effably intuited. Further conclusions about the divine Reality are drawn to a high degree of probability as the rational mind evaluates the revealed phenomena in nature, man himself, and providence. But the orthodox tradition likewise insisted that the fundamental knowledge of God thus acquired is perverted by the sinner's darkened mind and repressed by his selfish heart. Consequently, no sinner ever attains eternal felicity by reliance on his natural powers alone. Saving knowledge is mediated exclusively through God's supernatural self-disclosure in Christ as attested in Scripture. Sinners come to know God in no other way than through Christ's atoning work on the cross.

The eighteenth and nineteenth centuries, however, brought a frontal assault on the prevailing theological consensus. Various strands of European Enlightenment thought challenged the necessity and validity of special revelation, holding that such would involve God in a senseless interruption of the natural order. Moreover, denying the darkening effects of sin on the mind, Enlightenment scholars affirmed that human resources were adequate to ferret out ultimate truth. Natural man possesses the strength of mind and will both to know and to actualize the good. In the eighteenth century, then, the predominant outlook of the Enlightenment was rationalistic. In the following century, however, the sterility of a purely rationalistic approach to religion gave birth to the subjectivist romantic movement centered in the school of Schleiermacher.

Initially, the theological Enlightenment sought only to articulate a more reasonable faith. But gradually the tension between revelation and reason eroded with the latter finally usurping the primacy. Thus Enlightenment thinkers postulated that by the process of observation and reflection man could attain religious truths independently of any supernatural disclosure. Some within the Enlightenment tradition doubted the validity of any supernatural revelation whatsoever. Others argued that revelation involved merely a "republication" of elemental religious truths that had been obscured by the addition of superstitious accretions. An expanding scientism, stimulated by the discoveries of Kepler, Galileo, and Newton, gradually removed the shroud of mystery from the cosmos, disclosing a universe whose workings followed strict physical laws. Enlightenment thinkers thus concluded that the scientific method provides the means by which to penetrate the ultimate secrets of the universe. Hence the old Aristotelian-Thomistic natural theology gave way to a new theology of immanence grounded in a mechanistic view of the universe. The natural was held to be the reasonable, and the reasonable was held to be the natural. Moreover, exploration of new regions of Asia, Africa, and Oceana disclosed masses of peoples untouched by Christianity, yet ostensibly living fulfilled lives. Suddenly the Christian tradition was recognized as a minority movement in the world. These and other factors led to the gradual supplanting of traditional Christian beliefs based on a purported supernatural revelation. In the new humanistic climate, biblical statements about special revelation were reduced to affirmations of universal general revelation in nature. Enlightenment confidence in the competence of man's natural faculties led to the rise of a purely natural religion shaped by the data of ordinary experience. In lieu of the contradictory claims of the positive religions, natural religion embraced only those core convictions commonly held by all people through the honest exercise of reason. Bonhoeffer summed up the Enlightenment outlook with the observation, "Everywhere the thinking is directed towards the autonomy of man and the world."[1]

The philosophical foundations for Enlightenment theology's inflated estimate of natural man's knowing powers was provided in large measure by Descartes. Before examining in greater detail Enlightenment estimates of revelation and the knowability of God, the seminal contribution of this key figure must be briefly considered.

The Cartesian Contribution

René Descartes (1596–1650), French Roman Catholic mathematician and philosopher, is justly acclaimed the pioneer of modern philosophical and theological rationalism. In Descartes's polemic against scholasticism, rational thinking was upheld as the supreme instrument of truth and moral action. Independent of sense experience, reason assumed the role of the all-sufficient system builder. Descartes firmly believed that reason is capable of discovering the basic nature and structure of the universe. Reason provides the only ground of human certainty. Truth in the Cartesian scheme is relative to the knowing human subject. In propounding these ideas, Descartes inaugurated a new era in philosophy and theology.

Descartes's rational quest for truth involved two operations. First, by the faculty of intellect (viewed as a divine bestowal), the knower directly and immediately intuits truth. The resultant clear and distinct ideas, or first principles, are self-attesting and, because independent of sense experience, are identical for all people. Thus Descartes argued that by reflecting on the content of his mind, man discovers elemental truths that are immediately recognized as valid.[2] Thus far Descartes stands broadly within the aprioristic Platonic-Augustinian tradition.

Descartes in turn applied the method of intuited knowledge to establish the reality of the self. The significance of the cosmos may not be clear by the process of observation and inspection, but the reality of the thinking man cannot be denied. His argument is encapsulated in the classic formula, *cogito, ergo sum*, "I think, therefore I am." One cannot deny that he is thinking without thinking. But essential to the act of thinking is a subject that thinks. Hence the reality of the thinking self is established. *Cogito, ergo sum* emerges as an indubitable certainty, a clear and distinct idea.

Following proof of the reality of the self, Descartes sought to prove the existence and character of God by modifying Anselm's ontological argument. The idea of God as an infinite, perfect, all-knowing, and all-powerful Being is directly intuited. The finite self could not have produced such a notion, for a cause must be at least as great as its effect. Indeed, only a perfect being could have produced such an idea. But since existence is an attribute of perfection, such a being must necessarily exist. Descartes supports this latter contention with the assertion that just as the equivalence of the three angles of a triangle with two acute angles is a necessary property of a triangle, so existence is a necessary characteristic of a perfect being. Thus Descartes concludes, "In the case of God, . . . I cannot think of Him save as existing; and it therefore follows that existence is inseparable from Him, and that He therefore really exists."[3]

From clear and distinct ideas about the self and the world, Descartes proceeded to establish in strict Euclidean fashion the rest of his metaphysical system. Here the principle of Cartesian doubt is reintroduced with full force. Everything outside the thinking, perceiving, and feeling self is open to doubt. In fact, Descartes was committed to doubt everything that was not self-evident or that could not be logically deduced from self-evident premises.[4] Hence Descartes's second source of knowledge involves the logical deduction of truths in strict accord with the mathematical model. All knowledge must be as precise and certain as mathematical knowledge. To know is to be able to prove with deductive, syllogistic certainty. Whatever is proposed for acceptance, be it on the grounds of experience, religious authority, or revelation, must be subjected to rigorous rational scrutiny. Experience from the external world deceives; hence the judgments drawn from sense experience cannot be trusted. Thus, according to Descartes, truth is grasped not from the data of the space-time world, nor even from a supposed revelation from God, but exclusively through the act of thinking. In holding that knowledge is gained by deduction from first principles independent of sense experience, Descartes was a philosophical rationalist. By postulating a lofty view of man's natural rational powers, Descartes paved the way for the rationalistic spirit that surfaced in Spinoza and Leibnitz and that would dominate theology for at least the next one hundred and fifty years.

But Descartes's *cogito* stimulated, in addition, various subjectivist tendencies in theology. Descartes broadened the *cogito* beyond thinking and doubting to include feeling and ineffable awareness. According to this polarity, the starting point in the quest for knowledge is the human self-consciousness. On this showing, the universals of philosophy are subjectively apprehended. The subjectivist pole of Cartesian thought proved to be a stimulus to nineteenth-century romantic and twentieth-century existentialist systems. Thus we may conclude that Descartes's anthropocentric revolution led to a gradual drift away from evangelical belief. As one observer put it, "Cartesianism is thickly sown with the seeds of anti-Christian ideas."[5]

Unlike the earlier apriorists Augustine and Calvin, Descartes had a starting point that lacked grounding in the Creator-Preserver God who endows man's rationality with the gift of enabling grace. Without acknowledging the debilitating effects of sin on the human cognitive process, Descartes erroneously postulated that all knowledge could be ground out by the rational mind in strictly mechanical fashion. Or to put it another way, Descartes erringly held that all knowledge could be attained by Augustine's *ratio*, while ignoring the *intellectus* by which eternal truths are received. In this manner Descartes opened the door to later attempts to assert man's autonomy and independence from God. A further criticism of Descartes is that his idea of God was arrived at independently of divine revelation. The Frenchman's antiempirical stance allowed no room for the giveness of God's general revelation in nature, providence, and history. Moreover, his postulate of the sufficiency of human deductive reasoning overlooked the reality of special redemptive revelation as the only source for the full knowledge of God. The assumption of Descartes that man is competent to make his way to God apart from divine revelation cannot be sustained. By thus neglecting divine revelation in favor of a scheme of speculative philosophy, Descartes encouraged later generations of philosophers and theologians to pursue the quest for the knowledge of God either on the basis of discursive reason (rationalism), or ineffable subjective experience (romanticism, existentialism).

English Deism   The first major movement of Enlightenment rationalism was deism, which reigned as a dominant force in English religious life during the latter half of the seventeenth century and the first half of the eighteenth. While representing no well-defined doctrinal system, deism postulated the existence of a personal Creator-God who decreed that the universe should function in accordance with built-in natural laws. On this showing, God does not interfere supernaturally in the processes of the natural world. Less well known, perhaps, is the corollary that the deists subscribed to an exalted view of human nature. Orthodox convictions on original sin and the corruption of human nature were roundly rejected. Human reason, the chief element in the *imago Dei*, was ascribed with unlimited power and potential. One student of the movement concludes, "Deism was the working creed of many honest men who were persuaded that nature and reason provided all the truth that men could reasonably ask."[6] All beliefs must be justified at the bar of reason, where reason is defined as that faculty of the mind that perceives the truth, falsehood, probability, or improbability of propositions.[7]

The deists held that God at Creation gave a universal revelation of Himself in the natural world. This primal revelation, which was fully sufficient for man's religious needs, was seen as both interior and exterior to man. The deists identified the interior revelation as the voice of reason and conscience universally implanted in every human being. The revelation exterior to man was identified with the structure of the universe that discloses the nature and congruity of reality. Thus the deists affirmed that the natural light in man, which is analogous to the natural law (*lex naturae*) of the Greek and Roman Stoics, is adequate to establish the true and authentic "natural religion." This universal religion of reason and nature provides people of all times with sufficient light to live a life of practical morality pleasing to God. Jesus, the deists argued, taught the multitudes the law of reason and nature. Hence those who live by the dictates of conscience and reason are Christians.

It follows that the deists denied the possibility and the reality of supernatural revelation. Since the created order is a sufficient expression of God's mind, no further revelation is necessary. God's self-disclosure was limited to His initial activity in creating the universe and man. In lieu of special revelation, God gave man nature and the rule of his own conscience. No supernatural disclosure from without could supplant the plain, perfect, and unchangeable religion of reason and nature. Hence the Bible was viewed as a fallible secondary authority. Higher revealed truths and dogmas that deviate from the simple religion of natural morality represent the corrupt and superstitious accretions imposed by the priestly class. From this overview of the first expression of the Enlightenment spirit, we proceed to the thought of several leading deist thinkers.

Lord Herbert of Cherbury (1583–1648) is generally acclaimed the "father of English deism." Lord Herbert claimed that unaided human reason, independent of revelation, is capable of discovering the fundamental truths of religion. Bonhoeffer is correct in his observation that Lord Herbert "maintains that reason is sufficient for religious knowledge."[8] The rationally discoverable natural religion consists of five innate principles or universally acknowledged ideas that Lord Herbert in his essay *De veritate* promulgated as the "five articles" of English deism: "If we set aside superstitions and legends, the mind takes its stand on my five articles, and upon nothing else."[9] They are (1) that God truly exists; (2) that He is to be worshiped; (3) that piety and virtue lie at the heart of this duty; (4) that people need to repent of their sins; and (5) that the future life consists of rewards and punishments. If the adherents of the historic faiths would set aside their formal differences and stress only those core convictions attainable by reason, religious strife would be eliminated.

Lord Herbert believed that true religion is rooted not in special revelation, but in those truths that are naturally perceived by men everywhere. Eternal happiness is attained by assent to this universal religion of nature and reason. Lord Herbert's emphasis on the supremacy of reason over revelation established him as a link between the philosophical rationalism of Descartes and Spinoza and the formulations of the later deists.

Ecclesiastical support for the deist cause in England was provided by John Tillotson (1630–94), archbishop of Canterbury and prominent latitudinarian divine. Collins, a deist from the following generation, said that Tillotson was an authority "whom all English free-thinkers own as their head."[10] Like Lord Herbert, Tillotson held that reason is fully sufficient to establish the necessary truths of religion. In opposition to the traditional Christian claim that the transcendent mysteries of the gospel are received by faith, Tillotson affirmed that there is nothing in true religion repugnant to reason. The essence of Christianity is open to anyone who would utilize his God-given faculties of intuition and reason. Thus the bishop wrote, "All the duties of the Christian religion with respect to God are no other but what natural light prompts men to, excepting the two sacraments, and praying to God in the name and by the mediation of Jesus Christ."[11] Hence Christianity, the universal natural religion, is primarily a religion of common sense.

Yet Tillotson, the churchman, was reluctant to dismiss revelation altogether. The Christian doctrine of special revelation was interpreted as a republication or restatement of the primordial universal natural religion. By its promises of rewards and threats of punishments, Christian revelation reinforced those basic religious convictions of which all men are naturally aware. Nevertheless, revelation claims are accepted only insofar as they accord with the conclusions of reason. For Tillotson, natural religion and revealed religion exist side by side; but the primacy lies with natural religion.

Difficult to omit from the present discussion is the contribution of John Locke (1632–1704), the English physician, philosopher, and political theorist who is acclaimed by many as the intellectual ruler of the eighteenth century. Locke's thought proved to be one of the great shaping forces in the

Age of Reason. Later deists freely acknowledged their substantial indebtedness to John Locke.

In contrast to Descartes's negation of sense experience, Locke advocated an empirical approach to knowledge. In *An Essay Concerning Human Understanding* (1690), Locke denied the existence of innate ideas (the mind being rather a *tabula rasa*) and argued that induction from the data of sense experience is the only path to religious truth. Rejecting any ideas that do not correspond to actual facts and truth claims that cannot be tested by observable evidence, Locke became the father of the modern empirical tradition, which includes such noteworthies as Berkeley and Hume.

With other leading thinkers of the period, Locke wrestled with the relationship between Christian revelation and natural religion. In the end, he came down on the side of the autonomy of the human knower. Reason, reflecting on the data of the space-time world, is competent to unlock ultimate religious truths, including many of the truths traditionally ascribed to revelation. Christian revelation, however, imparts a modest fund of knowledge that is beyond reason's ability to fathom. Thus to some extent, natural religion must be supplemented by revelation. In making this assertion, Locke, unlike later deists, gave at least token assent to special revelation. But, according to Locke, Christian revelation discloses only a very few doctrines, for many traditional beliefs must be set aside as spurious dogmatic accretions. Locke proceeds to add that knowledge imparted by Christian revelation will never prove contrary to reason. Indeed, in his essay *The Reasonableness of Christianity* (1695), Locke rejects as out of hand tenets of the faith that in his judgment contravene experimental reason. In the final analysis, then, revelation claims must be capable of empirical verification. This, however, is but to affirm, in Locke's words, that "reason must be our last judge and guide in everything."[12] No other authority can usurp the primacy of inductive conclusions drawn from sense data.

The theme of natural religion plays an important role in Locke's system of thought. Natural law or natural religion is defined as the imprint of God's character and purpose in the structure of the universe and in the workings of the human mind. In its demonstration of God's existence and moral demands, natural religion is universally accessible to all. Consequently, those who lived before Christ or who never heard the Word of God cannot be eternally doomed. Argues Locke, "Nobody was or can be required to believe what was never proposed to him to believe."[13]

Wherein then lies Christianity's superiority to other religions? Why should Jesus be esteemed more highly than Plato or Socrates? Locke's answer is that the gospel is the most admirable exposition of the law of nature, and Christianity is the most reliable representation of natural religion. The religion of Jesus illumines and renders more explicit the light of reason and nature. In its fresh promulgation and codification of natural law, Christianity endowed the universal religion of nature with a new and compelling authority.

John Tolland (1640–1722) and Anthony Collins (1676–1729), two disciples of Locke, bring us to the heart of English deism. The titles of their major essays highlight the character of their views. Tolland affirmed the main assumptions of deism in his work *Christianity Not Mysterious: A Treatise Showing that there is nothing in the Gospel contrary to Reason nor above it, and that no Christian Doctrine can be properly called a Mystery* (1696). Collins likewise expounded the orthodox deistic position in such works as *An Essay on Reason* (1707), *A Discourse on Freethinking* (1713)—his *opus magnum*—and *The Grounds and Reasons of the Christian Religion* (1724).

Reason, the rational element of the *imago Dei*, abides in man unimpaired. In Tolland's words, "Reason . . . 'tis the Candle, the Guide, the Judge he has lodged within every man that cometh into this world."[14] Hence truth is attainable by the rational workings of the human mind. Reason becomes the only principle of certitude in religion. Its omnicompetence is reflected in Tolland's assertion that "reason is the only foundation of all certainty."[15] God never revealed anything reason was incapable of explicating. Freethinking, according to Collins, represents the surest method of attaining truth. The whole duty of man is summed up in the act of free thought.

> By free-thinking alone men are capable of knowing that a perfectly good, just, wise, and powerful being made and governs the world. And from this principle they know that he can require nothing of men in any country or condition of life but that whereof he has given them an opportunity of being convinced by evidence and reason in the place where they are. And that an honest and rational man can have no just reason to fear anything from him.[16]

Faith, in the deistic scheme, becomes synonymous with knowledge. In Tolland's words, faith is "entirely built upon ratiocination."[17]

Revelation, which may convey valid information, must conform to the judgments of reason. The so-called "truths" of Scripture must be validated by the process of human ratiocination. All Christian doctrines must agree with natural reason and common sense. There cannot be even the slightest appearance of a conflict between man's natural judgments and revelation claims. Unlike Locke, Tolland allows for no revealed truths that are above or beyond the scope of reason.

Since there is nothing in the gospel above reason, mystery has no place in true religion. As Tolland insists, "Religion must necessarily be reasonable and intelligible."[18] The mysteries propounded by the traditional Christian authorities must not be blindly accepted by modern freethinking man.

The essence of true religion, according to Tolland and Collins, resides in the natural religion that people of sound mind everywhere hold in common. Christianity happens to be an instance of the original religion of nature, culturally and historically conditioned. Thus Christianity can hardly be regarded as the exclusive vehicle of salvation. In truth, by the light of reason and nature, God from the beginning made perfectly clear to all people the means of securing blessedness.

V. HARROWING HEAVEN: THE ENLIGHTENMENT CHALLENGE

Matthew Tindal (1657–1733), lawyer and Fellow of All Soul's Oxford, represents the zenith of deistic thinking. Tindal's major work, *Christianity as Old as the Creation: or the Gospel a Republication of the Religion of Nature* (1730), is generally acclaimed "the deists' Bible." Tindal claims that through reason and conscience knowledge of God has always been within man's reach. These two faculties constitute the light or law of nature that God provided at Creation so that man might be directed to Himself. Tindal postulated "the all-sufficiency, absolute perfection, plainness, and perspicuity of the law of nature."[19] The light of nature is nothing other than the voice of God Himself. By illuminating the heart and mind, it persuades people that God exists, that He is a Being of infinite perfection, and that He is the source of life. The voice of nature declares to man all that God requires that he know by way of belief and duty.

Tindal goes on to say that as nature is clear and sufficient, so is the religion founded on nature. Natural religion Tindal defines as follows:

> By natural religion, I understand the belief of the existence of God, and the sense and practice of those duties which result from the knowledge we, by our reason, have of him and his perfections; and of ourselves, and of our imperfections, and of the relation we stand in to him, and to our fellow creatures; so that the religion of nature takes in everything that is founded on the reason and nature of things.[20]

Natural religion consists of those few simple truths discoverable by reason, which promote the common good. The parameters of natural religion are set forth in Jesus' Sermon on the Mount and in the teachings of Confucius. There is no difference, in fact, between the maxims of Confucius and those of Jesus Christ. The happiness of the rational creature is conditioned on living up to the clear and simple precepts of the religion of nature.

But what is the relationship between natural religion and so-called revealed religion? Tindal responds that natural religion differs from revealed religion only in the manner of its unveiling. There are not two kinds of religion, one natural and a higher one revealed. Rather, natural religion is an internal revelation of God's will, whereas revealed religion represents an external disclosure of the same unchangeable will. The latter constitutes a reduplication of the original revelation written on men's hearts. Natural religion and revealed religion must "like two tallies, exactly answer one another."[21] Hence special revelation adds nothing to the perfect, clear, and universal religion of nature. At the hands of Tindal, special revelation became practically superfluous. The Bible, laden with errors and absurdities and available to only a small segment of humanity, is no more than a secondary rule. Obedience to the light of nature is all that God requires of man. Tindal thus postulated a primal revelation in reason, conscience, and nature that is wholly adequate for man's religious needs. The revelation of God in nature fully equips people with a knowledge of the divine will.

Tindal grounds the perfection and permanence of natural religion in the nature of God Himself. Since God is good, wise, and unchangeable, the light of nature and reason, and hence the religion derived therefrom, must be the same at all times and in all places. True religion—namely, the religion of nature and reason—is as old as the Creation and as extensive as human nature. As the religion given by God at Creation, it requires no additions. True religion has not been recently unveiled to the human race, contrary to the claims of Christian orthodoxy. If true religion, Tindal argues, had first been disclosed in Christianity, God in effect would have abandoned the greater part of mankind to darkness for more than four thousand years. It would have been highly partial of God, if not immoral, to make salvation contingent on beliefs hidden from the greater part of mankind. God could not have disclosed to a few what He requires of all.

The Christian religion, in Tindal's view, is but one expression of the natural law given at Creation. Hence Christianity is merely the republication or restatement of that original religion founded on the eternal reason of things. In Tindal's own words, "The Gospel was the republication of the law of nature, and its precepts declarative of that original religion, which is as old as Creation."[22] Anything taught by Christianity beyond the simple truths of natural religion must be viewed as corrupt and superstitious accretions.

Tindal frequently extolled the virtue and morality of ethnic and national groups that were patently non-Christian. He regarded the Chinese people as the moral superiors of people in the Christian West. He brashly asserted that it was nothing short of providential that for centuries the Chinese had no contact with Christianity. In addition, the teachings of Confucius prove superior to the harsh and offensive elements in the law of Moses, and its precepts more worthy than those of the Sermon on the Mount. In short, Tindal held that Christianity is no more salvific than Hinduism, Confucianism, or Islam.

The goal of Tindal's religion of nature is practical morality, which alone ensures the happiness of the human race. Everything in religion that is not directly conducive to morality must be set aside. True religion, in effect, is defined as a religion of practical reason. In the deist Tindal, the scheme of deductive reason proposed by Descartes gives way to a theism of practical reason, which Kant would later develop in far greater detail.

The deistic assertion that God gave a perfect and sufficient revelation of Himself in the natural order at least is consistent with their central postulate—namely, that after creating the universe God retreated from direct involvement in its affairs. But by denying both the crippling effects of sin on the human mind and the reality of supernatural revelation, the deists demanded more of post-Fall man than he was able to deliver. Surely from the biblical perspective, natural man is not competent to discover the secret counsels of God apart from a special revelatory disclosure. Likewise, sinful man is not capable of living a life pleasing to God on the basis of his own resources. A special working of grace is mandated if man is to know God and walk with Him. In addition, the deistic stress on the divine transcendence violates the Bible's teaching on the divine immanence. But as Carnell points out, "A God without immanence is a God without relevance."[23] Thus it is not surprising that deism gave way to radical unbelief and atheism before coming to an end in the graveyard of reductionist theological systems. The modern scene hardly mourns the demise of the deistic movement, for a God who fails to relate to man and the world scarcely is missed.

French Naturalism   French naturalism, an offshoot of English deism, represents the second major Enlightenment movement to be considered. Like the deists, the French naturalists propounded a religion of nature and reason. Yet in their refusal to correlate natural religion with revealed religion, the French thinkers come to more radical conclusions than their English predecessors.

The chief spokesman of French naturalism was Voltaire (1694–1778), the first great historian of the modern era and a brilliant social and political theorist. The head of a group of critical philosophers known as the Encyclopedists, Voltaire is acclaimed by some as eighteenth-century France's greatest mind. Goethe hailed Voltaire as the greatest genius of modern times, perhaps of all times. During an extended visit to England (1726–28), Voltaire assimilated many deistic beliefs. The significance of this encounter led Mosley to observe that Voltaire went to England a poet and returned a philosopher.

In the tradition of Enlightenment skepticism, Voltaire rejected the doctrine of original sin as a crude Augustinian invention. With man's cognitive powers untarnished, reason became the omnicompetent guide in life. Through the cultured intellect, the things of God are made plain. With the elevation of human rationality, faith was correspondingly dethroned. "To believe in a wise Creator, eternal and supreme, is not faith, it is reason."[24]

In an attempt to work out a simple rational faith, Voltaire formulated two formal proofs for God's existence. He was persuaded that the burgeoning knowledge of the Newtonian universe fully justifies belief in a divine intelligence behind the cosmic order. In his *Traité de Métaphysique* (1734), Voltaire advanced traditional cosmological and teleological arguments for God's existence. Everything in the universe has its cause in something. If an entity exists through itself, then it always existed of necessity and thus would be God. On the other hand, if it received its being from something else, that from which it received its being must be God.

In his teleological argument, Voltaire draws on the classical argument of the watchmaker. The intricate design and mechanism of the watch points toward a skillful designer. Likewise, the remarkable complexity and adaptation of the human brain, nerves, muscles, and other organs is best explained by the existence of an intelligent mind. Remarks Voltaire, "I cannot conclude anything further than that it is probable that an intelligent and superior being has skillfully prepared and fashioned the matter."[25] Rational reflection on observable data leads Voltaire to conclude the existence of an infinite and intelligent Being who is powerful, good, and the original cause of all things. Relevant is Voltaire's now proverbial saying, "If God did not exist, He would have to be invented."

Through the influence of the deists, Voltaire became an enthusiastic devotee of natural religion. By natural religion, Voltaire meant the simple awareness of God and resultant practical morality, shorn of metaphysical subtleties, that derives from the clear and sufficient light granted man at the Creation. Thus Voltaire can say, "The only gospel that we ought to read is the great book of nature, written by the hand of God and sealed with his seal. The only religion that we ought to profess is to adore God and to be an honest man."[26] Voltaire's primitive natural religion consists of the simple worship of God and the practice of virtue, tolerance, and honesty. Again Voltaire speaks:

> Among all peoples who use their reason there are universal opinions that seem imprinted by the master of our hearts. Such is the persuasion of the existence of God, and of his merciful justice; such are the first principles of morality common to the Chinese, the Indians, and the Romans, and which have never varied while our globe has been thrown into confusion a thousand times.[27]

This natural religion of practical morality is necessary for the preservation of society. The loss of the values of goodness, morality, and justice inevitably leads to inhumanity, brutality, and painful social turmoil.

As a consequence of his rejection of supernatural revelation, Voltaire waged war on all revealed religion. During the last two decades of his life, Voltaire relentlessly strove for the destruction of institutional Christianity. "Crush the infamous thing!" became his famous cry. With its crude doctrines of Eucharist, Incarnation and blood Atonement, Christianity, said Voltaire, blasphemes the name of God. The dogmas of the church have led only to fanaticism and strife. Christian doctrinal disputes produced the barbarism of the Middle Ages. The history of Christianity is the history of superstition, bigotry, greed, and abuse of power and wealth. In the name of Christianity, ordinary people have been reduced to poverty, brutally tortured, and wantonly murdered. In Voltaire's own words, Christianity is "an absurd and bloody religion, supported by hangmen and surrounded with pyres."[28] Christianity therefore must be abolished, but not the primordial religion of practical morality, which is the one means by which the world will be delivered from moral blindness and strife.

Voltaire's comments on the validity of the world's religions approximate the deistic position. Christianity dare not claim superiority over the non-Christian religions for the following reasons. First, many religions, including those of the Indians, Chinese, Egyptians, and Chaldeans, are far more ancient than Christianity. It is inconceivable for Voltaire that God should eternally torment millions of His creatures who antedated the coming of "the truth." Second, Voltaire argues that adherents of the major non-

Christian religions often lived more virtuous lives than Christians. The Chinese religions are regarded as models of practical morality. And third, given their indifference to dogmas, the non-Christian religions prove less contentious than Christianity. All would be well if Christians would only follow the natural religion of Jesus, with its emphasis on practical morality, tolerance, and love.

A further advocate of natural religion was the Geneva-born philosopher, political theorist, and literary figure Jean Jacques Rousseau (1712–78), author of the famous *Social Contract* (1762). While a staunch proponent of the religion of nature, Rousseau showed considerably less hostility to Christianity than did Voltaire. Rousseau's denial of original sin reflects his basically Pelagian orientation. The Fall was viewed as a process of social maladjustment. Man was originally good until civilization corrupted his virtues and transformed him into a sinful and suffering being. In Rousseau's mind, man's natural goodness enables him to work out his own salvation apart from any supernatural disclosure.

With his broad appeal to reason, Rousseau dwelt within the camp of Enlightenment rationalism. The universal faculty of reason is a divine torch given to illumine man's path. Through reason, God speaks directly to man. "If I use my reason, if I cultivate it, if I employ rightly the innate faculties which God bestows on me, I shall learn by myself to know and to love him, to love his works, to will what he wills and to fulfill all my duties upon earth."[29] But Rousseau's reason should not be confused with the cool and calculating cognition of the rationalistic philosophers. Here Rousseau's naturalism diverges from the English deists and Voltaire. Reason in Rousseau is wedded to the powerful force of feeling. Rousseau's natural philosophy involved a profound correlation of reason and the religious sentiments.

Rousseau insists that if God is to be known, the intellect must be supplemented by the affections or feelings. God is not only seen in the magnificence of His works but He is also felt within the depths of the innermost self. The element of sentiment or feeling, which strongly shaped Rousseau's natural theology, should be understood as an intuitive disclosure in the form of an innate moral instinct.[30] Through the faculty of feeling, the reality of God is clearly and directly impressed on the human heart. The ultimate source for knowledge of God thus lies in the individual's personal subjective experience. Because reason has become infused with emotional experience, Rousseau has been called "the apostle of feeling," and his system of thought "emotional Deism." Rousseau's slogan thus is not, "I think, therefore I am," but "I exist, I sense, I feel, therefore I am."

Rousseau identified moral conscience as a special kind of feeling. Conscience is that primordial and unerring faculty in man that judges between good and evil and impels man to love the good. By this lively instinct, people of every culture, race, and nation discover the reality of God impressed on their hearts. "Conscience! Conscience! Divine instrument, immortal voice from heaven; sure guide for a creature ignorant and finite indeed, yet intelligent and free; infallible judge of good and evil, making man like God! In thee consists the excellence of man's nature and the morality of his actions."[31] Should reason fail in its duty, conscience will not fail to speak in clear tones.

In Rousseau, reason is supplemented with an inner, mystical mode of knowing. To find God, the coherent man has only to make good use of his inbred rational, religious, and moral faculties. Providence has provided the means by which all can find enlightenment. Nature without, but, more important, nature within—i.e., heart and conscience—conspire to disclose the reality of God. The life of moral action based on conscience, "which has neither temples, nor altars, nor rites, and is confined to the purely internal cult of the supreme God and the eternal obligations of morality,"[32] is the true and noble religion.

Given his commitment to natural religion, it comes as no surprise that Rousseau was critical of orthodox Christianity. The simple religion of Jesus was tragically corrupted by the later accretions of the church. Like Voltaire, Rousseau argued that the so-called revealed dogmas of Christianity have been the source of untold intolerance, cruelty, and misery in the world. The Christian faith is valid insofar as it conforms to the simple tenets of natural religion. Rousseau further judges that certain Eastern religions, such as Buddhism, Hinduism, and Sikhism, are worthy approximations of the primal natural religion. The Christian gospel cannot be the exclusive means of salvation, for the Book religion of Christianity is unknown by three-quarters of the world. Irrespective of religion or creed, whoever attends to the voice of God in his moral sentiments and who lives a virtuous life will receive the divine approbation.

Our earlier critique of deism, especially with respect to the negation of special revelation, sin, and redemption, is equally relevant to the French naturalists. In the final analysis, Voltaire was a skeptic and Rousseau a religious humanist. Rousseau, with his emphasis on human subjectivity as the locus of knowledge, was a precursor of Kant and the romantic movement. Fundamentally at odds with the revealed religion of grace and salvation, French naturalism was a powerful catalyst for various forms of irreligion in eighteenth century Europe and beyond.

German Rationalism   The third Enlightenment movement, German rationalism, represents the precipitate of the various strands of humanistic thought in eighteenth century Europe. Although influenced by the insights of the deists, theology in Germany was much more rationalistic than the empirical temper of English theology following Locke. The German rationalists broadly were guided by the first strand of the Cartesian dualism: knowledge of eternal truths is gained by rational inference. Religion, along with mathematics, law, or politics, can be deduced from clear rational principles. In other words, rational thinking is the fount of all theoretical knowledge and practical action. If revelation has any function at all it is merely to confirm the judgments of reason. In addition, the rationalistic theologians also placed considerable emphasis on the necessity of translating rationally derived beliefs into deeds of virtue and morality. Thus it could be said that reason represented the *formal* principle and virtue the *material* principle of eighteenth century German rationalism.

In the early stages of the development, Gottfried Leibnitz (1646–1716) and Christian Wolff (1679–1754) mediated between orthodox Lutheranism and the new rationalism by adopting a position described as "supernatural naturalism." In the Leibnitz-Wolffian philosophy, "reasonableness" was upheld as the primary criterion of truth. Only those articles of Christian belief that do not violate the conclusions of a deductive line of reasoning were upheld as valid. Dogmas antithetic to reason and common sense must be flatly rejected. Following Spinoza, Leibnitz insisted that spiritual freedom is achieved by following the light of reason, and servitude by following one's passions. As Leibnitz would have it, "our reason illumined by the spirit of God reveals the law of nature."[33] Convinced that the existence of God can be positively proved by reason, Leibnitz and Wolff advanced formal arguments for the existence and attributes of the supreme Being. The ontological argument of Descartes was set forth, as were the traditional cosmological and teleological proofs.

Leibnitz and Wolff did much to lay the groundwork for the rise of natural religion in eighteenth century Germany. People of all ages, guided by the light of reason, are led to the knowledge of God and morality that secures temporal and eternal happiness. Wolff insisted that if an atheist faithfully followed the law of nature, he would live as a Christian lives. The ultimate goal of religion is to lead man in the paths of virtue and morality.

Revelation, however, had not yet been made redundant. Truths discerned by reason may be supplemented by higher revealed truths, such as the Trinity, Incarnation, and grace. Revelation thus served to augment the contents of natural religion. Yet always the Christian revelation must harmonize with the simple tenets of natural religion. Hence Wolff could make the following assertion: "Scripture serves as an aid to natural theology. It furnishes natural theology with propositions which ought to be demonstrated. Consequently, the philosopher is bound not to invent but to demonstrate."[34] The function of Christian revelation is to propose propositions that the philosopher rationally validates or rejects. Although the early rationalists sought to uphold the Christian faith, the revelation-reason tension soon began to collapse in favor of autonomous reason.

The Leibnitz-Wolffian tradition regarded Christianity as a reasonable supplement to the universal natural religion. In terms of overall merit, Leibnitz held that the religions of the East are morally superior to Christianity. Buddhism, particularly, reflects a more profound wisdom in its freedom from metaphysical subtleties. Wolff praised the moral principles of Confucius as evidence that reason was capable of guiding non-Christians in the paths of virtue.

In the second phase of German rationalism, special revelation was swallowed up by natural religion and thus became virtually redundant. The supplanting of revealed religion by natural religion was accomplished by two sons of the Enlightenment—H. S. Reimarus (1694–1768), Professor of Oriental Languages at Hamburg, and G. E. Lessing (1729–1781), librarian of the Duke of Brunswick's library at Wolfenbüttel.

In his famous *Wolfenbüttel Fragments* (1774–78), edited and published by Lessing, Reimarus launched a frontal attack against revealed religion. The *Fragments* denied both the necessity and possibility of special revelation, particularly the Christian Scriptures. In an attempt to undermine revealed religion, Reimarus argued that the Bible was full of fallacies, absurdities, and crimes. Since Christianity stands or falls with the Bible, he declared that the Christian religion must be judged a fraud. In place of revealed truth, Reimarus postulated a purely natural religion based on a timeless revelation that is explicated by reason. The natural insights common to all people lead to knowledge of God, freedom, and immortality. Again, we meet the deist argument that true religion must be natural and universal, for it is inconceivable that God should provide special revelation for some and withhold it from others.

Lessing, the leading figure of the German Enlightenment, affirmed the autonomy and self-sufficiency of man without God. In his book *The Education of the Human Race* (1780), he redefined revelation as the continuous process of educating the human family. "That which education is to the individual, revelation is to the race. Education is revelation coming to the individual man; and revelation is education which has come, and is yet coming, to the human race."[35] By revelation man was taught more expeditiously truths that by reason he would have discovered himself.

Natural religion found a staunch ally in Lessing. Revelation was said to converge in the religion of nature and reason, by which man will be liberated from all sects, including Christianity itself. The universally accessible religion of nature and reason involves forming noble conceptions of God and then applying the resultant ideas in deeds of practical virtue. Morality, particularly love, constitutes the core of natural religion. He who loves his neighbor is a Christian. It was inevitable, in Lessing's opinion, that from the core of natural religion the positive religions should have developed. Christianity represents but one stage in the evolution of the true religion of nature, or the religion of all men of good will.

It follows, for Lessing, that the world's historical religions are equally true and equally false. Any given faith represents the adaptation of universal religious truths to a particular cultural context at a particular moment in the evolutionary advance. If a choice must be made, "the best positive or revealed religion is the one containing the fewest conventional additions to natural religion and [the one that] least limits the good effects of natural religion."[36] Throughout his life, Lessing was an implacable foe of supernatural religion. The story is told that when informed that the dying Voltaire had received last rites from a priest, Lessing replied, "When you see me dying call for the notary; I will declare to him that I die in none of the positive religions."[37]

German rationalism at the height of its development took leave of biblical faith by its insistence that man has no practical need of God. Its denial of the Fall and the crippling effects of sin on the intellect contravenes the plain teachings of the Word of God. Its repudiation of special revelation and its insistence on the sufficiency of the light of nature and reason violates the tenor of scriptural teaching. Neither Scripture nor the historic Christian consensus offers any ground for the rationalist claim that the final court of appeal in spiritual matters is man himself. The majesty and holiness of God together with the finitude and sinfulness of man suggests that many divine truths will transcend the workings of the human mind. The rationalist contention that man outside the church knows as much about God as man inside the church finds little support in the Word of God. Moreover, history offers little encouragement for the thesis that by following the light of nature and reason man will actualize virtue and morality in his daily life. In conclusion, the several rationalist movements in eighteenth-century Europe subscribed to an inadequate reductionist theology, namely, a theology within the bounds of reason only.

VI ASSERTING THE AUTONOMY OF MAN: FOUR LIBERAL AGENDAS

The rationalistic spirit in the church led to atheism and irreligion, while in society, through Voltaire, Diderot, and others, it led to the chaos of the French Revolution (1789–94). The cul-de-sac in which eighteenth-century Enlightenment rationalism found itself mandated a new tack that would avoid the sterility of a purely deductive approach to religious truth. Faith, many had come to believe, was a far richer reality than the attainment of conclusions through the process of syllogistic reasoning. Thus during the last quarter of the eighteenth century and the first half of the nineteenth, romanticism emerged as the dominant movement in theology, filling the gap voided by the deists, naturalists, and rationalists. Whereas the eighteenth century involved a revolt against revelation in the name of autonomous reason, the nineteenth century involved a revolt against autonomous reason in the name of ineffable religious feeling.

Romanticism, in fact, represents the subjective side of the Cartesian dualism; certainty was sought within the consciousness of the individual soul. As in the period of eighteenth-century rationalism, so in the romantic era theology remained essentially anthropocentric. Thus, independent of supernatural revelation, the reality of God was sought in the reality of man. Yet instead of seeking God in the external world, following the experimental reason of Locke, the romantics sought God within the aesthetic sensibilities of man himself, much as in the sentimentalism of Rousseau. To be sure, the romantic school of Herder, Fichte, Coleridge, Schleiermacher, and Maurice upheld the validity of natural theology; only now the data of natural theology was drawn not from without, but solely from man's inner religious awareness. "My experience is my proof" was the romantics' slogan. They thought it foolish that God should be sought by syllogistic reasoning when He is richly present in man's religious self-consciousness. Thus in romanticism we find liberal theology seeking to know God through the modality of religious experience.

The romantic school of theology, literature, and music was characterized by several common commitments. In the first place, a thoroughgoing subjectivity characterized the movement. Truth was seen to be a function of the inner world of ineffable self-consciousness. The romantics stressed the aesthetic rather than the intellectual side of human nature. Human imagination, feeling, and intuition disclose that there is more to reality than a mechanical universe operating according to fixed physical laws. In this regard, Wordsworth could speak of "sensations sweet, felt in the blood, and felt along the heart."[1] The almost sensual beauty of the natural world was an important theme in romanticism. Mountains, rivers, seas, clouds, and flowers represent a richly variegated phenomenon pulsating with life and splendor. Secondly, the romantic spirit focused on the element of mystery in experience. The *summum bonum* was posited in life's intangible realities that defy rational formulation. The romantic commitment involved an intuitive sense of nature's grand mysteries. Romanticism, thirdly, played on the fringes of pantheism. God was envisaged as "the vital Spirit immanent in all things, the creative eros in which everything moves and has its being."[2] The Infinite was perceived in every impulse of human consciousness, in every relationship and action. Finally, following the older deism, the romantic movement conceived of religion as variegated and diverse in its manifold expressions. Whatever the external shape of his creed or religion, man's most fundamental drive was to be in communion with the infinite Spirit of the universe. Two students of the movement précis the character of romanticism as follows:

> The mood of romanticism was one of reaction against the dry intellectualism of the rationalists; it pointed instead to imagination and to creative fancy, to freedom and individuality, to the spontaneity and mystery of life—i.e., particularly to those dimensions of the life of the spirit for which rationalism had no room.[3]

The Romanticism of Schleiermacher   Friedrich Schleiermacher (1763–1834), parish preacher who later held the chair of theology at Berlin, represents the dominant figure in nineteenth-century romantic theology. Raised in the pietistic tradition of the Moravian Brethren, Schleiermacher wrote two books that had a substantial impact on the religious world—*On Religion: Addresses in Response to Its Cultured Critics* (1799),[4] an apology for his system of religious experience, and *The Christian Faith* (1821),[5] the first systematic theology of the modern era. Schleiermacher, who was influenced by Kant, Spinoza, and Leibnitz, and who lived in the heyday of German idealism, has been acclaimed the greatest theologian between Calvin and Barth. Karl Barth himself declared that as the watershed of modern theology, "Schleiermacher . . . has no rival."[6] Schleiermacher's system of religious consciousness had a significant impact on the shape of theology in the nineteenth and early twentieth centuries.

Reacting against the rationalistic tradition, Schleiermacher established religious belief on the foundation of pious subjectivity. Man, he argued, is first and foremost a feeling rather than a thinking being. Providentially excited by God, man possesses the intrinsic capacity to sense and taste the Infinite. In Schleiermacher's scheme, higher truths are derived from religious feeling (*Gefühl*). More than mere human emotion, feeling is the intuition of immediate self-consciousness,[7] or that inner sense of continuity with the Spirit of the universe. As such, feeling overcomes the subject-object duality, as the subject unites with that which is set over against it. Moreover, he who penetrates deeply into his consciousness, Schleiermacher argues, will detect a sense of unqualified dependence on the Ultimate. But "to feel oneself absolutely dependent and to be conscious of being in relation to God are one and the same thing."[8] The "feeling of absolute dependence," or the universal element in self-consciousness, is noncognitive, mystical, and identical in all persons. "This feeling of absolute dependence . . . is therefore not an accidental element, or a thing which varies from person to person, but a universal element of life."[9] Man, then, is essentially a religious being (*homo religiosus*). People everywhere thus need only to attend to their inner religious feelings to establish contact with God, for consciousness of God involves "the direct inward expression of the feeling of absolute dependence."[10] At this point we may observe that, following Kant, man gains no knowledge of God as He is in Himself, but only knowledge of God's relationship to man.

With other romantic theologians, Schleiermacher argued that the classical "proofs" for the existence of God are entirely superfluous: "These proofs can never be a component part of the system of doctrine."[11] This is so because the feeling of utter dependence establishes the reality of God with certainty and finality. How far from the divine Reality, Schleiermacher argued, is the conclusion to a sequence of syllogistic reasoning! And how little does philosophical speculation contribute to the formation of true piety! For Schleiermacher, there is no substitute for the certitude provided by apprehension of God in the immediacy of one's sense and taste for the Infinite.

What kind of statements does Schleiermacher make about the object of one's feeling of absolute dependence? That of which man is immediately aware is God, the Universe, the Whole. Schleiermacher's God, however, is not a personal, transcendent Being distinct from the world. Stressing the unity and continuity of all reality, Schleiermacher envisages God as the Spirit of the universe or as the source of our feelings of utter dependence. God is beyond all the speculative conceptions of the philosopher or the theologian. Religion, in fact, has no special interest in God as a person, but only in man's experienced *relationship* with the Ultimate. Schleiermacher claims that we may even dispense with the term "God" and substitute for it any other term that adequately describes the universal factor encountered in human experience. Given the virtual identity of God with the totality of the universe, it is difficult to conclude that Schleiermacher's system is anything other than pantheistic.

Explicating further his system of religious subjectivity, Schleiermacher defines revelation as "every new and original communication of the universe and its innermost life to men."[12] Each combination of insight, perspective, and feeling constitutes for the individual a fresh revelation. It is clear that instead of requiring consciousness to be regulated by the Bible, Schleiermacher subsumed Scripture to the judgments of religious experience. Only those parts of the Bible consistent with one's religious feelings were accepted as valid. Schleiermacher firmly opposed the orthodox view of revelation as a deposit of timeless, objective truths. Likewise, Christ should not be regarded as a supernatural revelation, for He was no more than a man with his own feelings of absolute dependence on the Whole. In short, for Schleiermacher, man's knowledge of God derives very simply from his own religious consciousness.

Since Christianity is a life of piety and obedience, faith has little to do with traditional doctrines or dogmas. Theology's primary task is to provide a descriptive analysis of the self-consciousness or feelings of dependence experienced by the Christian community. Thus Schleiermacher could say, "Christian doctrines are accounts of the Christian religious affections set forth in speech."[13] Lest there remain any uncertainty on the matter, Schleiermacher added a further word: "The doctrines in all their forms have their ultimate ground so exclusively in the emotions that where these do not exist the doctrines cannot arise."[14]

Schleiermacher defined faith as "certainty concerning the feeling of absolute dependence."[15] Moreover, religion becomes the sum total of all such feelings of absolute dependence. "To seek and to find this infinite and eternal factor in all that lives and moves, in all growth and change, in all action and passion, and to have and to know life itself only in immediate feeling—that is religion."[16] Since the sense and taste for the Infinite is universal, it follows that all men by nature are religious. Of course, Schleiermacher recognized in people gradations of religion or piety. Godlessness or godliness are relative terms that signify a God-consciousness that is either arrested or properly cultivated. Where superstition or irreligion reign, the problem may be traced back to a God-consciousness that has not been properly sensitized. In the case of atheism, God-consciousness has been eclipsed by God-forgetfulness. But Schleiermacher adds that even where the moral condition of mankind is painted in darkest terms, as in Romans 1:18ff., the possibility of rekindling feelings of absolute dependence, and thus true piety, is ever present.

Borrowing the thesis advanced by the older deists, Schleiermacher insists that religion or piety exhibits itself in a variety of forms: "I certainly have presupposed the multiplicity of religions, for I find that multiplicity embedded in the very nature of religion."[17] The existence of the diverse religions of the world—animism, Islam, Judaism, Christianity, et al.—is due to the variety of ways in which the fundamental religious consciousness developed and was interpreted by man. Among peoples of diverse ethnic and cultural backgrounds, the religious affections have come to expression in richly variegated forms. Hence Schleiermacher concludes that one should speak of the world's positive religions not as true or false, but as more or less pure formulations of man's basic religious consciousness. In Schleiermacher's judgment, "The deity is to be perceived and worshiped in many ways."[18] Hence it is immaterial with which historical religion one identifies. "Each person may seek out religion in the church in a form best suited to nurture the inchoate seed of religion within him."[19] The real Schleiermacher thus stands up as a staunch proponent of religious pluralism.

But how does Schleiermacher, the Protestant theologian, esteem the Christian religion? Christianity provides the most adequate formulation of the experience of absolute dependence that lies at the heart of all religion. "Christianity . . . takes its place as the purest form of monotheism which has appeared in history."[20] In fact, Schleiermacher goes so far as to speak of "the exclusive superiority of Christianity."[21] Christianity's primacy rests on the unique character of its founder, Jesus of Nazareth. While denying the finality of Jesus' mediatorial work, Schleiermacher acknowledges that the power and clarity of the Nazarene's God-consciousness finds no equal among men. Hence the way of Jesus provides a particularly fruitful path to authentic religious experience and thus to the knowledge of God.

As a disciple of the German school of idealism, Schleiermacher departed from orthodox theology by denying the personality of God and His transcendence over the Creation. Since the romantic theologian seemingly merged God with the universe, Barth's designation of Schleiermacher as a pantheist appears valid. Moreover, Schleiermacher has taken leave of biblical faith by denying that revelation consists of saving deeds enacted on the stage of history and objective truths recorded on the pages of Scripture. In affirming that the locus of revelation is entirely within man himself, he has erroneously overlooked the several extrinsic modes of revelation by which God addresses man from outside his own internal world. Against Schleiermacher, revelation is more than the feeling of God's indwelling presence. Schleiermacher thus has little in common with the Reformation divines whose theological starting point was God's communication of intelligible, objective truths to man.

Schleiermacher likewise has erred in attempting to ground theology and piety in the shifting sands of subjective religious experience. Surely, a rational theology capable of being tested by logical consistency and coherence with the facts is superior to a private theology of mystical self-consciousness. Schleiermacher and the romantic school reacted so excessively against the sterile intellectualism of the rationalists that they conceded little power to cognition. They overlooked the biblical teaching that God has granted an enablement to the natural mind through universal common grace (John 1:9) and that God renews the believing mind by the operation of the Holy Spirit (Eph. 4:23; Col. 3:10). Classical theology, whatever its defects, at least was a theology characterized by a high degree of intelligibility. But Schleiermacher's theology of the inner life is mystical and ineffable. Schleiermacher rightly decried the autonomous intellect of the eighteenth-century rationalists, but he blindly overlooked the autonomous feeling on which his own system of theology is based.

In truth, the whole edifice of Christian theology cannot be derived, as Schleiermacher insists, from an analysis of human consciousness. In seeking to derive the truth of God from his own effable experience, one necessarily ends with a truncated theology. A nonrational theological apriorism, such as Schleiermacher advocates, operates under severe limitations. Thomas Aquinas was on far more solid ground in holding that his rational system of natural theology must be supplemented by an objective special revelation if such truths as the Trinity, Atonement, and Resurrection were to be attained. Indeed, when Schleiermacher views God neither as a person nor as a subject but as the ground of feelings of utter dependence, he seems to identify God with the experienced relation itself. Schleiermacher's epistemology thus creates a metaphysic in which the experience itself becomes God. But on this showing if man no longer experienced feelings of absolute dependence, then God would cease to exist. In this way the reductionist character of Schleiermacher's theology of subjective experience is pointed up.

Finally, Schleiermacher's system falls short of the biblical standard in its assertion that the end and goal of religion is not God but man. With its thoroughgoing anthropocentrism—where not God but man and his aspirations and anxieties occupy center stage—Schleiermacher provided a lively stimulus for various forms of experiential theology devised by generations of liberals to follow. Moreover, his thesis that piety springs not from eternal, objective truths but from subjective feelings laid the foundation for twentieth-century existentialist ethics.

Ritschl's Theology of Value Judgments   Following Schleiermacher's theology of religious feeling, and partially in reaction to it, there emerged in the latter part of the nineteenth century a new impulse pioneered by Albrecht Ritschl. The resultant Ritschlian school of theology, which included figures such as Wilhelm Herrmann, Julius Kaftan, Adolf Von Harnack, and the American spokesman for the social gospel, Walter Rauschenbush, was a potent force in the theological world from about 1875 to 1930. It is popularly believed that liberalism is a distinctly twentieth-century phenomenon. Yet the crucial theological struggles occurred decades earlier in the latter half of the nineteenth century. Thus, in reality, the Ritschlian theology may be regarded as the immediate forerunner of twentieth-century liberalism, both in Europe and in America.

The Ritschlian school rejected the romanticism of Schleiermacher and the idealism of Hegel by aligning itself with the philosophical and theological precepts of neo-Kantianism. Ritschlianism could be described as antimetaphysical, antimystical, and historical-empirical in character. Following Kant, the Ritschlian theologians insisted that what can be known is not the "thing-in-itself," but only its effect or felt value for the individual. The existence of God and other metaphysical problems lie beyond the domain of human ratiocination. The proper task of theology is not inquiry into metaphysics but regard for matters of practical religion. Moreover, in opposition to the mystics and romantics, the Ritschlian movement rejected the supposition that personal feelings constitute the heart of religion. Religion must not be viewed in terms of an individual's mystical relationship to God. Rather, religion involves the complex web of moral relationships that exist between God, man, and society. With his heavy emphasis on religious consciousness, Schleiermacher, Ritschl judged, was a dangerous subjectivist. Finally, loyal to the Kantian thesis that human knowing is limited to the phenomena of the space-time world, the Ritschlian school posited that spiritual truth is acquired by the process of empirical and historical interpretation. It adopted the functional viewpoint that what God *does* informs man of what God *is*.

Albrecht Ritschl (1822–1889), the chief pillar of the school that bears his name, studied under the neopietist Tholuck and the radical New Testament critic and historian F. C. Baur. Ritschl occupied the chair of theology at Göttingen for a quarter century (1864–1889) and developed into the model liberal theologian. Many authorities view Ritschl as the most influential theologian between Schleiermacher and Barth. Berkhof, for example, claims that "with the single exception of Schleiermacher, no one has exercised greater influence on present-day theology than has A. Ritschl."[22]

Ritschl's theological system is spelled out in his *opus magnum* called *The Christian Doctrine of Justification and Reconciliation*, published between 1870 and 1874.[23] Ritschl undoubtedly was motivated by the noble desire to vindicate religious belief in the modern secularized world. Moreover, he ostensibly sought to work within a broad biblical and Lutheran framework. Yet, however salutary his intentions, Ritschl came down firmly outside the bounds of the orthodoxy of Augustine, the Reformers, and the post-Reformation divines.

Ritschl's primary theological concern for the ethical side of the Christian religion—e.g., issues of sin, guilt, alienation, forgiveness, and freedom—is reflected in the title of his major work cited above. Whereas classical theology generally began with the study of God Himself, Ritschl imposed a new ordering by commencing the study of theology with the justification and reconciliation of the sinner, the two chief aspects of Christ's work. The former, justification, Ritschl defined as the forgiveness of sins and the restoration of fellowship with God. Through justification, man's guilt, viewed as deprivation of fellowship, is overcome. The latter, reconciliation, signifies man's identification with God and His purpose, chiefly through the practical doing of His will. Reconciliation, simply put, means "the realized ideal of human life."[24] Justification and reconciliation, the objective and subjective poles of salvation, are achieved through the moral influence of Christ on the life. It should be noted that Ritschl's soteriology allowed no place for the substitutionary atonement, the forensic imputation of Christ's righteousness, or the destruction of the power of indwelling sin.

Ritschl, moreover, viewed salvation primarily as a social experience. Faith works itself out not individually but corporately, as Christians together discharge their ethical responsibilities to society. As the church impacts the world with works of moral goodness, Ritschl argued, it will radically transform society and inaugurate the kingdom of God on earth. Indeed, the kingdom of God could be viewed as the key concept in Ritschl's theology. His definition of the kingdom, as other aspects of his theology, had a strong ethical ring to it. The kingdom of God signifies "the organization of humanity through action inspired by love."[25] Alternatively, the kingdom is an association of men bound together by the laws of virtue. In sum, then, Ritschl held that man's relationship to God in terms of justification and reconciliation, and God's relationship to the world in terms of the kingdom, are related as the two foci of an ellipse.

Ritschl concurred with Schleiermacher that the starting point of religion is the data of Christian experience. Yet in place of Schleiermacher's feeling of absolute dependence, Ritschl substituted man's total experience as a moral being. From this guiding principle, Ritschl developed a theology of moral values or value judgments. Ritschl's distinction between judgments of fact and judgments of value is crucial. Theoretical science, operating according to the critical reason, fails to carry the investigator beyond the level of bare facticity. But religious faith is grounded in value judgments (*Werturteile*) that involve the interpretation of the facts and their significance for the life of the individual or the group. Here Ritschl focused attention on knowledge that is of value and worth for the person. "Religious knowledge moves in independent value-judgments, which relate to man's attitude to the world, and call forth feelings of pleasure and pain in which man either enjoys dominion over the world vouchsafed to him by God, or feels grievously the lack of God's help to that end."[26] Ritschl's neo-Kantian orientation prompted distinterest in metaphysical speculation. But the concept of value judgment enabled him to focus on what he regarded as the truly relevant concern, namely, on the meaning and value of metaphysical realities for life. In this regard, Ritschl's religion was essentially pragmatic. Theoretical doctrines were devalued in favor of a lived life that leads to the highest end. Barth explicates Ritschl's concept of value judgments with the following observation:

> A value-judgment is a judgment in which a certain aspect of being is expressed concerning a certain object of human experience with regard to the value, i.e., the practical significance, which it has for man, a certain aspect of being which, apart from this practical significance, could not be expressed concerning the object.[27]

Ritschl, then, insists that all religious knowledge is founded on value judgments of faith.[28] Applied to the subject of the present study, God is known only in terms of His value for the individual. God is known not in a metaphysical sense through propositional revelation, but as a felt moral need. In pursuing this line of argument, we noted that Ritschl followed Kant, who argued that man knows things not as they are in themselves, but as he perceives them; namely, as he apprehends them in their relationship to and in their value for the person. Traditionalists argue that one must first know the nature of God before His worth for us can be ascertained. Ritschl totally reversed this order and insisted that the nature of God is known only in terms of His felt worth. Hence Ritschl flatly affirms, "Apart from this value-judgment of faith, there exists no knowledge of God."[29] It should be evident, in the first place, that Ritschl allowed for no innate knowledge of God or knowledge gained by rational reflection on Creation or providence. And secondly, the knowledge of God postulated by Ritschl is entirely subjective. Man knows of God only that which speaks to the problems of human existence in the world. God, in other words, is posited as a moral need. What God is in Himself cannot be known.

The historico-empirical character of Ritschl's system needs elaboration. Moral judgments are shaped not in a vacuum, but as the community of faith perceives the value of God's revelation in the history of Jesus Christ. The serious student of history insisted that moral judgments are inseparable from the historical data. God is known through his actions, particularly through the life, teachings, and deeds of Jesus of Nazareth. Ritschl's system thus is rigorously Christocentric. Collectively, the phenomena surrounding the historical person Jesus Christ constitute the divine revelation. Here Ritschl's corrective to Schleiermacher's mysticism is obvious. God is known not through ecstatic feelings that well up from within, but by means of value judgments made in respect of the New Testament witness to the divine revelation in Jesus.

Theology's task thus involves explicating the revelation embedded in the history of Jesus. Jesus, in Ritschl's opinion, is not ontologically God, but an unusual man among men.[30] Jesus' uniqueness resides in the fact that He was the first man to actualize in His life the kingdom purposes of God. Indeed, the character of God is unveiled in the firmness of Jesus' religious convictions, in the purity of His motives, and in the humility of His life. Faith, as it reflects on the life and works of Jesus of Nazareth, judges that God is pure and total love. In Jesus, man discovers that God is both a loving Father and a merciful Redeemer. In Jesus, man discerns that God extends to him forgiveness, restoration of fellowship, and personal freedom. Nothing demonstrates more clearly the value of the Godhead than the man Jesus. Insofar as Jesus most fully revealed God, Ritschl insists that the Nazarene possesses for man the *value* of God. Ritschl, of course, maintains that since the revelation of God is displayed in the history of the man Jesus, no special doctrine of biblical revelation is required. In sum, religious knowledge in the Ritsch-

101

lian scheme is gained not by assent to dogmas (orthodoxy), nor by reason (rationalism), nor by the religious self-consciousness (romanticism), but by value judgments made in respect of Jesus, the historical person.

It comes as no surprise that Ritschl, the neo-Kantian, was a staunch foe of all Roman Catholic and Protestant natural theologies that postulated a knowledge of God independent of historical revelation.[31] Inferences drawn from the observation of nature are of no worth in religion, since they are divorced from the history of Jesus. Moreover, conclusions drawn from the realm of nature are scientific judgments of fact rather than religious judgments of value. Theoretical knowledge and religious knowledge (value judgments) "are different functions of spirit, which when they deal with the same objects, are not even partially coincident, but wholly diverge."[32] The cosmological and teleological "proofs" at best afford only a theoretical and disinterested scientific knowledge. They fail to transport the seeker beyond the space-time world to the invisible realm. The ontological argument, likewise, is of little worth, since it involves the mere thought of God, as opposed to His existence and relevance *pro me*. All three "proofs" fail to convey God's value and worth for man the sinner. Ritschl sums up the value of the three classical arguments for God's existence as follows:

> The proofs for God's existence, whose construction is purely metaphysical, lead not to the Being the idea of which Scholastic theology receives as a datum from Christianity, but merely to conceptions of the world-unity which have nothing to do with any religion. This use of metaphysics, consequently, must be forbidden in theology, if the latter's positive and proper character is to be maintained.[33]

But Ritschl found a useful tool for developing his system of value judgments in Kant's moral argument for God's existence. Man is primarily an ethical being. As such, he is conscious of a supreme law that attests the reality of a divine Will that has created and ordered the world toward spiritual and ethical ends. Hence by means of practical reason rather than theoretical cognition, the existence and moral demands of a supreme Being are recognized. Here again, Ritschl makes room for a knowledge of God founded on judgments of value, which he perceives are of a totally different order than the objectives of theoretical science.

We now consider briefly how Ritschl's theory of knowledge works itself out in terms of the relationship between Christianity and the world's non-Christian religions. Ritschl conceives of religion ethically in terms of a life of practical morality predicated on value judgments. Humankind is intrinsically religious as it reflects on matters of ultimate value. Although all religions are based on revelation and mediate a relationship between God and man, not all religions are of equal value. Due to the progressive unfolding of divine revelation, there is an ascending series of positive religions. Since Jesus most fully reflects the value of God for man and thus mediates the fullest knowledge of God, Christianity is the highest religion. Said Ritschl, "Christianity transcends them all, and in Christianity the tendency of all the others finds its perfect consummation."[34] In the context of the evolutionary advance, Christianity represents the perfect embodiment of all that is noble in the older religions. Thus on the one hand Ritschl stresses the continuity that exists between religions, while on the other he exalts Christianity as the ideal to which all religions strive.

Unlike the optimism of Schleiermacher, Ritschl faced squarely the human realities of sin, guilt, and alienation. Likewise, he insisted that Christianity is no mere human creation. "The Christian religion has its origin in a special revelation,"[35] he maintained. Ritschl, moreover, must be commended for his profound interest in the historical Jesus and his commitment to the far-reaching implications of the Christian life. Ritschl reminds conservative Christianity that practical religion must not be neglected in its concern for orthodox theology. But there is little doubt that Ritschl's value judgment theology falls within the Enlightenment tradition.[36] Since the religious believer or the community of faith makes the judgments of value, Ritschl's system is no less subjective than Schleiermacher's scheme of religious consciousness, which he rejected. But like Schleiermacher, Ritschl made few references to propositional revelation, for in his system there were few transcendent truths that needed to be revealed.

Moreover, Ritschl's Christology diverges substantially from the biblical model. Whereas John and Paul, guided by the Holy Spirit, represent Jesus Christ as the externally divine Son who assumed the manhood of a Palestinian carpenter, Ritschl's Jesus was a mere man who bore the perfect revelation of God. In stressing the value of Christ's work for the community of faith, Ritschl overlooked the divine character of Christ's person. Falsely judging that God is pure love without any admixture of wrath, Ritschl argued that justification involves no placation of God and no removal of objective guilt. In this respect, he fundamentally misrepresented the Bible's teaching on justification and reconciliation. Thus, in reality, he violated the integrity of both the person and the work of our Lord.

Ritschl, the antimetaphysical theologian, exercised considerable influence on the theological school that bore his name and the subsequent history-of-religions school. Moreover, his explication of the kingdom of God as an association of men bound together by the rule of virtue provided a significant impetus to Rauschenbusch's man-centered social gospel in America. Theologians, both orthodox and neoorthodox, expressed concern about the deceptiveness of the religion of Ritschl. Brunner, for example, insisted that "the Ritschlian theology is a rationalistic system clad in supernatural garments."[37]

Wilhelm Herrmann (1846–1922), Marburg dogmatic theologian whose university lectures had a shaping influence on his pupils Barth, Bultmann, and Baillie, was a leading spokesman of the Ritschlian school. In addition to the impact of Ritschl, Herrmann was indebted to Kant's critical epistemology and to Schleiermacher's emphasis on religious experience as a means to knowledge of God. Although he found many points of agreement with

Schleiermacher's system, the neo-Kantian theologian Herrmann was closer to Ritschl than to the romantic school. Herrmann left a short posthumus work entitled *Systematic Theology*.[38] His chief contribution was an essay entitled *The Communion of the Christian With God* (1886).[39]

The highest concern of the religious life, according to Herrmann, is how a person can achieve communion with God. Negatively, in opposition to the scholastic tradition, Herrmann insisted that God is not to be found in nature or providence. Metaphysical speculation, including the traditional arguments in support of theism, are worthless. Indeed, all attempts to discover the reality of God in the existence, order, and harmony of the external world are doomed to failure. Herrmann thus claims,

> From the reality of the world which science can investigate, the attempt was made so to demonstrate the reality of God as to compel the assent of every thinking man. All such proofs are scientifically untenable, and the idea that a man can come to religion in this way is inconsistent with its essential nature.[40]

Moreover, contra Schleiermacher, knowledge of God does not emerge from feelings and emotions wholly interior to the soul. Herrmann argues against the romantic theologian, who says that what man apprehends in his consciousness may equally be Fate as the living God.

On the positive side, following Ritschl, Herrmann insisted that the quest for God must begin with data that are external to the soul and drawn from the working of God in the events of life.[41] That is, God crowds in on man's consciousness out of the reality of life in the space-time world. But although mediated through history, knowledge is something that man apprehends by direct communion with God Himself. Hence the fundamental focus of religion is man's own communion with God in the inner life. Thus Herrmann argues, "We cannot receive religious knowledge by having it proved to us, nor can we thus impart it to others. It must arise in each man afresh and individually."[42] Whereas Schleiermacher identified the core of religion as feeling (*Gefühl*), Herrmann acknowledged that the focus of religion is experience (*Erlebnis*) that flows out of a historical situation.

From this perspective, revelation was defined in experiential terms. Neither a corpus of objective truths nor a series of past historical events, revelation denotes the individual's inner experience of spiritual renewal and transformation. Herrmann identified as a revelation any experience in which the power of life is discovered. Revelation thus has no objective foundation but is grounded strictly in the religious affections. The movement in revelation is from man to God, and revelation occurs when man makes contact with a power higher than himself. Two concomitants of this emphasis on the experiential side of religion are worth noting. First, metaphysics in Herrmann is entirely eliminated. Even more rigorously than Ritschl, Herrmann rejected the role of metaphysics in religion. No metaphysical system can claim to affirm truths apart from the subjective experiences of the individual. In the second place, Herrmann abandoned all interest in formal theological doctrines. Herrmann said that doctrines are "worthless dreams which arouse useless strife."[43] Not only St. Thomas's *Summa Theologica* but also Calvin's *Institutes* must be relegated to the dustbin of outmoded approaches to the Christian faith. From the perspective of a theology of religious experience, much of traditional dogmatics has to be abandoned.

The source of the Christian's religious experience and the means of communion with God are found in the earthly life of Jesus as recorded in the Gospels. More specifically, Herrmann insists that the inner life of Jesus as interpreted by the Christian community is the means by which God is known. Through a sensitive reading of the Gospels, the transforming power of Jesus' inner life is impressed on the soul, and God Himself becomes a present reality in the reader's experience.

> The Person of Jesus becomes to us a real Power rooted in history, not through historical proofs, but through the experience produced in us by the picture of his spiritual life which we can find for ourselves in the pages of the New Testament. We gain here an experience that we would otherwise seek in vain, the impression of a unique Person who is able to hold us in the thraldom of utter surrender; we can no longer maintain an attitude of critical detachment, as we should do were we inclined to regard the tradition as a product of human imagination.[44]

Because the spirit of Jesus leaps out to the reader from the pages of the Gospels, "We through the man Jesus are first lifted up to a real communion with God."[45] Put in other terms, the objective historical record of Jesus in the Gospels represents a judgment of fact. But the individual's felt experience of Jesus' significance constitutes a far more important judgment of value. Indeed, the individual not only experiences communion with God through the significance that he derives from the presentation of Jesus' inner life but he is also set free from the limitations of self-centered, finite existence. However, by interpreting the significance of Jesus by exclusive appeal to personal experience, Herrmann has overlooked the objective testimony of Scripture to the permanent revelatory value of Jesus' person and work.

It follows that the sort of religious experience of which Herrmann speaks defies objectification. "The inner life of religion," he argues, "in the last resort is something secret and incommunicable."[46] Since the religious experience provides its own inner certitude and requires no objective formulation to confirm its validity, Herrmann insists that his noncognitive, experiential approach to the knowledge of God avoids the danger of mysticism. By grounding religious value judgments in the inner life of the historical Jesus, he felt that he had skirted the arbitrariness of the religious mystic. Nevertheless, by divorcing Jesus' significance from the objective Word of Scripture and by positing it as the personal valuation of an ineffable power impressed upon the soul, Herrmann has incontestably moved into the realm of religious mysticism.

With his developed system of Jesus-mysticism, one might expect Herrmann to be intolerant of the knowledge claims of other religions. But such is not the case. Indeed, Herrmann affirms that Jesus' inner life is the primary source of the knowledge of God for Christians. Nevertheless, since Israel possessed an authentic knowledge of God prior to the coming of Christ, we assume that other religious traditions also mediate a valid experience of God. Herrmann, in fact, claims that every religion mediates the experience of an exalted feeling and yearning for God. No heathen has ever lacked the capacity for instinctively recognizing God in the depths of his soul.

> We by no means wish to assert, even for a moment, that the savages of New Holland have no knowledge of God, no pulsations of true religion, and therefore no communion with God. But we do not know through what medium such knowledge and such communion reach them.[47]

Herrmann advances the old cultural argument of the deists to the effect that religion, defined as an experienced transformation of the soul, must assume different forms among peoples of different ethnic and cultural backgrounds. Truth necessarily manifests itself in a countless variety of forms. Moreover, people's religious imaginations become fixed in many different ways. Religion, therefore, must be given free rein to develop in accordance with the religious and moral consciousness of the individual worshiper. Even in the case of the Christian tradition, "The idea of dogma as a uniform doctrinal theory is contrary to the working of the Holy Spirit."[48]

In Herrmann and the Ritschlian school of theology, we find the classical liberal emphasis on subjective religious experience. As has been noted, the process of evaluating the significance of the inner life of Jesus is a highly subjective enterprise fraught with the possibility of self-deception and error. Inasmuch as Herrmann believed that the Gospels have been heavily redacted by later Christians, what guarantee is there that the Gospel portrait of the inner life of Jesus is reliable? Moreover, in Herrmann, faith was consistently defined as trust (*fiducia*), but rarely as knowledge (*notitia*). Contrary to Augustine's system of religious knowledge, where saving wisdom (*sapientia*) rests on factual knowledge about the Christ (*scientia*), Ritschlian faith is mystically mediated. Christian experience in Ritschl and Herrmann suffers by not being framed with cognitive truths. Karl Barth, for one, was pessimistic about the contribution of the romantic and Ritschlian schools. Said he in bold terms, "In the line of Schleiermacher-Ritschl-Herrmann . . . I can only see the plain destruction of Protestant theology and the Protestant Church."[49] Indeed, certain distinguished pupils of Herrmann—e.g., Barth, Bultmann, and Baillie—felt little constraint to perpetuate the Ritschlian theology, but rather opposed it as a reduction of revealed Christian truth.

Troeltsch and the History-of-Religions Focus
The so-called history-of-religions school (*religionsgeschichtliche Schule*), which flourished from

approximately 1875 to 1925, was less a theological school than a methodo-logical approach to the study of religion. Leading proponents of the method include Max Müller (d. 1900), Wilhelm Wrede (d. 1906), H. J. Holtzmann (d. 1910), Julius Wellhausen (d. 1918), Wilhelm Bousset (d. 1920), Ernest Troeltsch (d. 1923), Hermann Gunkel (d. 1932), and Rudolph Otto (d. 1937). In its insistence that truth is attainable from self-evident, rational principles, the comparative-religions movement represents the legacy of the theological Enlightenment. Its rise to prominence in the latter quarter of the nineteenth century was stimulated by a fresh understanding of other religions through anthropological research, by the discovery of the sacred books of the East, and by the application of Darwin's evolutionary hypothesis to religion.

The comparative-religions approach began with the postulate that reli-gion is a purely historical phenomenon that one investigates by the stand-ard methods of historical research. Through an analysis of religious phenomena, scholars sought to discover the origin of religion and the laws by which it operates. By studying the similarities and dissimilarities be-tween the various faiths, comparative-religions experts affirmed the unity of religion (in terms of an underlying common core) and the fact that the positive religions exist in various stages of development. Most history-of-religions scholars held that widely divergent groups of peoples, at bottom, subscribe to common patterns of religious belief and practice. Since particu-lar faiths exist as part of a complex web of religion, the task of theology is not to pass judgment on the truth or falsehood of specific religions. Con-sequently, assertions of finality or absoluteness based on alleged super-natural revelations were summarily ruled out of court.

Comparative-religions scholars sought to substantiate the validity of the world's major religions within the evolutionary continuum by replacing special revelation with a universal general revelation. A general and univer-sally valid self-disclosure of God was held to undergird the positive religions of the world. Most authorities within the movement held that the reality of God wells up within man as a fundamental and universal datum of reli-gious experience. Ernst Troeltsch, one of the leading proponents of the comparative-religions method, summarized its distinctives as follows:

> The movement signifies, in general, simply the recognition of the universally accepted scientific conclusion that human religion exists only in manifold spe-cific religious cults which develop in very complex relations of mutual contact and influence, and that in this religious development it is impossible to make the older dogmatic distinction between a natural and a supernatural revelation.[50]

According to the history-of-religions model, Christianity's claims to ab-soluteness as a supernaturally revealed religion can no longer be substan-tiated. Christianity takes its place as one element in the complex web of religion. Through a lengthy process of interaction and synthesis involving late Judaism, the Greek mystery religions, Gnosticism, and Stoicism, the Christian religion has evolved into its present form. Yet Christianity and contemporary world religions, through mutual interaction and enrichment, are destined to advance to more prefect representations of the truth of religion. Thus, in short, Christianity is a relativistic and syncretistic phenomenon that has become manifest at a particular point in the evolutionary ascent of the human spirit.

Ernst Troeltsch (1865–1923), philosopher of religion and theologian who lectured at the universities of Heidelberg and Berlin, is acclaimed the prominent theologian of the history-of-religions movement. While a student at Göttingen, Troeltsch bought into the neo-Kantian emphasis on noncognitive experience of God and the Ritschlian scheme of value judgments. Later associations at Göttingen with the historians of religion Bousset, Wrede, and Gunkel strengthened his interest in the historico-cultural approach to religion.

Throughout his life, Troeltsch was passionately interested in historical questions pertaining to the study of religion—e.g., the nature of historical knowledge, the role of religion in society, and the great diversity of religious forms. Moreover, in the tradition of Hegelian idealism, Troeltsch viewed history, culture, and religion as a single continuous whole. Since history is permeated by the progressively self-revealing activity of God, one cannot distinguish between sacred and profane history. One gains understanding of the complex phenomenon of religion by scientific empirical investigation of all the relevant historical, cultural, and anthropological data. In other words, the quest for truth must be pursued along the lines of the philosophy and history of religion. In Troeltsch's own words, "The investigation and assessment of Christianity is to find its place within the framework of religious and cultural history."[51]

From the central importance of historical research in religious studies, Troeltsch unfolded his estimate of the practical and experiential character of religion. Following Schleiermacher, Troeltsch defined religion as the direct feeling and apprehension of the divine Presence in the human soul. In Troeltsch's scheme, the human soul stands in an immediate knowing relationship to God. Nevertheless, the soul's direct experience of the Absolute lacks positive cognitive content. The "religious a priori," as Troeltsch labeled the experience, is nothing short of a mystical encounter between the human and divine subjects.

Troeltsch interprets the direct impress of the Absolute upon the human soul as revelation.[52] The divine revelatory disclosure involves no cognitive content, but merely the ecstatic, ineffable inner experience of God. By reflection on the soul's contact with God within a specific historical and cultural context, the experiencing subject shapes a set of religious beliefs and values. Plainly, then, a special redemptive revelation finds no place in Troeltsch's scheme of religion. The source and fount of religion is that general and universal disclosure given in the religious a priori. God's special revelatory acts through the living and written Word have been replaced by an all-sufficient mystical experience open to all with a modicum of religious sensitivity.

An immediate consequence of the foregoing development is the relativism of all religious teaching. Since religious beliefs represent the crystallization of an individual's subjective experience of the Absolute, truth is never fixed or final. By virtue of the fact that one's interpretation of religious experience is profoundly shaped by historical, cultural, and environmental factors, truth is polymorphous and variable. Thus Troeltsch argues that each world religion represents a valid manifestation of the pure spirit of religion in its particular milieu. Although the power of the divine Life operates in Christianity,

> this does not preclude the possibility that other racial groups, living in their entirely different cultural conditions, may experience their contact with the Divine Life in a quite different way, and may themselves possess a religion which has grown up with them and from which they cannot sever themselves so long as they remain as they are.[53]

By definition, religious convictions differ substantially for peoples of divergent ethnic and cultural circumstances. There is not one way to truth, there are many. As Troeltsch argues, "The very thought of setting forth any one historical religion as complete and final, capable of supplanting all others, seems to us to be open to serious criticism and doubt."[54] Troeltsch thus denies the finality of truth in religion on the basis of the social conditioning of each of the historic religions.

A second reason for the relativity of religious truth is what Troeltsch called the evolutionary factor in the history of religions. Absolutely basic to history are notions of change and becoming. As Troeltsch argues, it is

> an immeasurable, comparable profusion of always-new, unique, and hence individual tendencies, welling up from undisclosed depths, and coming to light in each case in unsuspected places and under different circumstances. Each process works itself out in its own way, bringing ever new series of transformations in its train.[55]

Since the universe and history are marked by growth and development, it follows that "the Divine Life, within history, constantly manifests itself in always-new and always peculiar individualizations."[56] Thus the history of religion, no less than the history of the earth's surface, is caught up in the inexorable process of evolutionary advance to novelty.

The implications of this assumption for the Christian religion are obvious and fatal. Like other historical religions, Christianity has been filtered through a specific historical and cultural grid. Hence Christianity has stamped on it the marks of individuality and relativity. By arguing along these lines, Troeltsch repudiated Harnack's explication of the essence of Christianity as set forth in the latter's book *What Is Christianity?* (1900).

There is no essence, no permanent core to Christianity, for the Christian religion is an open-ended historical development. "Nowhere is Christianity the absolute religion," asserts Troeltsch. "Nowhere is it the changeless, exhaustive and unconditioned realization of that which is conceived as the universal principle of religion."[57] Plainer still, Troeltsch concludes that "we cannot and must not regard it [Christianity] as an absolute, perfect, immutable truth."[58] In reality, Christianity contains only a fragment—a small fragment, at that—of the truth. Although not the universally absolute religion, Christianity circumstantially has become the normative faith for Western civilization. The conditions that have shaped Christianity in its peculiar individuality exist only in the bosom of European life and culture. Christianity "could only have arisen in the territory of the classical culture and among the Latin and Germanic races."[59] Again, Christianity "stands or falls with European civilization."[60] From a worldwide perspective, Christianity is one religion among many. Moreover, in the context of an evolutionary world it is possible, if not probable, that Christianity will be superseded by still higher forms of religion.

In his important essay, "The Place of Christianity Among the World Religions," Troeltsch repudiates the idea that Christianity stands on a higher plane than other world religions. God has been operative in the great philosophies (e.g., Platonism) and religions (e.g., Buddhism, Zoroastrianism) that have crossed the stage of history. "These too are all, in their own right, living religious movements in which God is at work."[61] Indeed, the principle of true religion is latent in all the historical religions as their ground and goal. Every religion mediates truth and salvation to its adherents. The differences that exist between religions are due, first, to diverse historical, cultural, and geographical factors; and second, to the depth, power, and clarity with which the ineffable spiritual experience has been conceptualized by its practitioners.

But how is man to choose between all the religious systems that compete for his allegiance? Troeltsch responds that one should engage in a careful scientific study of the world's religions and evaluate their interaction with the great issues of life. Yet the ultimate ground for selecting one religion over another is the Ritschlian value-judgment. Choice of a religion is a matter of a personal, subjective impression—a deep consciousness valid only for the individual. As Troeltsch insists, the choice between competing historical religions is "a personal, ethically oriented, religious conviction acquired by comparison and evaluation."[62] Thus on the basis of a universally valid general revelation, an Indian's choice of Hinduism or an Egyptian's choice of Islam are as valid as a European's choice of Christianity. Such is the limited and culturally conditioned nature of all historical phenomena.

Since, according to the insights of the comparative-religions movement, the higher primitive religions have their own authentic way of apprehending the Absolute, Christianity should not seek converts among adherents of the major non-Christian religions.[63] The Christian strategy *vis-à-vis* non-Christian peoples should be not proselytization or conversion, but contact, cross-fertilization, and programs of mutual enrichment. As Troeltsch argues, there should be "no conversion or transformation of one into the other, but only a measure of agreement and mutual understanding."[64] Hence the Western missionary enterprise with its bold commitment to evangelism should be brought to a speedy end.

Troeltsch's rejection of conceptual knowledge of God in favor of subjectivism and mysticism stems from his neo-Kantian perspective. Like the romantic and Ritschlian theologians who preceded him, Troeltsch's experiential approach to religion lacked all ontological grounding. His empirical approach to religious knowledge proved to be an impoverished substitute for the verities of revelation data. Troeltsch's definition of revelation as the excitation of man's religious spirit represents a humanistic distortion of the God-given reality. Troeltsch also erred by insisting that human nature is so culturally bound that even the so-called absolutes must be subsumed under the relativities of historical conditioning. A man, in Troeltsch's system, is so culturally imprisoned that he cannot for a moment break out of his relativistic mode of thinking. In the end, loyal to the Enlightenment tradition, Troeltsch allowed the critical judgments of the historian to nullify the truth claims of divine revelation. By so doing he relativized Christianity and denied its claims of uniqueness, finality, and universality. Ritschl at least viewed Christianity as a supernatural religion, but Troeltsch conceived of it naturalistically—as one human construct among many. But Christianity is more, as Troeltsch would have it, than a particular instance of the idea of religion. Indeed, the Christian gospel represents the pinnacle of truth whose sin-distorted images are reflected in the manifold non-Christian religions of the world.

Otto's Fascination With the "Holy"   Another scholar who worked within the framework of the history-of-religions movement is Rudolph Otto (1869–1937), the renowned Marburg systematic theologian. Otto's famous work *The Idea of the Holy* (1917)[65] went through some thirty editions and has become one of the most influential and widely read theological books of the twentieth century. A post-Kantian, antimetaphysical thinker, Otto had a high regard for Schleiermacher, whom he credited with the rediscovery of religion. Otto represents the culmination of the long line of subjective and experiential approaches to the problem of religious knowledge. For Otto, as for the subjectivist school, the Divine is apprehended through a profound inner religious awareness or ecstatic mode of perception.

In his phenomenological analysis of the religious consciousness, Otto fastened on the concept of the "holy." He envisaged the holy as a complex category consisting of rational and nonrational components. On the rational side, the holy includes moral goodness, personality, and purpose. However, the unique character of the holy resides in its nonrational or nonconceptual pole, which Otto designated as the "numinous." Claiming that conventional theology has overintellectualized religion and lost the experienced reality of the holy, Otto pleads for a rediscovery of the "wholly other," the inexpressible and ineffable element in religious faith and worship. As unconditioned, nontemporal, nonspatial, absolute Being, the numinous is itself totally unknowable. But whereas the reality of the numinous transcends rational concepts and human language, it can be pointed to by descriptive symbolism and imagery that Otto called "ideograms."

The nonrational pole of the holy—the numinous—represents an innate reality not derived from sense experience. It is present in the human spirit as an a priori cognition. That is to say, the numinous stems from "an original and underived capacity of the mind implanted in the 'pure reason' independently of all perception."[66] Adds Otto, "Like all other psychical elements, it *emerges* in due course in the developing life of human mind and spirit and is thenceforward simply present."[67] Otto continues that the human agent apprehends the numinous by an immediate experience of feeling or preconceptual cognition. Whereas Schleiermacher's feelings of absolute dependence are analogous to natural feelings of fear, love, and reverence, Otto stresses the unique character of the religious experience. Otto's perception of the numinous—the *sensus numinis*—thus is *sui generis*, a unique kind of religious perception. It involves the "faculty of divination," which Otto defines as a "faculty, of whatever sort it may be, of *genuinely* cognizing and recognizing the holy in its appearance."[68] The *sensus numinis*, then, is an elementary, nonreducible, and universal datum of religion.

Otto describes the experienced reality of the numinous by the phrase "*mysterium tremendum et fascinans*," the feeling of the presence of overwhelming Being. *Mysterium* underscores the "wholly other" character of the numinous reality, which can neither be conceived of in the mind nor expressed in words. In this vein, Otto speaks of "the wholly uncomprehended Mystery, revealed yet unrevealed."[69] *Tremendum* points to the awe, the dread, the fear, and the terror one experiences when confronted with the numinous Presence. The *tremendum* represents "the daunting and repelling moment of the numinous."[70] On the other hand, *fascinans* signifies the attractive, fascinating, and alluring feature of the numinous experience. In the presence of the holy, the creature finds himself both strangely daunted and fascinated, indeed both hauntingly repelled and attracted.

We have noted that the experience of the numinous represents a primal element in the psychical nature of man. All people of all times experience a profound and arresting noncognitive meeting of the soul with God. Otto clearly allows for no revelation save this general and universal encounter with the *mysterium tremendum et fascinans*. God is known not through any special revelatory disclosure, but solely through man's universal experience of the numinous. Thus Otto firmly supplants special revelation with a universal general revelation in the human psyche—a natural theology, one might conclude, of man's most intense religious affections.

Otto was a keen student of comparative religions, with a special interest in what he saw as the historical evolution of religions from the simplest to the most complex forms. Within the context of the evolutionary advance, Otto postulated the presence of the numinous in all religious systems, from the most elementary cult to Christianity. In the polytheistic cults of Greece and Rome, in the ethnic religions of China and India, in animism, fetishism, and totemism, in Buddhism, Hinduism, and Confucianism, there exists an irresistible awareness of the supersensible, the numinous, or the tremendous. As Otto insists, "From the time of the most primitive religions everything has counted as a sign that was able to arouse in man the sense of the holy, to excite the feeling of apprehended sanctity, and stimulate it into open activity."[71] Thus the adherents of the world's religions possess a consciousness of the holy in varying degrees of clarity and intensity. The final conclusion of Otto's comparative study of religions is that all religions and faiths mediate an authentic experience of salvation. The quest for redemption is a living and experienced reality especially in the higher religions of Buddhism, Judaism, Islam, and Christianity. Again, fully consistent with the conclusions of the history-of-religions method, religion is regarded as a relative phenomenon.

Otto, the Lutheran theologian, nevertheless, concedes that Christianity, as a vehicle of salvation, is equal to or perhaps higher than the great religions or the East. Christianity's superiority to other religions resides in the unique way in which the numinous elements (awe, majesty, beauty, etc.) combine with rational elements (personality, goodness, purpose) to provide symbolic representation of the wholly other that man encounters. Thus Otto concludes, "Christian religious feeling has given birth to a religious intuition profounder and more vital than any to be found in the whole history of religion."[72]

From Otto's own definition of mysticism ("the preponderance in religious consciousness, even to the point of one-sided exaggeration, of its nonrational features"[73]) we are obliged to posit the German scholar firmly in the camp of the religious mystics. His identification of religion with the *mysterium tremendum et fascinans* allows no room for a meeting of the soul with God on the rational level. At this point Otto has nothing in common with Augustine and other effable intuitionists. But religion is more than a state of mind or an awareness of ecstatic primal reality. Biblical Christianity affirms the existence of a personal Being describable in meaningful language independent of the emotional state of the worshiper. That is, God is known via an objective revelation whose content can be represented in truth-bearing analogical language. At rock bottom, Otto's vision of religion approximates the mystical pantheism of the leading Eastern systems.

Furthermore, Otto is idealistic in his insistence that man's ecstatic experience of the numinous affords an adequate saving knowledge of God.

The Scripture plainly teaches that the light of moral experience in the end serves only to condemn. The ignorance, superstition, and immoral practices of non-Christian peoples provide historical support for the claim that this general and universal revelation in ecstatic religious experience must be supplemented by a special, saving revelation that addresses man at the level of his cognitive faculties.

In sum, then, nineteenth- and early twentieth-century liberal theology postulated the immanence of God in man and the radical "have-ability" of the divine (i.e., God readily appropriable) in human experience. At the hands of several generations of liberal theologians, God had been rendered virtually indistinguishable from man and the universe. Moreover, human emotions were uncritically identified with the voice of the living God. Christianity was stripped from its position as the definitive embodiment of truth and reduced to the level of just another religion. Thus in the broad liberal tradition, God was gradually edged out of theology and the church and was replaced by man as the focus of religion. But social and political developments in the early decades of the twentieth century prompted the growing conviction that the liberal program had blasphemed God and imperiled man. Thus advocates of the "theology of crisis" arose to challenge the humanistic drift of religion and summon the church, in the name of the living and transcendent God, back to the foundations of the faith.

VII YAHWEH vs. BAAL: THE BARTHIAN BACKLASH

Neoorthodoxy made its mark as a movement that staunchly opposed the reductionist tendencies of theological liberalism during the second and third quarters of the twentieth century. In its quarrel with liberal theology, neoorthodoxy ostensibly sought to recover the doctrinal distinctives of the Reformation. The extent to which it achieved this goal will be assessed later in the chapter. Nevertheless, it is clear that neoorthodoxy waged war against modernism's humanization and desupernaturalization of the Christian faith. It met head-on the liberal assumption that knowledge gained by bare reason or pious experience is the same as knowledge given by revelation. It did battle with liberalism's emphasis, inherited from philosophical idealism, on the immanence of God in human consciousness. It rebelled against modernism's substitution of the word of man for the preached Word of God. In clarion tones neoorthodoxy proclaimed that God is known not by human striving, but only as the sovereign God in free mercy and grace chooses to reveal Himself.

Neoorthodox theology directly opposed the romantic emphasis on the immediate "have-ability" of God in human consciousness. The supposition that man gains immediate access to God by analysis of his subjective experiences violates the radical otherness of the divine Majesty. To the subjectivist claim that the creature apprehends the Creator by looking within, neoorthodox theologians retorted with the cry, "Let God be God and man be man!" A second liberal movement against which neoorthodoxy struggled was the history-of-religions school. Neoorthodoxy insisted that far from being an isolated phenomenon in the evolutionary advance of religion, Christianity represents the unique vehicle of the divine transcendent revelation. In the third place, the neoorthodox movement opposed the entire spectrum of medieval scholastic theology. Barth, Brunner, and other neoorthodox theologians had little sympathy for the Thomistic postulate of reason's ability to make its way to God. Said Brunner, "We do not begin our inquiry with reason and then work up to revelation, but, as a believing church, we begin our inquiry with revelation and then work outwards to reason."[1] The scholastic juxtaposition of man's approach to God and God's approach to man suggested that the creature could gain an adequate knowledge of the Creator independent of a special revelatory disclosure. In any case, knowledge gained from nature would represent a knowledge formed in propositional assertions rather than the warmly personal knowledge gained by the soul's existential encounter with God Himself.

Barth and Brunner in Dialogue

Karl Barth (1886—1968) and Emil Brunner (1889—1966) represent the two founders and leading pillars of the dialectical or neoorthodox school of theology. Barth, the Basel-born pastor trained under the leading liberal scholars of his day, made a radical breach with liberalism in his watershed commentary on Romans (1919). While a professor at Göttingen, Münster, and Bonn in the 1920s and 1930s, Barth was a leading proponent of the new theology of crisis. Deprived of his chair of theology by the Nazis, Barth launched a distinguished career at the University of Basel (1935—1962), where he prepared his *opus magnum*, the massive *Church Dogmatics* (1935—67). Brunner, a parish pastor and later professor of theology at Zurich and Tokyo, was second only to Barth as a dialectical theologian of the Word. Influenced by Kierkegaard's bipolar dialectic and Martin Buber's "I-Thou" personalism, Brunner made a radical breach with his compatriot Barth on the issue of the validity of general revelation as a source for knowledge of God.

The debate in neoorthodox circles regarding the scope and efficacy of general revelation was shaped by the theologians' understanding of the radical transcendence of God and the pervasive sinfulness of the creature. Early in his career Barth appropriated from Kierkegaard the thesis of an infinite qualitative difference between man and God. According to the early Barth, eternity and time are two mutually exclusive realms, lacking any natural connecting links. God, the ruler of eternity, is wholly other and thus unlike anything in the space-time world. As the radically transcendent and hidden Deity, God remains ineffable and incomprehensible. Although Brunner made much of the "I-Thou" personal relation between creature and Creator, he too affirmed the incommensurability of the divine Majesty. God in both Barth and Brunner is the hidden God (*Deus absconditus*), who cannot be known save by faith in His act of self-revelation. No thinker before Barth stressed so thoroughly the total otherness of God and the inadequacy of human resources to apprehend Him. Thus Barth, especially, carried to the extreme the Reformed dictum "The finite cannot grasp the infinite" (*finitum non capax infiniti*).[2] The infinite, wholly other God cannot be known save by the decisive act of His self-disclosure in the Word. God, who inhabits eternity, breaks into the temporal realm in Jesus Christ like a vertical line intersecting a horizontal plane. From the perspective of radical transcendence, Barth characterizes the God of the Bible as "the God to whom there is no way and bridge, of whom we could not say or have to say one single word, had he not of his own initiative met us as *Deus revelatus.*"[3]

Not only man's finitude but also his fallenness militates against a general and universal knowledge of the divine Holiness. Both Barth and Brunner affirm the radical corruption of the sinner and the utter lostness of the lost. Barth's attitude, however, toward the possibility that sinful man (*homo peccator*) can acquire a general knowledge of God is one of unqualified pessimism. As an incorrigible sinner, fallen man finds himself totally incapable of knowing through the light of nature and reason even that God exists. As Barth argues, "Man's capacity for God . . . has really been lost."[4] The possibility of a general knowledge of God by natural man has been obviated by the total annihilation of the *imago Dei* through sin. "*Homo peccator non capax verbi Domini.*"[5] Because the image of God in man was obliterated by the Fall, the chief point of contact between creature and Creator no longer remains. Hence Barth asserts, "What is possible from the standpoint of creation from man to God has actually been lost through the Fall."[6] Since no traces of the *imago Dei* remain in *homo peccator*, reason is unable to acquire a valid knowledge of God. Consequently, the hope of a natural theology has become a total illusion. Unless, Barth intones, the *imago* is restored by the grace of re-creation in Christ, God cannot be authentically known. Only the divine revelation in Christ restores to man his original capacity to know God through the Creation. Barth sums up the matter as follows: "God—the living God who encounters us in Jesus Christ—is not such a one as can be appropriated by us in our own capacity. He is the One who will appropriate us."[7]

Brunner sought to do justice both to the radical character of the Fall and to the biblical assertion of human responsibility by postulating a twofold distinction in the *imago Dei*. What Brunner called the formal aspect of the *imago* consists of the rationality and personality with which man was endowed at Creation. God formed man to be a thinking, responsible subject superior to all other living creatures. Man's rationality and personality not only survived the Fall, but remain intact even in his state of sinful rebellion. However, Brunner regards the material aspect of the *imago*, the pristine condition of the soul at its creation, as having been totally effaced. In his post-Fall condition, man remains a sinner through and through. There is nothing in fallen man that has not been defiled by sin. Yet Brunner insists that by virtue of the retention of man's formal likeness to God, a point of contact (*Anknüpfungspunkt*) exists in the sinful creature for God's grace. Through universal general revelation, natural man gains a knowledge of God, albeit a knowledge partial and imperfect. Thus Brunner's anthropology preserved for fallen man the possibility of an authentic, nonsalvific knowledge, which the rebel in turn proceeds to distort through the darkness of his sin-clouded mind.

Although Barth and Brunner were united in their opposition to the immanency and relativism of liberal theology, a widely publicized rift developed between them on the issue of general revelation. In his cataclysmic Roman commentary, Barth announced his commitment to the overthrow of all forms of natural theology. Brunner's initial reaction to Barth's theological thunderbolt was enthusiastic and supportive. Brunner continued the dialogue with Barth in his 1934 essay, *Nature and Grace*. The debate came to a head with the publication in the same year of Barth's heated rejoiner entitled *Nein!* in which the latter charged Brunner with the resurrection of scholastic Thomism, if not outright capitulation to the liberal theologies of Schleiermacher, Ritschl, and Herrmann. It had become clear to Barth that Brunner was less radical than himself in repudiating all forms of natural theology. Said Barth of his Swiss colleague, "What is certain is that on *this* road things can only become worse and worse, i.e., he cannot but move further and further away from the postulates of evangelical thought which he himself has set down at the beginning of his essay."[8] A closer look at the positions of Brunner and Barth on the nature, scope, and validity of general revelation will now be undertaken.

Brunner on General Revelation   For his part, Brunner vigorously opposed all natural theologies that were constructed without regard to special revelation. In this sense, he argues, "bibical and natural theology will never agree; they are bitterly and fundamentally opposed."[9] On the other hand, Brunner accused Barth of irresponsibly swinging the pendulum to the opposite extreme by denying all knowledge of God except that mediated by Jesus Christ, the Word become flesh. Brunner purportedly sought to return to the position of the Reformers, who affirmed the reality of general revelation but denied the possibility of a salvific natural theology. "It is the task of our theological generation to find a way back to a true *theologia naturalis.* And I am quite convinced that it is to be found far away from Barth's negation and quite near Calvin's doctrine."[10]

Brunner, of course, is well known for promoting the notion of truth as encounter. Guided by Buber's "I-Thou" personalism and the existentialist understanding of truth of Keirkegaard, Brunner viewed special revelation not as the communication of facts but as God's unique disclosure of Himself. His theory of "personal correspondence" envisaged revelation as a personal confrontation between God and man in which the subject-object split is overcome. Hence Brunner maintains that "the antithesis between object and subject, between 'something true' and 'knowledge of this truth' has disappeared and has been replaced by the personal meeting between the God who speaks and the man who answers."[11] In special revelation, God gives Himself in an act of love, and man receives God's offer in an act of faith and obedience. But Brunner adds that Jesus Christ Himself is the self-communication of God with men. "The incarnation of the Word, the entrance of God into the sphere of our life, the self-manifestation of God in His Son—this is the real revelation."[12] For Brunner, *biblical* revelation, or the revelation that saves, involves a living communion between persons rather than the formal communication of truths. As an aside, many interpreters have noted that Brunner's encounter model emphasized the subjective character of revelation to the exclusion of its noetic and objective content. With this judgment we entirely agree.

But the chief point we wish to make is this: In addition to postulating personal truth mediated by encounter, Brunner allowed for rational truths that deal with objects and things. The God who revealed Himself in Christ is the same God who fashioned the world. Hence Brunner insists that there exists a divine revelation in the Creation or a primal revelation, independent of the historical manifestation of Jesus Christ. Moreover, man created in the image of God explicates the general revelation by the faculty of reason. Thus in the face of the Barthian skepticism, Brunner insisted that God has made a valid self-disclosure through the modalities of nature, history, and human conscience. Biblical texts such as Romans 1:18−21; 2:15; John 1:4−9; Acts 14:17; and 17:26−27 plainly teach a universal general revelation of the Creator-God. Argues Brunner, "The fact that the Holy Scriptures teach the revelation of God in His works of creation needs no proof."[13] The texts in view mandate the conclusion that God revealed Himself to men before Christ and apart from the direct revelation of Christ. The postulate of general revelation is eminently reasonable, for whenever and wherever God is operative, the character of His being is impressed upon His works.

God then has made a valid self-disclosure of Himself in the works of Creation. Insofar as the physical universe bears the marks of its Maker, it represents a valid revelation of the existence and character of the Creator. The arrangement, order, purposefulness, and permanency of the universe, Brunner argues, attest the reality of God. Three times in the first chapter of Romans (vv. 19, 21, 32) Paul asserts that the Gentiles gained from the visible cosmos a factual knowledge of God. Such knowledge is not a remote future possibility, but an actual present possession. The judgment levied by Paul against the Gentiles is that they "suppress the truth by their wickedness" (Rom. 1:18). But how, Brunner rightly argues, can one hold down or suppress a knowledge that does not exist? Moreover, Brunner insists that anyone willing to employ right reason will discover God's preserving and guiding hand in the ebb and flow of human history. The historical continuum bears direct witness to the existence, wisdom, and power of God. In sum, Brunner maintains that God is both the subject and the content of the universal general revelation in nature and history.

On the subjective side, Brunner insists that the existence and moral demands of God are disclosed within man himself through conscience, which he defines as "the consciousness of responsibility."[14] In the beginning, God inscribed on the human heart His eternal law, which none can avoid. We should note that Brunner regards the moral law within as part of the general revelation in the Creation.[15] But he adds, "Scripture clearly testifies to the fact that knowledge of the law of God is somehow also knowledge of God."[16] Hence through the compelling voice of the conscience, no one can excuse himself by saying he never knew God. The tragedy of the matter is that sinful man refuses to permit the knowledge of God afforded by conscience to have its full effect. The sinner spurns the knowledge of God mediated by his conscience and hence bears full responsibility for his isolation from the fount of life.

Brunner adamantly insists that man's ability to recognize God through the cosmos and his conscience has been adversely affected but not totally destroyed by sin. Since fallen man is a creature shaped in the image of God and not a brute beast, he continues in epistemic contact with his Creator. Man, even fallen man, "has been so created by God that, by means of his reason, he can perceive God in His works."[17] Since God's revelatory disclosures are fully rational, the recognition of God through His works (both in nature and conscience) is part of man's destiny as a rational creature. Reason, the faculty that elevates man above the lesser creatures, is the means whereby even the sinner is enabled to discern in part the divine revelation in Creation. The assertion that this general knowledge of God is not destroyed by sin, Brunner insists, "is not a specifically Catholic, but a general Christian, doctrine; it is good Reformation doctrine, plainly Biblical, and common to the Christian Church as a whole."[18]

In his work, *Nature and Grace*, Brunner boldly describes the system of knowledge derived from Creation as a "Christian natural theology."[19] Contrary to medieval natural theology, which adopted reason as its starting point, Brunner postulates the priority of revelation without demeaning the function of human intelligence in the knowing process. In the face of heated protests from Barth, Brunner later retracted the label "Christian natural theology" and chose rather to speak of the doctrine of "revelation in the Creation."[20]

While mediating a knowledge of God's existence and chief attributes, the light of general revelation is beset with severe limitations. In the first place, as soon as the sinner perceives God as the sovereign Creator and lawgiver through the data of the cosmos, he immediately represses that knowledge and transforms it into an illusion. In his sinful rebellion, man turns his back on the knowledge of the true God and stoops to fashion idols of wood and stone. In the words of Paul, sinners "suppress the truth by their wickedness" (Rom. 1:18), thus preventing it from taking root in their minds and hearts and transforming their lives. Man confronts the knowledge of God in the Creation but stubbornly refuses to embrace and cherish it. The process by which sinners spurn the truth of God and delight in lies constitutes man's great "fatal exchange."[21] As Brunner so descriptively put it, "The sinful human being is a vessel in which the lees of sin transform the wine of the knowledge of God into the vinegar of idolatry."[22]

The second and more decisive limitation of general revelation, a limitation that follows from the first, is that it fails to prove salvific. The light afforded by general revelation is incapable of freeing man from the shackles of sin. Since man in his course of stubborn rebellion spurns the elemental knowledge of God and deliberately worships idols, it is inconceivable that he should press on to that fuller knowledge of God that saves. God never failed to leave man with an adequate witness to Himself (Acts 14:17). Nevertheless, sinners fail to embrace the God-given light in such a way that He becomes to them eternal salvation.

Brunner continues by saying that the general revelation, though insolently spurned, chiefly serves to establish man's responsibility before God. Did not the apostle Paul, after certifying man's rejection of the light of general revelation, draw the conclusion that "men are without excuse" (Rom. 1:20)? Without an objectively valid universal revelation, man could not be constituted a sinner. "They *are* all sinners, simply and solely because they 'hold down in unrighteousness' the revelation in the Creation which has been presented to them as the truth of God."[23] With the Reformers, Brunner insists that he who would deny the reality of a valid, universal self-disclosure of God eliminates the basis for man's responsibility before God. But man *does* apprehend God in Creation, conscience, and history, and thus he *is* pronounced guilty for failure to respond to the light that he has. As Brunner argues,

> The denial of such a 'general revelation' preceding the historical revelation of grace in Jesus Christ can appeal neither to Paul nor to the Bible at large. It contradicts the fact of responsibility. If man did not know God, how could he be responsible? But he is responsible, for he knows about God on the strength of the divine self-revelation.[24]

In contrast to the unbridled optimism of the humanistic history-of-religions movement, Brunner envisaged the non-Christian religions as shaped by the suppression and distortion of the divine general revelation. The world's religions undoubtedly involve the recollection of a primal awareness of God and a longing for the divine Light and Love. But fundamentally, the non-Christian religions must be viewed as the product of the confused and blinded sinful mind.

> From the standpoint of Jesus Christ, the non-Christian religions seem like stammering words from some half-forgotten saying. None of them is without a breath of the Holy, and yet none of them is the Holy. None is without its impressive truth, and yet none of them is the Truth; for their truth is Jesus Chrst.[25]

Since self-centered man tends either to make finite or to depersonalize Deity, "the God of the 'other religions' is always an idol."[26] Human religion, in fact, involves the twin poles of demonic distortion of the truth and man's vain attempt to escape God. Brunner singles out Buddhism, with its negative Nirvana mysticism, as an expression of "religious atheism."[27] All human religion, insofar as it distorts the divine general revelation, is "false religion," "illusion," and "unreality."[28] Brunner adds, "Viewed in His light, all religious systems appear untrue, unbelieving, and indeed godless."[29] Brunner, in fact, excludes Christianity from the general category of religion. Because it rests on the unique foundation of the Word made flesh, Christianity is qualitatively different from the "other" religions. Whereas they are false systems, Christianity is the one true faith. Thus Brunner concludes, "Jesus Christ is both the Fulfillment of all religion and the Judgment on all religion."[30]

The key issue for Brunner is not the validity of general revelation, but the relationship it sustains to the message of God's grace in Jesus Christ. The divine unveilings in nature, history, and conscience represent necessary preparatory revelations to God's ultimate disclosure in Christ. Only through the preliminary modalities of general revelation can God be recognized as God. Only thus, as we have seen, is man constituted a sinner morally responsible before God. Hence, "the general revelation does not compete with the particular, historical revelation, but is its presupposition."[31] Brunner argues, on the one hand, that general revelation cannot be ignored or omitted, for in the divine plan it constitutes the prolegomenon to the gospel message. Nature and grace are continuous, the one with the other, rather than discontinuous. On the other hand, neither is the universal general revelation sufficiently extensive to lead the sinner to an experiential or saving knowledge of God. In this sense, Brunner insists that the Bible "denies the possibility of a *theologia naturalis* as a basis for a complementary *theologia revelata.*"[32] Thus in Brunner's scheme, general revelation represents the necessary preliminary to special revelation. But the general revelation in Creation in no way invalidates the need for biblical revelation and special saving grace.

Barth on General Revelation   Karl Barth, as we have noted, broke with Brunner, claiming that the latter had betrayed the transcendent theology of the Word. Far more severely than his Swiss colleague, Barth boldly asserted the discontinuity of nature and grace, of reason and revelation. Since time and eternity represent mutually exclusive realms, nothing in the space-time continuum could possibly serve as a point of contact between finite, sinful man and the transcendent, holy God. Barth envisaged the quest to apprehend God from created effects as "an attempt to unite Yahweh with Baal."[33] Barth regarded as an "invention of the Antichrist"[34] the concept of a similarity or an analogy of being (*analogia entis*), whereby Thomas, the Schoolmen, and others claimed to achieve a formal knowledge of God independently of His grace. Because of the destruction of the *imago Dei* and the incompetence of human reason in things divine, all rational arguments and philosophical "proofs" for God are invalid. If the classical arguments lead anywhere they lead not to the God of the Bible, but to an idol. Barth's attitude to the autonomous human quest for God clearly was one of resolute opposition.

Barth thus pleaded for the total repudiation of all natural theology. In whatever form it might appear, natural theology is pointless and sinful. Every appeal to a universal general revelation, whether external or internal to man, must be judged null and void. No divine revelation is mediated "in reason, in conscience, in the emotions, in history, in nature, and in culture and its achievements and developments."[35] The usual methods of scientific and historical research tell us nothing about the reality of God. Barth argues that general revelation is an illusion, for God is known not in the abstract but concretely in an act of faith and obedience. "Knowledge of God," as Barth expressed it, "is obedience to God."[36] General revelation is a mirage, for God is not known except in the totality of His being. As Barth insists, unless God is known in His trinitarian nature, true knowledge is not gained. "We either know God Himself and therefore entirely, or we do not know Him at all."[37] Since general revelation fails to produce either the obedience of faith or recognition of God as triune, nature, conscience, and history mediate no knowledge of God whatsoever. All systems of natural theology commit the fatal error of presuming that God can be known independently of His special grace.

It needs to be said that Barth's flat rejection of general revelation was motivated by a profound concern for the integrity of God's special revelation in Christ. He believed that the liberal Protestant and Roman Catholic synthesis of general and special revelation inevitably leads to a compromise between the authority of God and the authority of man. When natural theology and revealed theology are accepted as equals, the former overwhelms and conquers the latter. Barth's fears along these lines were legitimately aroused during the Nazi era, when many Christians perceived in Hitler's rise to power in 1933 a new revelation of the will of God. National Socialism committed the tragic error of shaping a natural theology based on a supposed divine revelation in the historical process. The gravity of developments in Nazi Germany was for Barth proof of the fact that the issue of natural theology was a matter of life and death for the church. Barth thus concluded that there could be no possible compromise between human culture and the divine address through the Word.

> The logic of the matter demands that, even if we only lend our little finger to natural theology, there necessarily follows a denial of the revelation of God in Jesus Christ. . . . And to give it place at all is to put oneself, even if unwittingly, on the way which leads to this sole sovereignty.[38]

Man apprehends God in no other way than by faith in His radical Word of supernatural communication.

To maintain consistency, Barth was compelled to reinterpret radically the apostle Paul's teaching on general revelation in Romans 1. Indeed, Barth argues that he who accepts the traditional interpretation of Romans 1:18–20 has sold his soul to Thomism or liberalism. The Romans text, according to Barth, teaches nothing about the Gentiles acquiring a natural knowledge of God's invisible nature. "We cannot understand it as an abstract statement about the heathen as such, or about a revelation which the heathen possess as such."[39] When the text says, "What may be known about God is plain to them, because God has made it plain to them" (Rom. 1:19), Barth appeals to the immediately preceding context (vv. 15–17), which deals with the apostolic preaching of the gospel of God's grace. Thus the revelation Paul speaks about in verses 18–20 is not a general disclosure in nature; it is the message of God's supernatural revelation in Christ. "We cannot," Barth argues, "isolate what Paul says about the heathen in Romans 1:19–20 from the context of the apostolic preaching, from the incarnation of the Word."[40] Barth is thus emphatic in his denial that the pagan has gained the slightest remnant of a natural knowledge of God.

Yet in what sense does Barth maintain that the pagan "knows" God through His special disclosure in Christ? The pagan, or the man-in-the-cosmos, *theoretically* knows God on the basis of God's universal election of mankind in Christ, even though *in actual fact* he is not conscious of such knowledge.[41] Here again surfaces another leading Barthian paradox. Man at one and the same time both *knows* and does *not know* God. Natural man's great problem is that he does not know that he knows God! The pagan "is a witness of divine revelation, although unconsciously, involuntarily, and without affirming it as such in his thought and in his conduct."[42] The ambiguities of the paradox of election aside, Barth's thesis concerning revelation is unmistakable. There is no other source for knowledge save that which has been given once for all in Jesus Christ. Only he whose eyes have been opened by the divine unveiling in Christ is capable of interpreting the data of the created order. Man is accounted guilty before God solely on the basis of his rejection of God's redemptive revelation in Christ.

In contrast to all human attempts to apprehend God, Barth insists that God is known only when and where He chooses to reveal Himself. The meeting between God and man can be actualized only from God's side. "God can be known only through God, namely in the event of the divine encroachment of His self- revelation. There can be no question of any other *posse* [potentiality], i.e., a *posse* which is not included in and with this divine encroachment."[43] In other words, "The fact that we know God is His work and not ours."[44] Barth clearly restricts all revelation to the Word of God, which is God Himself speaking. "God gives Himself to man to be known in the revelation of His Word through the Holy Spirit."[45] The Word, however, assumes three different forms: (1) the Word of God preached (gospel proclamation), (2) the Word of God written (the Bible), and (3) the Word of God revealed (Jesus Christ). Yet these three polarities of the Word of God, by which God speaks to man, constitute no less a unity than the three persons of the Godhead.

Fundamentally, for Barth, God's sole revelation and only means of communication with people is Jesus Chrst. "If God had not descended so far into these depths that He met us as one of ourselves in all the distance and nearness of a human form, there would be no revelation."[46] Simply put, "Revelation means the Incarnation of the Word of God."[47] God radically breaks into our world in the person of Jesus Christ, confounding all human aspirations and religiosity. The revelation resides not in the historical Jesus but in the moment of crisis and decision when the Word overwhelms the heart and engenders faith. Here Barth stresses the personal, paradoxical, and noncognitive character of the divine revelation. In the act of self-disclosure God reveals not formal objective truths, but His very Self. Yet even as He confronts man, God remains *incognito*—hidden in the man Jesus. Barth clearly joins hands with Brunner in insisting that revelation is dynamic, personal, and nonpropositional. But Barth refuses to share Brunner's view of revelation as an encounter between divine and human persons. For Barth, revelation involves the radical self-presentation of God to man in Jesus Christ through the power of the Holy Spirit, rather than an "I-Thou" dialogical encounter in the tradition of Buber.

The point Barth attempts to make is that God discloses Himself only in the gracious act of reconciliation, where the sovereign initiative lies entirely with God Himself. The bottom line reads that God is not known save through His reconciling grace in Christ. "We must learn again to understand revelation as *grace* and grace as *revelation* and therefore turn away from all 'true' or 'false' *theol. naturalis.*"[48] Any purported disclosure that does not involve the unveiling of grace to the sinful heart is not a true revelation. The shortfall of natural theology is that it attempts to know God apart from His saving grace and mercy.

It is crystal clear, then, that at the height of his career Barth passionately pled for the exclusion of both general revelation and natural theology (the corpus of truth about God built on general revelation). Yet there are signs that later in life Barth softened somewhat his hostility to a revelation of God in the cosmos. The first hint of such theological mellowing appeared in his *Shorter Commentary on Romans*, based on lectures given during the early years of World War II. Just as in his earlier classic treatment of Romans, so in this later reflection on the epistle, Barth viewed the Romans 1:18ff. text within the context of the righteousness of God revealed in the gospel (Rom. 1:16−17). Thus Barth could write of Paul: "He is speaking of the Gentiles as they are now confronted with the Gospel, whether they know it or not, and whether they like it or not. They are confronted with the Gospel . . . since the proclamation of his name has been taking its course throughout the world."[49] Knowledge of God, for Barth, still is limited to that mediated through God's threefold Word of address. And yet without warning, Barth immediately adds the following concerning the Gentiles:

> God has in fact . . . since the creation of the world been declaring and revealing himself to them. The world which has always been around them, has always been God's work and as such God's witness to himself. Objectively the Gentiles have always had the opportunity of knowing God, his invisible being, his eternal power and godhead. And again, objectively speaking, they have also always known him.[50]

Barth fortunately elaborates on his new emphasis (but not entirely con-sistent with the above) in the third part (first half) of the fourth volume of the *Church Dogmatics*, which was published in 1959.[51] Subordinate to Jesus Christ, the one true Word and Light of life, the Creation includes numerous lesser lights that display the glory of God. The witness of these lights of Creation has not been extinguished by the noetic effects of sin. The chief function of the lights of Creation is to illumine the stage of history for the coming of Jesus Christ and His light and His Word. While thus speaking freely of the luminosity of the created order, Barth cautions that we should avoid use of the expressions "revelation of creation" or "primal revelation."[52] For Barth, Creation is a luminosity, a host of lights, but not revelation as such. Adds Barth, "One reason why we might perhaps refrain from speaking of these guaranteeing lights as 'revelation,' is that no faith is needed to grasp them, but only an obvious and almost inevitable perception, only the good but limited gift of common sense."[53] Thus even though Barth later in life made concessions to the illuminatory value of Creation, he did not deviate from his lifelong conviction that God reveals Himself to sinners only through the Word in its threefold form. This conclusion is reinforced by the fact that in his 1962 theological summary, *Evangelical Theology*, Barth made no men-tion of God's revelation through the created order. His theology remained uniformly a theology of the Word.[54]

Barth went on to draw a clear distinction between theology and religion. Theology is not talk about God (for God is not a legitimate object of human discourse), but the human response to the Word of God's address. Barth contemplated theology as *ministerium verbi domini*—the service of the Word of God. Its task is to assess the measure of agreement between the church's proclamation and the revelation witnessed to in Scripture.

Religion, on the other hand, is viewed as a totally human enterprise—the fruit of man's sinful rebellion against God. In the second part of the first volume of the *Church Dogmatics*, Barth devoted a lengthy section of some fifty thousand words to the theme "Religion as Unbelief."[55] Religion rep-resents man's blind and groping quest for God. It represents the feeble, defiant, and hopeless attempt to do what man cannot do, namely, to ap-prehend God in Himself. "We begin by stating that religion is unbelief. It is a concern, indeed, we must say that it is the one great concern, of godless man."[56] Continues Barth, "From the standpoint of revelation religion is clearly seen to be a human attempt to anticipate what God in His revelation wills to do and does do. It it the attempted replacement of the divine work by a human manufacture."[57] From the Barthian perspective, revelation to-tally contradicts religion, and religion contradicts revelation. The autono-mous human quest of the Divine, which lies at the heart of religion, must be brought to a speedy end.

Since God has revealed Himself exclusively in Jesus Christ, Barth insists that the non-Christian religions are devoid of truth. At rock bottom, the non-Christian faiths are expressions of paganism.[58] The Word of God stands totally and irrevocably opposed to all pagan and idolatrous ideologies. "Now that revelation has come and its light has fallen on heathendom, heathen religion is shown to be the very opposite of revelation: a false religion of unbelief."[59] According to Barth, the existence of the world's religions is strictly a matter for divine forgiveness. Barth could say of Islam, for example, "The God of Mohammed is an idol like all other idols."[60] Every claim that the non-Christian religions embody the truth of God must be rooted out and destroyed.

By way of critique, Barth and Brunner performed an invaluable service by exposing many of the fallacies of liberal theology and by calling the church back to its biblical roots. In the area of anthropology, Barthianism justly challenged the prevailing humanism by portraying man as finite and radically sinful. Biblical faith is encouraged by its devastating critique of the progress and perfectability of man through self-effort. In the area of revelation, neoorthodoxy forthrightly opposed the liberal notion that knowledge of God naturally wells up within man's subjective consciousness. The message needed to be sounded that knowledge of the human subject must not be confused with knowledge of God. Indeed, the Barthian movement infused considerable fresh air into the religious scene by summoning Christendom back to the life-giving Word of God. In the area of salvation, neoorthodoxy must be commended for opposing the dominant spirit of relativism and for upholding the absoluteness of the Christian faith. Both Barth and Brunner faithfully extolled the centrality of Jesus Christ for salvation. In contrast to the eclecticism of the history-of-religions movement, neoorthodoxy boldly proclaimed that God is savingly known only through the Christian gospel. Barth rightly rejected as unworthy of the name Christian the old liberal assertion that all religions are noble expressions of the divine will.

In spite of its many positive contributions, neoorthodoxy must be faulted at certain fundamental points. Barth, particularly, was plagued with an inordinate dose of Kantian skepticism *vis-à-vis* the knowability of God. Kant's assertion, appropriated by Barth, that God cannot reveal Himself through either nature or man himself, and that God therefore is beyond the reach of human knowing, must be rejected. In the epistemological realm, the Kantian bifurcation of noumenal and phenomenal cannot be fully assumed. The biblical Christian therefore must distance himself from Barth's claim that the visible order of nature mediates no significant information about God.

In particular, the neoorthodox postulate of the infinite qualitative distinction between God and man must be viewed as an unwarranted exaggeration. God, indeed, is the supreme transcendent Being. But the fact that the God of the Bible is also immanent nullifies the suggestion that He is wholly other. In sum, the transcendental theology of Barth and Brunner overstated the distance between God and man. The exalted and majestic God who inhabits eternity is also mysteriously close at hand, as saints down through the ages testify. Likewise, Barth overstates the truth when he argues that the image of God in man was totally annihilated by the Fall. The fact that man has not been reduced to the level of the beasts suggests that the *imago*, while defaced, has not been altogether destroyed. Although man is a sinner through and through, the Bible acknowledges that he is a rational creature with whom God can communicate on the intellectual level. Thus God's invitation to man at large is recorded in Isaiah 1:18: " 'Come now, let us reason together,' says the LORD." According to Psalm 32:9, for man to refuse to use his mind to think about God is totally contrary to the will of the Creator. Moreover, New Testament texts such as Ephesians 4:24 and Colossians 3:10 assure us that a valid point of contact does exist at the epistemic level between God and man. Hence God the Creator can in some measure be perceived and known by man the created being. For these reasons, it is not strictly true that the finite is not capable of apprehending the infinite.

The neoorthodox restriction of revelation to a nonpropositional personal encounter with God similarly fails to do justice to the full range of biblical teaching. Although the Word represents the highest form of the divine self-disclosure, Scripture scarcely limits God's revelation to this important modality. That the several modes of general revelation possess validity (as Brunner insists) is substantiated by both the Old and New Testaments. Instead of being destroyed by grace as Barth would have it, general revelation, in fact, represents the necessary prolegomenon to the pinnacle of God's grace revealed in the Word.

However, it is Barth's exegesis of Romans 1:18ff. that is particularly misleading. Rather than following the established procedures of historical-grammatical exegesis, Barth engaged in eisegesis by permitting his theological presuppositions to shape his understanding of the text. Barth's interpretation of Paul's claim that the Gentiles "know God" in the sense of man's universal election in Christ sniffs of an arbitrary theologizing. In fact, in Barth we observe the familiar pendulum syndrome at work. In reacting against liberalism's radical inflation of general revelation, Barth swung the pendulum to the opposite extreme by denying altogether a revelation in the Creation. Liberal theology's monism of nature was exchanged for a no less extreme monism of the Word. However, Barth's fears that acknowledgment of general revelation will signal the demise of special revelation are quite groundless.

Brunner's theological foundations, on the other hand, are hardly less shaky than Barth's. He too has bought into the Kantian bifurcation between eternity and time and between God and man, with resultant theological difficulties and inconsistencies. Yet on the issue of general revelation, Brunner came up right and Barth wrong. But the fact that Brunner has reached correct conclusions while working with faulty (Barthian) assumptions suggests that he has argued his case inconsistently and thus inadequately. All factors considered, it is clear that neither Barth nor Brunner has said the last word on the issue of the validity and utility of general revelation.

Kraemer's Missiological Focus   A twentieth-century scholar whose views on revelation and world religions, though defective, can hardly be overlooked is the Dutch theologian Hendrik Kraemer (1888–1965). Kraemer served with the Dutch Reformed Church in Indonesia as a linguistics and Bible-translation consultant, occupied the chair of the history of religions at Leiden, and directed the ecumenical study center at Bossey, near Geneva. As an aside, tiny Netherlands was the first country to establish university chairs for the comparative study of world religions. The Dutch scholar's most famous work, *The Christian Message in a Non-Christian World*,[61] emerged out of the third World Missionary Conference at Tambaram in 1938.

Kraemer's theological position is broadly Barthian. Postulating with Barth and Brunner the absolute qualitative difference between God and man, Kraemer held that religious truth is patently paradoxical. Since the divine order of life disclosed in Jesus Christ differs radically from human life and discourse, theology refuses to be bound by logical, rational coherence. Hence Kraemer acknowledged the intrinsically dialectical character of the Christian faith, where truth is captured only in the synthesis of affirmation and negation. Moreover, consistent with the Barthian scheme, truth is never conceived of as intellectually demonstrable propositions or as supernaturally communicated doctrine. Truth is defined relationally and existentially as a *living* communion between two personal centers. It follows that revelation is not a series of objective truths but a life-relationship between the divine Self and human selves. The Bible, on this showing, is not a deposit of universal and timeless formulae, but a human witness to God's saving acts in history. Finally, Kraemer insists that Christianity's truth-claims are validated not by rational argumentation, but solely by the inner certification afforded by faith. Religious convictions never rest on the conclusions to a formal line of reasoning but are always actualized by radical choice and decision. From Kraemer's perspective, Athens must bow before Jerusalem.

The overarching problem Kraemer addresses in all his writings is how man, shaped in the image of God and yet fallen and rebellious, comes to know God in a saving relationship. Moreover, he is keenly interested in the extent to which God is revealed in the religious life of the world's non-Christian faiths. Kraemer acknowledges at the outset the bewildering complexity of the relationship between revelation and human religion. The vexing problem of the knowability of God begins to unfold in what he calls "the free atmosphere of Biblical realism."[62] At the heart of Kraemer's biblical realism is the vision of revelation as the aggregate of God's mighty acts, by which he confronts man and commands faith. The Dutch scholar parts ways with the liberal understanding of revelation as the emergence of religious insights and intuitions from the depths of the human consciousness.

129

Revelation derives entirely from the divine initiative and action. The knowledge of God and the destiny of man lie within the domain of the sovereign God. "Revelation means God doing redemptive and saving acts to realize the restoration of mankind and the world."[63] Biblical revelation centers about the divine movement through the person and work of Jesus Christ. The truth of God is not . . . a lofty conception about His being and nature, monotheistic or mystic or what not, but is the incomprehensible fact that He became flesh in Jesus Christ, that God is self-giving, self-forgetting love, as was manifested in the scandal of the cross.[64] It follows that revelation, as an act of divine grace for a forlorn world, must not be confused with religion. Religion represents man's sinful reflections about God, whereas revelation concerns God's decisive action and speech toward man.

But if God is revealed primarily in the Word made flesh, the issue arises whether He can be known in any other way. Are nature, history, and conscience authentic vehicles of revelation through which the practicing Muslim, Hindu, or Buddhist gains a personal knowledge of God? As Kraemer himself posed the problem, "What answer can be given to the question: Does God—and if so, how and where does God—reveal Himself in the religious life as present in the non-Christian religions?"[65] The solution to this problem hinges on his estimate of the character and scope of general revelation. Here again, the Dutch scholar's view of general revelation is shaped by what he calls the inexorable dialectic of biblical realism.

Concerning the validity of general revelation, Kraemer responds, on the one hand, with a firm "Yes!" Biblical realism affirms both that God created the world and that He continues to work in His world. God's eternal power and deity, as Romans 1 teaches, are visibly and intelligibly perceived through nature, history, and providence. Moreover, human nature is indelibly stamped with a *sensus divinitatis*, or a *sensus religionis*, as Calvin put it, that yields a valid apprehension of God. In other words, man knows God by the faculty of intuitive perception. Thus with Brunner and against Barth, Kraemer wants to talk about "a critical and right kind of natural theology."[66] Nevertheless, the dialectician's "Yes!" is immediately qualified by an opposing "No!" The modalities of general revelation, in fact, conceal God even more than they reveal Him. The philosophical "proofs" purporting to demonstrate God's existence and character prove nothing. The fact is that general revelation becomes intelligible only in the light of special revelation. Kraemer agrees with Barth that the divine disclosure in nature, history, and conscience makes sense to fallen man only from the perspective of God's righteousness in Christ. The various modalities of general revelation are integrally related to the one central revelation in Christ. Isolated and detached from the Word made flesh, they become meaningless generalizations. Thus Kraemer observes:

> The only thing that should be said is that the central or focal revelation is the revelation of the righteousness of God in Christ . . . and that the other modes are

all of them revelations of God's righteousness in their own specific way, are all related to the central one, and yield their true significance through it, because they all happen through Christ and to Christ.[67]

From the negative side of the dialectic Kraemer regards general revelation as a highly misleading and confusing term that the church would do well to abolish. Neither Paul nor the other biblical writers teach the doctrines of general revelation and natural theology.

Kraemer's dialectic allows him to eat his cake and have it too. With respect to the teaching of Scripture and the historic church on the validity of general revelation, Kraemer can add his firm "Yes!" But to the protest of the Barthian school, concerned that general revelation signals a concession to the autonomy of sinful man, Kraemer wants to add his firm "No!" But we judge it preferable to flee the relativistic jungle of dialectics and to postulate an objectively valid self-disclosure of God in nature, history, and conscience, for man, created in the *imago Dei*, perceives God's self-disclosure but radically suppresses and distorts it.

Kraemer applies the dialectical method not only to revelation but also to world religions. The dialectical scheme of radical realism says "Yes!" to the loftiest heights and "No!" to the basest depths of the world's faiths. All religions are a mixture of the divine and demonic, whether we have in mind Islam, Buddhism, Hinduism, or Christianity. And it is the virtue of the dialectical method that allows one to see clearly the ambivalent divine-demonic character of each religion.

Concerning the world's non-Christian religions, Kraemer initially speaks approvingly. One finds noble insights, experiences, and accomplishments in the great world faiths. Kraemer extols the richness of the religious and ethical values manifested in these systems. The non-Christian faiths, in his judgment, undoubtedly lead people into deep and satisfying religious experiences. Adherents of Hinduism, for example, display evidence of sincere and genuine devotion that gives meaning to such concepts as sin, grace, and forgiveness. The science of comparative religion has shown that in many respects the non-Christian religions prove superior to Christianity. Many achievements of other faiths, says Kraemer, are of higher value for mankind than the accomplishments of Christianity. Thus Christians can and ought to learn from the non-Christian religions. Kraemer judges that these conclusions are reasonable, since God has disclosed Himself and continues to work in the non-Christian religions. They represent "a field in which we can trace God's own footmarks."[68] On the "Yes!" side of the dialectic, Kraemer can say of the non-Christian faiths: "In their nobler aspects they aspire to Jesus Christ; and in many if not in all respects they point to Him who is 'full of grace and truth.'"[69]

But on the negative side of the dialectic, Kraemer contemplates the world's religions as a mixture of perversion, evil, falsehood, and sheer absurdity. In their blind and deluded search for God, they prove to be idolatrous and adulterous expressions of the divine wrath. The religions of mankind thus express the creature's proud and unbelieving resistence to God, rather than willing response to the divine revelation. When one examines carefully the life and experience of the non-Christian religions, "they are shown to be religions of self-redemption, self-justification, and self-sanctification and so to be, in their ultimate and essential meaning and significance, erroneous."[70]

Kraemer's so-called dialectic of biblical realism applies not only to revelation and the non-Christian religions, but also to Christianity. On the negative side, the science of comparative religion allegedly has shown that historical or empirical Christianity often proves as degrading as non-Christian religion. Historical Christianity must "be viewed largely as a specimen of human effort in the field of religion, and therefore to be brought into line with the other religions as expressions of human spiritual life."[71] Thus Christianity as a historical phenomenon stands on the same plane as the other major religions of the world. Like Buddhism and Hinduism, it is passing away, as all things human pass away. In this sense, one cannot speak glibly of the superiority or absoluteness of Christianity, for such talk is both untrue and offensive. In practice, historical Christianity stands open to correction and enlightenment from such rival systems as Islam, Buddhism, and Marxism.

But on the positive side of the dialectic, Kraemer declares that Christianity towers above all other religions by virtue of its role as custodian of the divine revelation in the person of Jesus Christ. In spite of all its deplorable sins, Christianity is the "best" religion because through it the gospel is proclaimed. The Christ of Christianity represents the visible, tangible revelation of the sovereign God of heaven. He holds the preeminence over Buddha, Confucius, Muhammad, and all other religious figures. Christ, who is the wisdom, power, and righteousness of God, represents "the Crisis, the Caller in question, of all religion."[72] In the light of Christ, the religions of the world appear as clumsy and halting evasions. Hence Christianity, the religion of Christ, is uniquely the religion of reconciliation and atonement. Only through Christ, and thus only through Christianity, is the new order of eternal life inaugurated. There is no basis for viewing Christianity as the flowering or fulfillment of world religion. Jesus Christ does not fulfill the non-Christian religions; He absolutely annihilates them. God's revelation in Christ is entirely *sui generis.*

Kraemer's approach to the issues of revelation, the knowledge of God, and the validity of the world's religions is obviously dialectical through and through. His so-called dialectic of biblical realism purports to preserve both the radical antithesis and the radical synthesis of nature and grace. In my opinion, the dialectical method utilized by neoorthodoxy is a device of convenience that permits assent to the confessions of orthodox faith on the one hand, and the conclusions of critical scholarship on the other. But we judge that it is biblically unsound and pragmatically unrealistic to suppose that one can simultaneously please those who postulate the unqualified lord-ship of Christ and those who affirm the full equality of the world's religions. One cannot have it both ways and live within the law of noncontradiction. At a more basic level, the assumption that general revelation is intelligible only in the light of special revelation violates, as we have seen, the clear teachings of Scripture. Especially open to criticism is the view that the Christian faith is an expression of *human* effort and *human* religiosity. The historical or empirical Christian movement chronicled in the New Testament and church history, while tainted with human failings, was nevertheless an obvious manifestation of the grace and the power of God. And the same can be said in the modern world where the church is true to its calling and true to its Lord.

"LET GOD BE GOD":
VIII ALTERNATIVE REFORMED APPROACHES

The present chapter explores the influential Dutch school of theology that fastened on the pessimistic strand of Calvin's teaching relative to general revelation and the knowability of God. No figure had a greater influence on Dutch theology in the twentieth century than Abraham Kuyper (1837–1920). In his insistence that general revelation is of little practical value to the sinner and that knowledge of God is mediated only by special revelation, Kuyper served as a catalyst to the confessional method of Berkouwer and the presuppositional approach of Van Til.

The Amsterdam Theology of Kuyper   Kuyper was trained at the University of Leiden (D. Theol., 1862), where he assimilated the critical and rationalistic outlook then regnant at the university. During his first pastorate in the village of Beesd, Kuyper was led by certain godly parishioners to embrace a biblical faith in the Reformed tradition. On the basis of his belief in the full sovereignty of God, Kuyper longed to bring all areas of human endeavor under the Lordship of Christ. Kuyper thought through the far-reaching implications of the Christian faith for science, politics, education, and the arts. His overriding vision was that the divine ordinances would reign supreme in the home, school, church, and state for the glory of God and the good of the people. In 1880 Kuyper founded the Free University of Amsterdam, where he held both the chair of theology and of arts. While teaching at the Free University, Kuyper prepared his *opus magnum*, the *Theological Encyclopedia* (1893–94).[1] Kuyper's political career reached its zenith in 1901 when he was elected prime minister of the Netherlands, which office he successfully discharged for a period of four years. Not unjustly, Kuyper has been acclaimed "Holland's greatest Calvinist," and "the greatest Calvinist since Calvin."[2] As a pastor, theologian, educator, politician, and statesman, Kuyper was one of the most versatile and talented men of modern times.

Kuyper's views on the scope and utility of general revelation were determined to a great extent by his understanding of the nature of man. In the first place, the Dutch scholar rejected the postulate of an analogy of being between God and man. "Standing before God you do not find an analogy in your own being to His Being, because He is God and you are man."[3] So vast is the gulf between the finite creature and the infinite Creator that man is no measure of the reality of God. Second, the grave rational and moral incapacity of the sinner renders him incapable of apprehending God in His works. Natural man untouched by saving grace exists in an abnormal and deprived condition. Objectively, due to sin, a "disturbance has convulsed nature to cloud the transparency of God in the cosmos."[4] And subjectively, within the heart of the sinner, the "Divine impulse encounters an evil cataract, which prevents the entrance of light."[5] The stark reality of sin opposes man's determined search for God. Before God can be known from His works, the sinner's rational incapacity and moral bias must be remedied by the power of regeneration.

As a Calvinist, Kuyper held that God has sown in all men's hearts the unfailing seed of religion. Or to alter the analogy, God so strikes the strings on the harp of the soul that an inescapable *sensus divinitatis* wells up from within the depth of man's being. This subjective illumination of the soul persists in the fallen sinner by virtue of common grace and accounts for the universal phenomenon of religion. But Kuyper insists that these inner perceptions of the sinner ("innate theology") fall short of what he calls the "true" knowledge of God. The divine operations on the sinner's heart produce only vague "perceptions, impressions and feelings,"[6] which amount to little more than a mysticism of the emotions. Instead of leading the sinner to the living God of the Bible, the natural light of the soul affords only "a mere superficiality."[7] Sin, in a word, has effectively cut off the natural man's reception of divine revelation. Or as Kuyper expressed it in his own words, "As soon as sin had entered in, revelation had to work without inward, since sin had fast bolted the door which gave manifestations of God in the soul."[8]

Unlike Barth, Kuyper postulated a revelation of God in the objective cosmos. He believed that Creation and history manifest numerous truths about the sovereign God. In the plan of God, innate theology was intended to be enriched by acquired theology as soon as man entered into a conscious relationship to the world around him. The darkening effects of sin, however, vitiate the objective revelation no less than the subjective revelation. The divine self-disclosure in the external world makes no sense at all to the sinner. Although man displays a curiosity about what lies behind nature and history, "He can never attain to a positive knowledge, nor ever produce anything that falls outside of the scope of philosophy."[9] God's revelation in the objective cosmos thus undergoes a degenerate development. The masses fall into debauchery and idolatry, while the finer minds indulge in false philosophies and equally false morals. The only fruit that revelation in the external world bears is the false theology of paganism. In sum, then general revelation produces no "true knowledge" of God in fallen man. As Kuyper comments, it is absurd to suggest "that the *natural* knowledge of God without enrichment by the *special,* could ever effect a satisfying result."[10] The hard fact is that "natural theology of itself is unable to supply *any* pure knowledge of God."[11]

The crucial point in Kuyper's theology is that fallen man can perceive God's general revelation only through the superadded light of special revelation. If God is to be truly known, there must occur a modification in revelation of the same magnitude as the modification that took place in man due to sin. The nature of the change that governs the one must also govern the other. Hence in the post-Fall state, a higher, brighter light must beam on the sinner if any knowledge whatsoever is to arise. As Kuyper puts it, "This knowledge, given us by nature in our creation, has been veiled *from* and darkened *in* us by the results of sin. Consequently, it now comes to us in the form of a *special revelation.*"[12] Kuyper's position regarding the practical utility of general revelation is clear: "It is only by the *special* knowledge that the *natural* knowledge becomes serviceable."[13]

Revelation is modified, first of all, by the fuller disclosure of the divine will in the written Word of God. As man gropes about in the dark night of sin, a brighter light beams forth from God's Holy Word. Concerning the experience of the sinner, Kuyper remarks, "Outside the Scripture, he discovered only vague shadows. But now as he looked upward, through the prism of the Scriptures he rediscovers his Father and his God."[14]

The second sin-mandated modification of revelation centers on the mighty initiative of God from *without* in the form of the enfleshment of the Son. The vain display of God in the sinful soul gives way to the rich display of God in sinless flesh. The "self-manifestation had to be transferred from the mystery of the soul-life to the outer world, with the incarnation as its central point."[15] Kuyper's point is that valid knowledge of God must include what God is willing to be to the sinner. Anything less than the truth-content that emerges from faith in Christ simply is not "true knowledge" of God.

Kuyper firmly believed that natural man's noblest contemplations of the universe avail nothing. A key word he returns to repeatedly is *palingenesis* (regeneration). Only through *palingenesis* is the lamp of the knowledge of God, which sin had extinguished, rekindled. Only through *palingenesis* is the human consciousness enabled to assimilate divine revelation. If true knowledge of God is sought, *palingenesis* must be acknowledged as the only valid starting point. Only those who have been regenerated by the Spirit of God can begin to assess the identity of those vague strivings in the depths of the human soul. Only those who approach nature and history from the perspective of *palingenesis* find the cosmos to be a legible book. Only those who have been "enlightened" truly know God. As Kuyper sums up the matter, "In our sinful state we could never attain to a true theology, i.e., a true knowledge of God, unless the form of revelation were soteriological."[16] Clearly, then, general revelation avails none but the regenerate.

Kuyper's views represent the basis for the various forms of presuppositionalism that would greatly impact twentieth-century theology. From Kuyper's perspective, the theological task is not to demonstrate that there is a God, but to proclaim to the world the fact that God exists and that He can be known by a faith-reception of His Word. Short of the presupposition of the God of the Bible, the data of Creation, history, or the experiences of the inner life prove worthless. Given the bedrock necessity of presupposing biblical theism, theology "cannot itself start out from doubt, nor can it spend itself in the investigation of religious phenomena, or in the speculative development of the idea of the absolute."[17] If the God of theism is appropriated by faith as the one great presupposition, the need for general revelation and natural theology immediately falls away.

How shall we respond to the theology of Kuyper? His emphasis on the sovereignty and holiness of God and the depravity of man must be heartily commended. His insistence that true religion is soteriological religion and that salvation is secured only by a faith-reception of God's revelation in Christ posits him squarely within the historic Christian faith. His assertion, against modernism, that a complete system of theology can be constructed only on the basis of the written Word of God is entirely correct. His claim that the theologian, however astute he may be, must participate in the experience of *palingenesis* is a theme that needs to be sounded clearly in our day. Moreover, generations of theologians are indebted to Kuyper for his thorough explication of the realtionship between common grace and human achievement in the fields of science, government, and the arts. Yet in spite of substantial agreement with many aspects of Kuyper's theology, we must take issue with his treatment of general revelation as a source for knowledge of God.

First of all, when Kuyper insists that sin renders man incapable of acquiring any significant knowledge of God, he tends to exaggerate the effects of the Fall on man's cognitive powers. Or more accurately, he attributes little potency to the common operation of the Logos by which the sinner's ability to think meaningfully about God is partially restored. With Kuyper, we agree that sin extinguished man's ability to intuit the reality of God and to draw right conclusions about God from the created order. But with the apostle John (John 1:4, 9), Augustine, and Calvin we must postulate a general illumination through the Logos that enables man, made in the image of God, to arrive at right judgments about God's existence, character, and righteous demands. By universal common grace, man is enabled not only to think logically but also to reach certain rudimentary truths about God Himself. Kuyper asserts that common grace curbs the destructive power of sin and makes possible the sinner's reception of special revelation.[18] But if common grace opens the door to special revelation and regeneration, as Kuyper maintains, surely it is capable of the more modest operation of enabling the creature to think right thoughts about his Creator. In sum, Kuyper denies man the Logos-enabled rational ability that Scripture appears to concede. Hence it is not true, with respect to divine things, that man can know nothing apart from the illumination of regeneration. Kuyper erringly posits all illumination in the category of special, saving grace.[19] More faithful to Scripture is the view that common grace restores to the sinner the ability not only to intuit the reality of God, but also to attain by discursive reason additional valid conclusions about the Creator.

If we believe that common grace enables man to make sense out of general revelation, if we are persuaded with Augustine that a general illumination of general revelation enables the creature to attain *sapientia* and *scientia* ("all truth is God's truth"), then the degenerate condition of humanity must be due largely to the perversity of the sinful will. The primary problem thus resides not at the level of human cognition (which has been restored in part by illumination of general revelation), but with fallen man's perverse response to the rudimentary knowledge of God that he possesses. With the apostle Paul in Romans 1:19−25 and 2:14−15, we judge that man actually acquires an elemental knowledge of God; but instead of cultivating that knowledge, man in the darkness of his heart and the stubbornness of his will spurns the knowledge of God and tramples it underfoot. The chief problem of man, who is touched by the Logos-illumination of his mind, is not so much rational inability as pervasive moral corruption. Contrary to Kuyper's development, then, general revelation does serve man qua man over a limited range of the knowledge spectrum, affording him some knowledge of God's existence, character, and moral demands.

In the second place, Kuyper encounters a difficulty shared by all who disallow the mediation of elemental knowledge of God via general revelation. The problem focuses on how guiltworthiness justly can be pronounced on those who have failed to embrace what they did not and, indeed, could not know. In his discussion of revelation and the knowability of God in *Sacred Theology*, Kuyper says little about the basis of the sinner's condemnation. But the apostle Paul plainly links man's condition of moral accountability before God with his stubborn rejection of the rudimentary knowledge acquired from general revelation (Rom. 1:20). The fact is that there must be sufficient light in nature and conscience (short of regeneration) for one who has made no profession of Christ to be justly damned. Let us follow Paul and his teaching that man is judged guilty because he stubbornly refuses to honor and obey the God he knew in a rudimentary way through the several modalities of general revelation.

A further criticism of Kuyper (and certain of his followers) is that he appears to use what Charles L. Stevenson in *Ethics and Language* (1944) called "persuasive definitions." Stevenson said:

> Our language abounds with words which like "culture" have both a vague descriptive meaning and a rich emotive meaning. The descriptive meaning of them

all is subject to constant redefinition. The words are prizes which each man seeks to bestow on qualities of his own choice. Persuasive definitions are often recognizable from the words "real" or "true"....Since people usually accept what they consider true, "true" comes to have the persuasive force of "to be accepted." This force is utilized in the metaphorical expression "true meaning." The hearer is induced to accept the new meaning which the speaker introduces.[20]

Flew continues in the same article on "definition":

When Adolph Hitler claims that "National Socialism is true democracy," and when the Communist governments of North Korea or East Germany maintain that they preside over real democracies, attempts are thereby being made, usually with some appearance of reason given, to annex a prestigious word. A similar exercise in persuasive definitions can also be seen in Book IX of the *Republic*, where Plato argues that only approved pleasures count and that those of disfavored activities are not real and true pleasures.[21]

Kuyper phrased a persuasive definition in stating, "It is unquestionably true that in our sinful state we could never attain to a . . . true knowledge of God, unless the form of revelation were soteriological."[22] The same applies to his saying, "Natural theology of itself is unable to supply *any* pure knowledge of God."[23]

The point is that expressions such as "true knowledge" and "pure knowledge" are emotive, noncognitive forms of persuasion. What person in his right mind would argue with a statement that appeals to "true," "pure," or "real" knowledge? Consequently, the theologian should avoid emotively freighted terms such as "true" or "pure" knowledge and define precisely what kind of knowledge he has in mind. By resorting to persuasive definitions, Kuyper has failed to define with sufficient precision what he actually means by knowledge of God and also the truth content contained in the "sense of divinity" or "seed of religion." In fact, several of his statements dealing with the knowability of God are either confusing or plainly contradictory. For example, we have noted Kuyper's statement to the effect that "natural knowledge of itself is unable to supply *any* pure knowledge of God."[24] And yet on the very next page Kuyper adds an apparent contradiction, saying, "It is upon the canvas of this natural knowledge of God itself that the special revelation is embroidered."[25] In the latter instance, Kuyper postulates a knowledge of God, whereas in the former he denies knowledge. Elsewhere, Kuyper both affirms and denies knowledge in the same statement: "Even though revelation in us on the one hand, and the working of our faith on the other hand, have so advanced that at length we have perceived God in us and consequently *know* God, we have as yet no knowledge *of* God, and hence no theology."[26] If Kuyper, following Calvin, had defined the first instance of knowledge in the above statement as knowledge of God as Creator, and the second instance as knowledge of God as Redeemer, then his assertion would be logically consistent and thus meaningful. A similar criticism could be levied against his use of Calvin's terms "seed of religion" and "sense of divinity." Through the operation of the Logos, the "seed of religion," to cite an example, appears to be invested with some kind of truth content. In Kuyper's words, "The purest confession of faith finds ultimately a starting-point in the seed of religion."[27] And yet in the light of Kuyper's frequent rejection of the natural knowledge of God, what can these terms signify other than an empty potential?

Finally, although Abraham Kuyper and Karl Barth in many respects were poles apart theologically, the two theologians converge in rejecting the utility of general revelation. Both insist that man's rational capacity to know God has been destroyed by sin. Both maintain that only through a supernatural experience is man capable of knowing God in any sense. Both argue that no natural point of contact exists between sinful man and the transcendent and holy God. Kuyper, of course, granted what Barth would not concede—namely, that God has made a valid self-disclosure in His works. I do not suggest that Kuyper was a proto-Barthian. But it may not be an overstatement to suggest that on the issue of general revelation and the knowability of God, Kuyper was closer to Barth than to Augustine or Luther.

The Confessional Method of Berkouwer

G. C. Berkouwer (b. 1903), who is associated with the Reformed Churches of the Netherlands, held for some years the chair of systematic theology at the Free University of Amsterdam. His *opus magnum* is the widely read multivolume series *Studies in Dogmatics.* Berkouwer is a leading advocate in Reformed circles of the confessionalist method in theology. In establishing a case for Christianity, the confessional theologian appeals primarily not to any empirical data but to the biblical witness and to the historic creeds and confessions of the church. "It stands written" is the patented cry of the confessional school.

On the issue of sources for man's knowledge of God, Berkouwer rightly opposes the inflation of general revelation effected by Catholic scholasticism and Protestant liberalism. By supplanting special revelation with general revelation, liberal theology boldly asserts that a way can be made to God independently of Scripture and Christ. In the liberal scheme, natural revelation swallows up special revelation, or at best allows the latter only an augmenting function. The tragic end of this development is the triumph of a rationalistic, Christ-rejecting theology. But Berkouwer also trains his heavy weapons on the classical Roman Catholic position that placed an inordinate emphasis on man's ability to obtain extensive knowledge of God by the natural light of reason. Berkouwer regards as unworthy of the name Christian the assertion that God can be known apart from Christ, and the claim that the existence of God can be proven by a line of formal reasoning.

Berkhouwer argues that Scripture speaks to the issue of a general and universal knowledge of God from the created order infrequently and incidentally. The only Scriptures that deal with the relationship between the divine revelation and the pagan's knowledge of God are Acts 17 and Romans 1. The character of the revelation and the resultant knowledge of God affirmed by these texts needs to be unfolded. But in Berkouwer's mind, the main thrust of the biblical teaching on the subject is clear: The heathen lack a knowledge of God as God. The apostle Paul speaks of the unsaved as those "who do not know God" (1 Thess. 4:5) and he describes the heathen on whom the judgment of God is poured out likewise as "those who do not know God" (2 Thess. 1:8). Writing to the Galatian converts Paul could say, "Formerly, . . . you did not know God, . . . But now . . . you know God" (Gal. 4:8−9). The judgment of the New Testament, according to Berkouwer, is clear; the constitutional condition of the heathen is thoroughgoing ignorance of God (Acts 17:30; 1 Cor. 1:19−20; Eph. 4:18; 1 Peter 1:14). "The picture is bleak: emptiness of mind, ignorance, estrangement. The darkness is sharply contrasted with the light of the Gospel."[28] Conversion to Christ involves a radical transition from darkness to light, from ignorance to knowledge.

But how does Berkouwer square the Pauline intimations of knowledge of God in Acts 17 and Romans 1 with the allegedly dominant New Testament teaching on ignorance? "Do the heathen according to Romans 1 and 2 have more knowledge than the heathen according to Galatians or Thessalonians?"[29] Berkhouwer asks. Is the problem resolved by postulating the existence of dialectic in Paul's thought? Berkhouwer firmly rejects the suggestion than any knowledge/ignorance dualism exists in the apostle's teaching. He judges the so-called optimism vis-à-vis a universal natural knowledge of God to be fully consistent with the overriding pessimism of the New Testament on the subject.

Turning to Paul's preaching on the Areopagus (Acts 17:22−31) and particularly to his remark concerning the alter inscription—"TO AN UNKNOWN GOD"—Berkouwer judges that the apostle's point of contact with the Greeks was their *ignorance.* Paul proclaimed to the pagan philosophers the one whom they did not know. "Now what you worship as something unknown, I am going to proclaim to you" (Acts 17:23). Granted the heathen were confronted with God's universal general revelation, but they opposed and distorted the light, exchanging the truth of God for lies. Thus Berkouwer fails to find in this text in Acts support for an alleged fund of knowledge the Greeks acquired from general revelation. "There is no knowledge of God that lies interspersed in heathen religions which is later incorporated into the body of faith. The antithesis looms large in every encounter with heathendom."[30] The apostle viewed heathen religion and the gospel of Christ as radically antithetical. On the issue of knowledge of God, there is no common ground and no *rapprochement* between heathen religiosity and Christian faith.

But does not Romans 1, at least, indicate that the Gentiles "knew God"? Berkouwer argues that the knowledge attributed to the pagans in Romans 1 likewise fails to contradict the ignorance spoken of in the rest of the New

Testament. In the Romans passage, Paul focuses on the darkness, foolishness, and perversion of the heathen's response to the divine revelation. Because mankind has "exchanged the truth of God for a lie, and worshiped and served created things rather than the Creator" (Rom. 1:25), "the wrath of God is being revealed from heaven against all the godlessness and wickedness of men who suppress the truth by their wickedness" (v. 18). As the apostle views the heathen world, his field of view is filled with human vanity and ignorance coupled with the divine wrath. But still the text affirms, "What may be known about God is plain to them, because God has made it plain to them" (v. 19). In addition, the general revelation is "clearly seen" (v. 20). And finally, "they knew God" (v. 21). But the knowledge here predicated of the heathen, Berkouwer argues, must be interpreted as man's inescapable *contact* and *confrontation* with God's revelation through His works. The divine revelation is so clear, so evident, so inescapable that Paul speaks hyperbolically of the heathen as "knowing" God. From man's encounter with natural revelation there thus occurs a "seeing" and a "knowing" that are murky rather than clear, distorted rather than genuine. As Berkouwer concludes, "There is contact with revelation, but a contact which fails to lead to a true knowledge and acknowledgment."[31] General revelation affords man a kind of knowledge that falls short of "the clear color of true knowledge."[32]

Although denying that God can be authentically known from nature, conscience, and history, Berkouwer does not wish to repudiate the reality of general revelation. Through the modalities of general revelation, God's eternal power and divinity are plainly set forth. On the basis of Romans 1, the church dares not abandon its doctrine of general revelation. The universal revelation is an indisputable datum: It is unmistakably "there." Its reality is a reminder that God has not abandoned the world. But motivated by darkened and brutish minds, fallen men immediately move to oppose God's universal self-disclosure. In daily contact with general revelation, the sinner in his unrighteousness distorts, corrupts, and nullifies the truth. He turns his back on the living God and with his hands shapes lifeless idols. Thus as Berkouwer puts it, "The kernel of religion bears sour fruit."[33] Hence a radical disjunction exists between the divine revelation and man's practical response to that revelation. A valid general revelation, yes! But a personal knowledge of God that issues forth in service for God, no! Insists Berkouwer, "The Christian Church, in speaking of general revelation, never intended to assert that *true* knowledge of God is possible through the natural light of reason."[34]

In failing to respond positively to the disclosure of God in His works, natural man seals his own doom. A clear feature of Romans 1 is the connection between revelation and guilt. Man's guiltworthiness resides in the fact that when confronted with general revelation ignorance never passes over to knowledge. Following Kuyper, Berkouwer maintains that natural man comes in contact with general revelation and even acquires vague perceptions, but he never attains knowledge. For this refusal to cultivate knowledge man is condemned.

But if general revelation proves condemnatory for all who are in Adam, it proves salvific to all who are in Christ. Those whose eyes have been opened through the grace of Christ clearly perceive God in the created order. Berkouwer insists that nature in the Old Testament is never viewed in isolation from Yahweh's salvific activity. The poets' discussion of nature is always set in the context of His saving work on behalf of His people. As a result, the Old Testament nature psalms (e.g. Pss. 8, 19, 29, 65, 104, 147) offer no basis for an independent natural theology constructed by empirical investigation and rational reflection. Rather, these psalms represent the songs of the saints who, with spiritually renewed faculties, behold their God in sea, wind, and storm. Israel perceived her God in Creation, but the pagan nations walked in utter darkness. As Berkouwer sees it, "The knowledge of the nature Psalms is faith knowledge."[35] "Faith in Israel's God . . . opens up the windows of the world, and man once again discovers the works of God's hands."[36] Berkouwer thus maintains that general revelation is intelligible only in the light of special revelation. "This understanding, and seeing, and hearing, is possible only in the communion with him, in the enlightening of the eyes by the salvation of God, and by the Word of the Lord."[37] Or to put it otherwise, knowledge of God as Creator is possible only on the basis of prior knowledge of God as Redeemer. As he looks back on history, Berkouwer is concerned, with Kuyper and Barth, that nature may become an idol, and natural religion a means of spiritual seduction. He was legitimately concerned that by positing nature as a source of knowledge, biblical theism would be swallowed up by a closed world view of mechanical causality.

It should be clear by now that from Berkouwer's perspective the existence of God cannot be proved,[38] and the reality of God cannot be known by rational reflection on the created order. Natural man is incapable of drawing right conclusions from the cosmos, since his thinking and judgments are controlled by sin. As has been intimated, Berkouwer argues that there is no "true knowledge" of God apart from Christ. Knowledge of God is always knowledge of God in Christ. The power, majesty, and wisdom of God set forth in His works are inseparable from the love, grace, and mercy of God displayed in Christ. Both must be taken together. Only by the Spirit in an act of faith does man perceive the reality of God. And the object of that faith is Jesus Christ. Berkouwer argues that the entire biblical witness stresses the exclusiveness of the divine revelation in Christ. Christ is "the light of the world" (John 8:12; 9:5), "the gate" to God (10:9), and "the way and the truth and the life" (14:6). The knowledge of God, which is at the same time eternal life (17:3), is secured solely through faith in Christ. Since Scripture speaks in such exclusive terms of the divine self-disclosure in Christ, it is counterproductive, if not dangerous, to postulate another, more general revelation alongside the Word made flesh.

VIII. "LET GOD BE GOD": ALTERNATIVE REFORMED APPROACHES

It follows from the foregoing discussion that Berkouwer has few illusions about the validity and integrity of the world's religions. Against claims that each religion in its own way mediates an experience of God, Berkouwer regards the non-Christian religions as expressions of man's sinful rebellion against the revelation of God in His works. Religion, in fact, proves to be "a reaction to the revelation of God, a reaction defined by disobedience and apostasy."[39] The common element in all false religions is man's corrupted natural knowledge of God. Cultural, historical, and dispositional differences, superimposed on man's fundamental distortion of the light of God in nature, produce the myriad variations that exist amongst the non-Christian religions. Berkouwer concurs with Barth's view of religion as an affair of godless man. But unlike Barth, Berkouwer is no advocate of an unoffensive universalism. The finality and exclusiveness of Christianity rightly dominates the horizons of his theology.

Berkouwer's deep concern to uphold the divine revelatory initiative as the solution to sinful man's dilemma is heartily applauded. As a watchman over the house of God, he rightly warns of liberalism's attempt to reinstate a new and more subtle form of natural religion. Justifiably, he is worried that new revelations might arise to challenge God's definitive revelation in Christ. One must be vigilant for the relentless tendency of general revelation to level and supplant special revelation as the primary source for saving knowledge. Likewise, we sympathize with his criticism of scholastic Roman Catholic teaching that man is capable of approaching God and constructing a natural theology on his own. But we judge it irresponsible to abolish altogether a valid concept (a natural, albeit distorted, knowledge of God from the Creation) on the grounds that it has been abused. Theology must avoid the pendulum syndrome, whereby in reacting against an extreme position (Thomistic and liberal optimism) it swings to the opposite extreme (inordinate Barthian skepticism). The church should not scuttle a valid concept because it has been abused, but ought to purify the concept by rooting out the abuse.

It must be added that Berkouwer's treatment of the nature psalms is not entirely convincing. We acknowledge that a great many of the psalms affirming a divine revelation in nature flow from the faith consciousness of the Israelite worshiper. The teachings of Psalms 29, 65, 104, and 147, for example, are presented from the perspective of faith. Moreover, Berkouwer is correct in his observation that these psalms reflect the pattern of praise of God for salvation (e.g., Ps. 65:1–5), accompanied by a recognition of God in Creation (e.g., Ps. 65:6–13). However, this is but to recognize that the redeemed in the Old Testament (as in the New) extolled God both as Creator and as Redeemer. In their hymnody, the saints of old praised God for His operations in the physical Creation and for His working in spiritual recreation. But other psalms, such as Psalm 19, are plainly more didactic than devotional. David in Psalm 19 makes several positive statements to the effect that *all* men (not just the saints) behold God's operations in the visible

Creation. Thus the created order mediates a "knowledge" of God that is continuous ("day after day . . . night after night," v. 2), universal ("into all the earth, . . . to the ends of the world," v. 4), and independent of linguistic differences ("there is no speech or language where their voice is not heard," v. 3). In this didactic psalm, nature is presented as a source of light that all behold and that none can avoid, and as a book from which all are able to read off something of the reality of God. In Psalm 19, at least, Berkouwer ignores the propositional content or teaching asserted by the believing writer concerning God's witness to Himself through the created order. A remarkable correspondence, in fact, exists between the teachings of Psalm 19 and Romans 1.

In addition, Berkouwer misrepresents the force of the so-called "ignorance" texts (Gal. 4:8; 1 Thess. 4:5; 2 Thess. 1:8; et al.) when he alleges that they allow the sinner no knowledge of God from nature. When Paul charges the pagans with ignorance, he asserts that in their natural, unconverted state they did not know God *redemptively*. From the created world without and the testimony of conscience within, the heathen knew God as the all-powerful, wise, and just Creator and Sustainer of the universe. But from these same sources they knew Him not as Savior, Father, and Friend. Because sinful man refuses to submit himself to God, he fails to know God in the fullness of light, hope, and salvation (Eph. 4:18).

Unfortunately Berkouwer closes his eyes to the plain meaning of Romans 1 and Acts 17 when he insists that man as man gains no knowledge of God from the cosmos. However, he agrees with Paul in Romans 1 that the general revelation is objectively given (v. 19b) and clearly seen and perceived (vv. 19a, 20). But whereas Berkouwer attempts to explain the "known" in terms of man's mere contact with the revelation, Paul goes beyond the "given" and the "seen and perceived" to posit, in addition, that God's invisible nature and attributes are "known" as a proper truth content. In this respect Berkouwer has driven a wedge between perception and knowledge. General revelation is perceived, but it does not register as knowledge. Paul's indictment against the heathen world is that although they "knew God" as the true God of heaven and earth, they failed to honor and obey Him as God, pledging rather their loyalty to inert idols. Similarly, in the Acts 17 passage we recall Berkouwer's judgment that heathendom deliberately opposed and distorted the knowledge and the truth of God given by general revelation.[40] But is it reasonable to suppose that one can deliberately oppose that of which he is ignorant? Guilt, we insist, presupposes actual knowledge.

At the philosophical level, Berkouwer's rejection of general revelation as a source for the knowledge of God may also be rooted in his suborthodox view of truth. Truth, according to Berkouwer, is never conceptual or propositional. Commending a relational, existential view of truth, he argues that it is not possible to describe in formal terms who God *is*. One merely encounters God in the context of a personally experienced relationship.

Since knowledge is a function of one's own experience or involvement with a subject, it is impossible that nature should disclose truths about God such as His divinity, eternal power, wisdom, or goodness. By viewing truth not as propositional but in terms of an "I-Thou" personal encounter, Berkouwer has moved in the direction of a neoorthodox understanding of revelation and knowledge. This trend is particularly evident in his later work, *Holy Scripture*, where revelation is said to occur primarily in the experience of salvation.[41]

Similar to Kuyper, but less extensively, Berkouwer lapses into the use of persuasive definitions. The most that general revelation affords is a veiled form of pseudoknowledge. Only special revelation provides man with what Berkouwer calls "true knowledge."[42] If Scripture and Christ alone lead sinners to a knowledge of God, then logically general revelation effects no knowledge. But in such a case the justice of God would be impugned for condemning a person on the basis of ignorance. As indicated in our discussion of Kuyper's theology, the most satisfactory resolution of the problem is to postulate with Calvin a twofold knowledge of God. Through general illumination of natural revelation, man gains a knowledge of God as Creator. But through special revelation, he is graciously enabled to know God as Redeemer. Thus, in sum, we can commend the Christomonism of Barth and Berkouwer as regards salvation, but not their Christomonism as it relates to revelation.

The Presuppositional Apologetic of Van Til   From the confessional approach of Berkouwer we pass to the presuppositional method of Cornelius Van Til (b. 1895). The Dutch-born scholar, who served on the faculties of Princeton and Westminster theological seminaries, has become one of the most prominent Reformed theologians and apologists of the twentieth century. A leading disciple of Abraham Kuyper, Van Til has excelled in exposing the fallacious presuppositions of the leading non-Christian philosophical and apologetic systems. Van Til is generally regarded as the father of presuppositionalism in America.

Van Til argues that there are only two kinds of philosophy, or schemes of viewing reality: the Christian and the non-Christian. The former postulates as its ultimate referent the self-contained God of the Bible, the latter rebellious, autonomous man. Van Til views modern humanistic philosophy as shaped by antitheistic thinking that moves in a line from the ancient Greeks through the European Enlightenment. In spite of token references to God, Greek thinking asserted the ultimacy of the natural order. It postulated autonomous man's ability to apprehend all finite facts independently of God. Moreover, by sheer ratiocination, Greek thought also claimed the ability to investigate the reality of God. Building on this base, eighteenth- and nineteenth-century Enlightenment thinkers promulgated the dogma of the autonomy of natural man and his competence to function as judge over all reality. With his militant antitheistic orientation, Enlightenment man declared open war against the God of the Bible.

Van Til insists that when it comes to the interpretation of reality, there are only two possible reference points: God and man. Reformation Protestantism faithfully posits as its ultimate referent "the self-contained ontological Trinity."[43] The triune God who created, sustains, and providentially controls all things is necessarily the ultimate principle of interpretation in the universe. A fact is true when it receives its interpretation from the triune God of the Bible. From Van Til's perspective, if God be God, "then no fact is a fact apart from God and has a full and valid interpretation apart *from Him.*"[44] Van Til defines the kind of reasoning employed by the Christian who posits God as the ultimate reference point of predication as *analogical* reasoning. Only when human knowledge is analogical of divine knowledge, only when the former is subordinate and the latter determinative, is the attainment of truth possible. But the sinner, seeking to be like God, postulates himself as the ultimate reference point in the universe. In his fallen, rebellious condition, man refuses to think God's thoughts after Him, but chooses instead to posit himself as the normative principle of interpretation. Autonomous man thus proceeds either to eliminate God entirely or to allow God to coexist on his own terms. Van Til calls *univocal* reasoning that mode of thinking in which man arrogates to himself the final point of interpretation and predication. By thinking univocally, autonomous man ends up with a distorted vision of reality and at best an immanent God that is indistinguishable from nature. The ultimacy of God and the autonomy of man represent the two rival options in the history of philosophy.

From the foregoing, it follows that in principle the sinner is incapable of any knowledge in the proper sense, either in the spiritual or in the scientific realms. In Van Til's scheme, facts must be correlated with universals. Hence apart from God, by whom all things are created and through whom all things derive their meaning, intelligent understanding and predication about anything is impossible. Without presupposing the universal of the ontological Trinity, there is no facticity, no truth. In other words, "only *theistic* facts are possible. We definitely maintain that for any fact to be a fact at all, it must be a theistic fact."[45] In discarding God, the ultimate universal, fallen man has discarded everything. Thus the consistent natural man knows nothing truly. But the sinner rescues himself from this extremity by lapsing into inconsistency. While rejecting God, the ground of all knowledge, he nevertheless as a matter of expediency slips into theistic thinking. In sum, then, Van Til emphatically rejects every attempt to ground knowledge in any other datum but God.

Van Til, however, draws a distinction in man's interpretive activity between what is metaphysical and psychological and what is epistemological. Van Til insists that psychologically there are no atheists. Man possesses within him the knowledge of God (a knowledge, indeed, suppressed) by virtue of having been created in the image of God. To this point we will return shortly. Nevertheless, from the perspective of epistemology every sinner is an atheist. By rejecting the ultimate principle of interpretation, sinful man has lost the capacity to attain right conclusions about God and His saving purposes. Epistemologically, no common ground exists between believer and unbeliever. In Van Til's own words:

> To look for a point of contact with the unbeliever's notion of himself and his world is to encourage him in his wicked rebellion and to establish him in his self-imposed delusion that he is "free," i.e., independent of the control and counsel of God, and that the "facts" about him are also "free" in this way. He may pretend to be "open-minded" and ready to consider whether God exists. But in being so "neutral" he commits the same sin as Adam and Eve.[46]

By affirming that God and man have nothing in common at the epistemological level, Van Til sides with Tertullian, who abhorred the speculation of the Greeks and polemicized against "the stupidities of philosophy." Every student of theology recalls Tertullian's classic rhetorical question, "What has Athens to do with Jerusalem?" Athens, the domain of self-sufficient, autonomous man whose god is nature, and Jerusalem, the domain of biblical theism, are two irreconcilable realms. Moreover, since God is infinite and perfect in knowledge and man is finite and sinful, it is folly to expect that the truth of Christianity should appear reasonable to the sinner. Hence Tertullian declared, "I believe because it is absurd" (*credo quia absurdum*). Armed with the basic perspective of Tertullian, Van Til develops further his case for a fideistic apologetic.

Because autonomous human reasoning leads nowhere, Van Til asserts that the Christian must address the sinner by way of presupposition. Since there is one system of reality that centers on the self-contained God, all thinking and predication must begin by acknowledging the triune Creator and Sustainer-God who speaks with absolute authority in Scripture. The presentation of isolated facts adduced from nature or history independent of God, the ultimate referent, is a futile venture. According to Van Til,

> Unless he will accept the presuppositions and with them the interpretations of Christianity, there is no coherence in human experience. That is to say, . . . unless one accepts the Bible for what true Protestantism says it is, the authoritative interpretation of human life and experience as a whole, it will be impossible to find meaning in anything.[47]

That is, only as one boldly begins with the idea of the self-contained God does the data of the space-time world become intelligible and reason become a reliable interpretative tool. A sound and convincing case for biblical theism cannot be constructed by the traditional empirical, rational, or verificational systems. The commonly employed empirical-historical method guarantees the overthrow of biblical Christianity. "The only 'proof' of the Christian position is that unless its truth is presupposed there is no possibility of 'proving' anything at all."[48] Against detractors, Van Til insists that the true Christian philosophy presented presuppositionally is anything but arbitrary and subjective. Rather, the truth of the gospel promulgated on the authority of Scripture is always self-authenticating and self-validating. Apart from any line of deductive or inductive reasoning, the individual who allows himself to be confronted with the living Word of God becomes existentially persuaded of its truthfulness.

But for Van Til, all of these considerations do not gainsay the fact that God has given a valid revelation of Himself in the natural order. With St. Paul and Calvin, Van Til declares that from the very beginning God has never left Himself without a witness. There are signs of God's power and divinity on every hand. The universe as a divine Creation plainly displays God as sovereign Maker, Preserver, and Judge. Given the abundance, clarity, and inescapable presence of the evidence, man, quite apart from special revelation, *ought* to have recognized God as such. If man had only reasoned *analogically*, he would have been led from nature to nature's God. If man had recognized God as the ultimate referent, the ontological, cosmological, teleological, and moral arguments would have given birth to an experiential knowledge of God.[49]

The chief problem, however, is that the sinner, untamed by grace, does not reason analogically. By positing his own ultimacy, natural man chooses to reason univocally. By adopting the false principle that he himself is the ultimate referent, natural man suppresses and nullifies the idea of God. Thus pleading his own autonomy, the sinner is anything but neutral with respect to the evidence for God's existence and character. When confronted with God's witness to Himself in nature and history, carnal man reacts with total opposition. As the covenant-breaker that he is, the sinner refuses to keep God in remembrance. Motivated by satanic hostility to God, he deliberately strives to efface every trace of the knowledge of God. When the facts force themselves in upon him, the sinner avoids the conclusion of theism by interpreting the data immanently. Thus Van Til argues:

> Man by his sinful nature hates the revelation of God. Therefore every concrete expression that any sinner makes about God will have in it the poisoning effect of this hatred of God. His epistemological reaction will invariably be negative, and negative along the whole line of his interpretive endeavor. There are no general principles or truths about the true God . . . which he does not falsify.[50]

In sum, then, general revelation affords the sinner no light. In Van Til's own words, "The natural man is as blind as a mole with respect to natural things as well as with respect to spiritual things." In short, "The natural man is spiritually blind with respect to everything."[51] By reasoning univocally over the data of the space-time world, natural man draws the wrong conclusions about God's existence and being. Consequently, the natural order affords no knowledge of God. Apart from a special, supernatural disclosure, the God of the Bible could not be known.

Whereas epistemologically no common ground exists between God and man, Van Til proceeds to argue that psychologically and metaphysically common ground cannot be denied. Because man thinks univocally, God can never be known by rational reflection on the data of the natural world. But because man is created in the image of God, he bears within his psychological constitution the realization that God is the Creator and Preserver of all that is. These intuitions that well up in man's consciousness in spite of his sinful nature are innate rather than acquired. That which Van Til calls "innate knowledge"[52] thus proves similar to Augustine's effable intuition and Calvin's "sense of Deity" or "seed of religion." This innate knowledge may also be viewed from a metaphysical perspective, for "to not know God man would have to destroy himself."[53] Man's knowledge of God at the psychological and metaphysical levels forms the necessary presupposition for man's ethical opposition to God. Thus Van Til concludes, "All men know God, the true God, the only God. They have not merely a capacity for knowing him but actually do know him."[54]

But rather than cherish and cultivate this natural knowledge, fallen man deliberately stifles the Father's voice in his heart and strives to efface every trace of divine knowledge from his mind. Confronted with the reality and truth of God at the center of his being, man asserts his own ultimacy and chooses the path of the covenant-breaker. In short, man knows God psychologically and metaphysically, but he deliberately moves to suffocate that knowledge in his consciousness.

Turning to the Epistle to the Romans, Van Til concedes that the apostle teaches that natural man possesses a knowledge of God. Van Til has few problems with Romans 2, where Paul details a divine revelation in the depths of man's psychological constitution, namely, within his conscience. But he has greater difficulty squaring his overall system with Paul's teaching in Romans 1 concerning a knowledge of God derived from the date of nature. As has been noted, the foundational premise in the Van Tilian scheme is that man sees the truth only by adopting the presupposition of the self-contained ontological Trinity. No valid interpretation of the empirical data is possible, short of presupposing the reality of the God of the Bible. The only true fact, Van Til holds, is a theistic fact. We recall his bold assertion that the sinner is as "blind as a mole" with respect to both natural and spiritual things. Also we remember Van Til's claim that natural man's knowledge of God is not intellectual but psychological. He who seeks to interpret reality by evaluating the data independently of the theistic presupposition fuctions as an atheist. Thus in order to remain consistent, Van Til argues that man's knowledge of God in Romans 1 has nothing to do with his intellect, but is strictly psychological and is given by virtue of man's creation in the *imago Dei*. But it is difficult to avoid the conclusion that Paul plainly teaches in Romans 1 that man gains rudimentary knowledge of God's existence and character by rational reflection on the created order. The vastness, order, and beneficence of the cosmos serve as objective pointers to the great God who created and sustains all that is. Paul, unlike Van Til, envisages the realities of the space-time continuum as *indicia*, on the basis of which theistic conclusions are actually drawn. Paul, Van Til, and this writer all agree that fallen man acts perversely with respect to the elemental knowledge that he possesses. But it seems an injustice to the Pauline teaching in Romans 1 to argue that natural man's knowledge of God is strictly psychological and not also intellectual. Although he subsequently distorts the truth of God, natural man nevertheless draws valid conclusions about God by reflecting in some way on the data of the visible order.

As has been noted, Van Til wants to retain the idea of general revelation even though, broadly speaking, it fails to lead natural man to a knowledge of God as Creator. General revelation condemns the sinner rather than pointing him in the direction of God. Van Til, in fact, argues a case for the unity of general and special revelation:

> God's revelation in nature, together with God's revelation in Scripture, form God's one grand scheme of covenant revelation of himself to man. The two forms of revelation must therefore be seen as presupposing and supplementing one another. They are aspects of one general philosophy of history.[55]

From Van Til's perspective, only after God gives man a new heart and a new mind is he able to apprehend the Creator in nature. The created order thus becomes revelatory at a practical level only for the believing Christian.[56]

Van Til sees serious dangers in the traditional method that allowed for the mediation of a preparatory knowledge of God apart from special revelation. Anytime, he argues, that human capability is admitted in one area without restrictions, larger areas of human capability are assumed. Such a process invariably culminates in the total ascendency of man and the complete demise of God. As Van Til argues, "If the natural man's eyes (reason) enable him to see correctly in one dimension, there is no good reason to think that those same eyes will not enable him, without further assistance from without, to see correctly in all dimensions.[57] In our view, the claim that no epistemic capability should be ascribed to man as man is a harsh judgment that fails to enjoy the support of Scripture. Rather, God enjoins natural man to examine and weigh the evidence so as to come to right conclusions about God and His demands.[58] To invite man as a rational creature of God to think critically within bounds is not equivalent to acknowledging his autonomous independence of God over the whole range of human thought. Common grace enables man qua man within a limited band of the intellectual spectrum to think God's thoughts after Him.

Thus as a matter of practical apologetics, Van Til places little store in any serious appeal to the data of general revelation. The starting point for his Christian proclamation *vis-à-vis* unregenerate man is the self-attesting Christ of inspired Scripture. A truly Christian epistemology postulates the subordination of man's knowledge to God's knowledge as revealed in

Jesus Christ. Van Til insists that the Christian must argue by way of presupposition:

> The Christian offers the self-attesting Christ to the world as the only foundation upon which a man must stand in order to give any "reasons" for anything at all. The whole notion of "giving reasons" is completely destroyed by an ontology other than the Christian one. The Christian claims that only after accepting the biblical scheme of things will any man be able to understand and account for his own rationality.[59]

The Reformed apologist thus proclaims the facts of special revelation and challenges the non-Christian to accept them as the means to a knowledge of God and to a proper understanding of all other facts.

Van Til and his followers are to be commended for unmasking the antitheistic presuppositions of autonomous man in philosophy and theology. Few apologists have pointed up as effectively as Van Til the true character of the unbeliever's first principles. He has built a convincing case for natural man's radical inability, the failure of all humanistic systems, and the sinner's need for divine grace. Above all, Van Til has been a staunch advocate of the unqualified uniqueness and finality of the Christian gospel. Christianity is unrivaled by any world religion or ideology. Van Til must also be commended for recognizing more clearly than Kuyper or Berkouwer that man made in the divine *imago* possesses a knowledge of God that is innate. On this basis, he rightly asserts that all men know God naturally. Indeed, it is this possession of innate knowledge of God that provides a point of contact for the presentation of the gospel to non-Christians.

But on the other side of the ledger, Van Til fails to do justice to the fact that, in addition to his innate knowledge of God, man made in the *imago Dei* and blessed with general illumination of the Logos acquires further knowledge of the Creator by reflecting on the works of God's hands. Van Til's presuppositionalism does not square with the fact that the apostles in their missionary preaching to non-Christians called for belief on the basis of arguments drawn from nature and the providential flow of history (Acts 14, 17). The early Christian evangelists appealed to such matters of common knowledge as God's dominion over heaven and earth, His provision of the means by which all life is sustained, and the divine ordering of the boundaries of the nations. In the affairs of daily life, God has granted to all men a compelling testimony to Himself. Likewise, in Romans 1 it is difficult to sustain Van Til's judgment that the knowledge Paul refers to is fully explicable by the innate factor in man's psychological constitution. No, the apostle teaches that "since the creation of the world God's invisible qualities—his eternal power and divine nature—have been clearly seen, *being understood from what has been made*" (Rom. 1:20, italics added). The vastness, precision, beneficence, and beauty of the created order prompts the Logos-illumined mind to draw conclusions about God's character and moral demands. Philip Edgcumbe Hughes, writing in the Van Til *Festschrift*,

Jerusalem and Athens, likewise maintains that natural man gains a knowledge of God by intellectual apprehension of the external data of God's Creation. Comments Hughes:

> The whole cosmic system points incontestably to the truth that there exists a Creator of all who is unique in the eternity of his sovereign divinity. This knowledge is obvious to man as a rational creature. The rationality of the whole, itself a witness to the rationality of the Creator, is a truth from which man cannot rationally dissociate himself.[60]

That is, the apostle Paul, against Van Til, firmly believed that common ground exists between God and natural man not only at the psychological level but at the epistemological level as well. Van Til erroneously interprets Romans 1:19−20 in the sense of Romans 2 rather than in the sense of the first half of Psalm 19.

Many interpreters of Van Til have pointed out the fundamental circularity of his presuppositional apologetic. Given the impossibility of reasoning from nature to God, one must, in fact, reason from God to God. As Van Til would have it, the most reliable proof of God's existence is the indispensable character of God's existence. But the form of reasoning in which the conclusion is embedded in the premise begs the question and proves nothing. Why an outsider should accept Van Til's circle of reasoning and not a rival circle of reasoning is not clear. The circular form of argument that Van Til commends extends an open invitation to the twin dangers of subjectivism and mysticism.

But the most questionable of Van Til's theses is the assertion that apart from acknowledgment of the ontological Trinity man knows nothing truly at all. Without presupposing the existence of God, he argues, man cannot know a single fact. An implication of this assertion is that man is hopelessly blind to the witness of nature and history. However, it seems more responsible to argue that since the *imago Dei* has not been totally effaced, natural man retains the capacity to attain rationally at least some valid conclusions. Whereas man needs special grace to perceive redemptive truths, common grace enables the sinner to apprehend nonredemptive truths. From Scripture we have seen that God holds natural man responsible for making responsible judgments by interpreting and evaluating the data from his environment (Deut. 13, 18). Moreover, from experience it is difficult to sustain the judgment that apart from the theistic presupposition man knows nothing at all. Can it not be said that quite apart from acknowledging God natural man knows that $2 + 2 = 4$? Do the sinner and the saint mean two different things when each asserts that the leaves on the tree in the garden are green? Is it accurate to insist that man shifts from antitheistic to theistic thinking when he reaches such conclusions? On the basis of God's common grace extended to man qua man, much truth, beauty, and insight into reality may be found in human thought and activity. Luther argued as much when he developed the notion of natural reason. As long as it operates in the mundane realm, natural reason is one of God's good gifts to man. Biblically and experientially, it is not true to assert that unless one consciously acknowledges the ontological Trinity, he is devoid of all knowledge. As Gordon Lewis rightly argues, when Van Til attempts to show the unbeliever that Christianity makes sense out of life, he violates his own foundational premise that the unregenerate can make no sense out of reality.[61] For Van Til himself argues, "The Christian-theistic position must be shown to be not as defensible as some other position, it must rather be shown to be *the position which alone does not annihilate intelligent human experience.*"[62] The relationship between sin and human knowing is represented more accurately by Emil Brunner in his "law of the closeness of relation."[63] Brunner theorizes that in the arena of human endeavors the closer one moves toward the core of the religious life, the greater become the distorting effects of sin. Thus the believer and the unbeliever come to virtually identical conclusions in the disciplines of mathematics, physics, and astronomy. But in the areas of psychology, philosophy, and theology, serious differences emerge because of the operation of the sin principle in the heart. We agree with Brunner that, preserved in the image of God and illumined by the Logos, man is able to think rightly without consciously presupposing the ontological Trinity revealed in Holy Scripture.

As a disciple of Augustine and Calvin, Van Til makes the bold assertion that all Reformed thinkers who renounce presuppositionalism are inconsistent Calvinists. The consistent Calvinist, Van Til argues, postulates the absence of epistemic contact between creature and Creator and rejects all natural knowledge of God. But did Calvin himself subscribe to such a position? Prior to Calvin, Martin Luther plainly taught that on the basis of general revelation natural man acquires a knowledge of God as Creator, Sustainer, and Judge. While the knowledge of God from His works does not save, it nevertheless informs man that God exists and that He is all-powerful, wise, just, and good to all who call upon Him.[64] But Calvin's explication of general revelation and knowledge of God closely follows that of his fellow Reformer. In order to show that the nonpresuppositionalist who posits a natural knowledge of God from general revelation is the rightful heir of Calvin's thought, we make the following four observations.

First, against Kuyper, Calvin's sense of divinity or seed or religion is not an empty potential. Calvin did not resort to persuasive definitions, but definitively stated that man possesses a knowledge of God's existence and certain of His perfections by the power of effable intuition. That which by common grace is engraved on the human heart is properly called knowledge of God. Second, general revelation, according to Calvin, is intended for all people and not merely for the saved. Calvin argued that God gave a revelation in nature, in man himself, and in providence so that all might worship Him and obtain the hope of eternal life. Third, Calvin postulated that all people possess a knowledge of God as Creator. Calvin plainly taught what Kuyper, Berkouwer, and Van Til deny, namely, that on the basis of general revelation in the external world, all people gain a knowledge of God as the Creator, Preserver, and Judge of all. God's self-disclosure in the heavens, in the providential flow of history, and in the constitution of man mediates to the creature a body of truth about Himself. And finally, again against all three Reformed theologians, knowledge of God as Creator is realized independently of the experience of regeneration. Calvin made the point very clearly that there is a knowledge of God as Creator and a higher knowledge of God as Redeemer. The former is realized from the several modalities of Logos-illumined general revelation, and the latter through faith in the Christ of Holy Scripture. Regeneration clarifies, but does not originate, the knowledge of God as Creator in man, the image-bearer of God. In sum, those who postulate that by Logos illumination of general revelation man qua man gains a knowledge of God as Creator may well be the consistent Calvinists. Although profoundly appreciative of the contributions of evangelical colleagues who subscribe to confessional and presuppositional theologies, I conclude that they fail to explicate fully the relationship between general revelation and man's natural knowledge of God in a way that adequately accounts for the data of Scripture and human experience.

BEYOND THE GOD
IX OF THEISM:
THE NEOLIBERAL QUEST

The classical liberal theologies of Schleiermacher, Ritschl, and Raus-chenbusch were dealt a mortal blow by the powerful Barthian backlash in the 1940s and 1950s. But with the ebb of neoorthodoxy's influence in the ensuing decades, a more sophisticated and chastened liberal movement emerged from the ruins to challenge evangelicals for leadership in the theological world. Thus the 1960s and 1970s gave birth to a bewildering variety of existentialist, process, liberation, and secularist theologies. In the modern world, a burgeoning scientism prompted theologians to de-mythologize the biblical cosmology and to reinterpret radically the teach-ings of Scripture. Not only the three-decker universe but also the biblical picture of God was eclipsed in the name of scientific modernity. A growing antimetaphysical bias created a reluctance to speak about God as He is in Himself. Personalist philosophy prompted the redefinition of God's tran-scendence in terms of the relationship between divine and human persons. And finally, the classical model of God as a transcendent yet immanent Person distinct from the Creation gave way to neoclassical alternatives, the most prominent of which is the panentheistic vision: God is in everything and everything is in God.

A legacy of modern scientism is the omnipresent spirit of secularism. In contemporary Protestant circles, the classical discipline of theology ("the queen of the sciences") has given way in large measure to the science of religion. In a secular age, the study of God has been supplanted by the study of man. Reflection on God's character and will has yielded to an existential analysis of man's anguish and aspirations. Along the same lines, traditional natural theology, which sought God in the external world, has been ex-changed for a natural theology of mystical awareness within the depths of the human psyche. The historic quest for formal proofs to support theism has been replaced by the all-sufficient proof of ineffable subjective experi-ence. In its belief that God is an inescapable datum of human consciousness, contemporary neoliberalism boldly postulates the validity and equality of all the world's religions. Convinced that a loving God could not condemn any of His creatures to eternal punishment, modernism propounds an unoffensive theory of universal salvation. The task of missions, on this showing, is not evangelization or proselytization, but creative dialogue and cooperation in the social, economic, and political arenas.

Toynbee the Historian   Although not a professional theologian, Arnold Toynbee (1889–1975), former London University professor and the most influential philosopher of history in the twentieth century, interacts extensively with the issue of the knowability of God and the validity of the world's religions. His breadth of knowledge, literary productivity, and commanding influence have led one authority to describe Toynbee as "the Barth of historical science."[1] Toynbee's monumental work, the twelve-volume *Study of History* (1934–1961), examines in great detail the genesis, growth, and disintegration of the world's great civilizations. Of the twenty-six identifiable world civilizations, only one, Western European culture, remains intact. Yet because of its failure to creatively respond to challenges posed to it, Toynbee argues, Western society faces an inevitable future decline. Although civilizations rise and fall in a recurrent cyclical pattern, Toynbee believed that a linear development takes place in the sphere of religion. In asserting that religion moves in a continuous upward line, Toynbee was influenced by twentieth-century evolutionary theory and process philosophy. Although the British historian was steeped in the Anglican tradition, the prevalence of evil in the world led him to question the existence of the personal and benevolent God of the Bible. Confessed Toynbee, "When I am thinking rationally, I am a religious agnostic. I do not know whether there *is* a living God, and, on the whole, I think this is improbable, if the word 'God' implies a humanlike personality."[2] On balance, Toynbee's writings portray a man attracted to the undogmatic simplicity of Mahayana Buddhism.

Spiritual light is not the exclusive prerogative of any one faith, but, on the contrary, represents the common property of the world's higher religions. Appealing to the familiar Johannine teaching that the Logos is "the true light that gives light to every man" (John 1:9), Toynbee insists that man in the universe is enveloped by an ineffable and infinite spiritual presence. The higher religions—Buddhism, Hinduism, Judaism, Islam, and Christianity—facilitate the creature's experience of discovery, enlightenment, and mystical apprehension of absolute Reality.[3] Toynbee himself claimed to have had three mystical experiences of ultimate Reality in which his moral consciousness was suspended and he was caught up into the presence of the transcendent All-in-All.[4] Consequently, in Toynbee's scheme, God is apprehended by feelings of omniscient enlightenment and all-inclusive intuition—a process that the renowned historian freely acknowledged to be no more than a fitful "groping in the dark."[5] Thus similar to Buddhist teaching, Toynbee regards the knowledge of God as a function not of special revelation, but of mystical enlightenment and discovery. In the sense that the symbols and sacraments of the higher religions facilitate man's experience of the Absolute, it may be said that each of these faiths serve as vehicles of enlightenment. Although Toynbee frequently quoted the Bible, the Christian Scriptures are no more revelatory than the sacred writings of the other higher religions. The Bible merely chronicles *one* way in which man has sought to discover God behind earth's phenomena. Although a collection of myths and fables, the Scriptures document in part man's evolutionary ascent to more perfect perceptions of transcendent reality.

Toynbee maintains that there is a basic agreement between Buddhism, Hinduism, Judaism, Islam, and Christianity. These five higher religions, which dominate the present age, amount to four variations on the same theme. No one religion sets forth the final and definitive explication of religious truth; all, in fact, are partial representations of the way to God. As Toynbee expresses it, "Absolute Reality is a Mystery to which there is more than one approach."[6] The assertion that *my* vision of reality, *my* religion is the sole purveyor of truth represents a condition of sinful pride, blasphemy, and megalomania.

> Since self-centeredness is innate in human nature, we are all inclined, to some extent, to assume that our own religion is the only true and right religion; that our own vision of Absolute Reality is the only authentic vision; that we alone have received a revelation; that the truth which has been revealed to us is the whole truth; and that, in consequence, we ourselves are "the chosen people" and the "children of light," while the rest of the human race are gentiles sitting in darkness. Such pride and prejudice are symptoms of original sin.[7]

Judaism, Christianity, and Islam, with their concept of the "jealous God," are especially guilty of intolerant claims of finality.

Clearly, then, for Toynbee Christianity is not the unique and absolute religion. The fact that God loves the whole of mankind provides the assurance that a valid revelation is made to people of all faiths in forms appropriate to their particular cultural heritage. Thus of the higher non-Christian religions Toynbee can say, "They too are light radiating from the same source from which our own religion derives its spiritual light."[8] Nevertheless, in the evolutionary ascent of the human spirit in the world, religious diversity is bound to give way to uniformity. Through a process of peaceful competition, those religions that offer the clearest vision of God and the fullest measure of grace will win the allegiance of the entire human race. Yet the other religions will not altogether perish, since their highest virtues will be absorbed into the dominant systems to form a syncretistic faith suitable for the future of the race. Thus the future unification of world cultures into a vast single family will be paralleled by a similar coalescence of world faiths. In fact, in Toynbee's scheme, the pagan no less than the Buddhist, the Hindu, or the Christian has ultimate salvation within his grasp.[9] Any soul who makes the best of his spiritual opportunities, who opens himself to the light that radiates from one of the higher religions, qualifies for salvation, which Toynbee viewed as present communion with the Absolute and future passage to the next life.

Toynbee's outlook rightly has been described as an amalgam of Christianity and Mahayana Buddhism. His insistence that man apprehends ultimate Reality by a process of mystical enlightenment bears greater affinity to the Buddhist scheme than to the Judeo-Christian tradition. Toynbee errs in supplanting a cognitive knowledge of God with the concept of ecstatic, mystical encounter. Moreover, Toynbee's attempt to eliminate the offense of the gospel by reducing religion to the lowest common denominator betrays the outlook of Jesus and the New Testament writers. In his appeal for religious tolerance and broad-mindedness, Toynbee makes a powerful appeal to the relativistic and syncretistic spirit of the age. Yet this uncritical acceptance of all religious viewpoints blurs if not destroys altogether the concept of truth. Similarly, his emphasis on religion in the singular blindly overlooks the contradictions that exist between the world's historic religions. Rather than the harmony and unity Toynbee envisages, there are sharp differences of substantive belief on such fundamental matters as the nature of God, the person and work of Christ, and the mode of salvation. Understanding and respect are important virtues, but a firm discrimination between true and false propositions certainly is the most responsible and loving course of action for one to adopt. In sum, then, the brilliant English historian embraced and promulgated a system of religion quite unlike the faith of the apostle Paul, Augustine, the Protestant Reformers, and those who faithfully follow in their train.

Tillich and the Ground of Being   Paul Tillich (1886–1965) is acclaimed, along with Barth and Bultmann, one of the three towering figures in twentieth-century Protestantism. After receiving the doctorate in philosophy from the University of Breslau, he lectured in philosophy and theology at several German universities. In 1929 Tillich became professor of philosophy at the University of Frankfort and served until 1933, when he was forced to leave Germany because of his opposition to Hitler and National Socialism. From 1933 to 1955, Tillich served as professor of philosophical theology at Union Theological Seminary in New York. After retiring from Union, he taught at Harvard (1955–1962) and the University of Chicago (1962–1965). Tillich insisted that his purpose in writing theology was to "make the tradition [i.e., the classical expression of Christian doctrine] understandable."[10] Yet except for those well versed in the systems of Kant, Hegel, Schelling, and twentieth-century existentialism, much of Tillich's writings remain difficult if not abstruse.

Tillich refused to be linked with the pragmatic empiricism of the modern liberal tradition and with the supernatural biblicism of Barthian neoorthodoxy. Instead, he sought to forge a mediating position between supernaturalism and naturalism, between traditional theism and atheistic humanism. Tillich's "existential-ontological theism"[11] synthesizes insights from the idealism of Hegel and Schelling, the romanticism of Schleiermacher, and the existentialism of Kierkegaard and the early Heidegger. From his doctoral research on Schelling (d. 1854), Tillich bought into the pantheistic scheme involving an ontological union between subject and object, self and the world, man and God. The whole of the universe is united in Being-itself, or the ground of Being. Moreover, from Schleiermacher's "feeling of absolute dependence," Tillich laid stress on man's immediate awareness of the transcendent and the unconditional. In concert with Schleiermacher, Tillich explored the world of ineffable religious experience that transcends empirical verification. Finally, from twentieth-century existentialist thought, Tillich learned that truth is derived from an analysis of the total range of human existence. Theological understanding, rather than being rational and objective, is rooted in the subjective realities of human experience.

Tillich makes the bold assertion that God is not a being alongside other beings, for in that case Deity would be a creature of time and space. Whatever God may be like, His nature is beyond the limiting categories of existence. In this vein Tillich argues, "God does not exist. He is Being-itself, beyond essence and existence. Therefore, to argue that God exists is to deny him."[12] Moreover, "It is as atheistic to affirm the existence of God as it is to deny it."[13] As the ground of Being, God infinitely transcends that of which He is the ground. Against supernaturalism, Tillich maintains that God is not a being who dwells in a superworld of divine objects (the classical *deus ex machina* concept). God is not "out there" as a celestial person whose character and demands one seeks to ascertain by rational reflection. Tillich equates the truly immanent God with the dynamic process of temporal existence. Thus, as Tillich sees it, what one must affirm in the modern world is the "God beyond God,"[14] or the "God above the God of theism."[15]

Tillich's existentially based ontology, utilizing the language of medieval metaphysics, describes God as Being-itself (*ipsum esse*), or the ground and power of Being. Here Being represents the most universal concept, the most inexhaustible reality, the mental mirroring of what most fundamentally is. Replacing spatio-temporary imagery with the idea of self-transcendence, Tillich envisages God as present to the creature not as any special being, but as the source and ground of all Being, infinitely full and inexhaustible. The infinity of Being is continuous with human finite being and vice versa. Following Schelling and Hegel, Tillich's God transcends the subject-object dichotomy prominent in Descartes. Thus "God is not Another, an Object which we may know or fail to know, but Being-itself, in which we participate by the very fact of existing."[16] By the symbol "God" Tillich means the Abyss, the Other, the inexhaustible Depth of all reality. More than this no man can say.

Revelation, for Tillich, is a thoroughly human activity facilitated by the Logos, the uncreated light present in the human soul. Via the indwelling Logos, man discovers Being-itself reflected in his own finite being. Hence revelation is not the communication of information, but a person's ecstatic experience of the Unconditioned, or of the ground and power of Being.[17] It is the manifestation of what concerns man ultimately. It is an immediate mystical awareness of that inexhaustible primal Reality, or the Abyss, that transcends the classical subject-object duality. Thus God is not arrived at by a process of discursive reasoning; rather God is apprehended in a moment of lived insight and intuition. Through this immediate, prereflective awareness, human eyes are opened to "the abysmal element in the ground of Being,"[18] thereby overcoming "ontological shock"[19] or "the threat of non-being."[20] Tillich describes this moment of gnostic insight, this direct awareness of the Unconditional, as "phenomenological intuition."[21] Revelation, therefore, does not break into man's life perpendicularly from above; rather, it wells up from within as a profound inner awakening or illumination.

In other terms, God is known through the experience of being grasped by "ultimate, unconditional, total, infinite concern,"[22] a concept similar to Schleiermacher's "feeling of absolute dependence." When a person is engaged with what is of ultimate concern for his life, when he has plumbed the depths of his soul and the source of his being, *then* God is experientially encountered.[23] Via the act of faith, namely the exercise of ultimate concern, man is grasped by the ground and power of Being and moves from existential estrangement to a relationship with Being-itself. Through this transforming union of finite being with that ground of Being beyond time and space, man finds meaning and value and is endued with the "courage to be."[24] Tillich concedes that his approach to knowledge is mystical, but in defense of his position he appeals to the fact that mysticism was a potent force in Christianity from the fifth century onwards.

The mystical intuition of Being-itself represents for Tillich the scope of primary revelation. All may encounter the reality of God, given the universal character of the mystical a priori. Man, in fact, experiences God in every encounter with reality. Anything can function as an instrument of revelation, since "everything participates in Being-itself."[25] The elements of nature, historical events, living beings, sexual acts, natural catastrophies, and death are but a few of the means through which the mystery of Being is manifested. Tillich seeks to avoid a lapse into natural theology by referring to the aforementioned not as sources for the knowledge of God, but as the media through which God is existentially encountered. In other words, "Revelation through natural mediums is not natural revelation."[26] Tillich thus emphasizes the radical have-ability of God, finding Him very much *in* the world rather than beyond the world.

Following Kant, Tillich dismisses the rational arguments for God's existence based on the empirical data of the objective cosmos. Far from leading one to truths about God, discursive reason merely formulates the question about the Mystery of Being. "The arguments for the existence of God neither are arguments nor are they proofs of the existence of God. They are expressions of the *question* of God which is implied in human finitude."[27]

There is no direct argument from the world to the ineffable, unconditioned Absolute. Natural theology, which attempts to give answers to the question of God, arrives at a stranger, if not an idol. Primary revelation provides answers to the questions posed not in the form of propositional truths but through the transcendental union of being with Being-itself. Why engage in a torturous rational quest for God, Tillich asks, when He is already the ever-present Ground of man's being.

Although the priority clearly lies with primary revelation, Tillich postulates the existence of a secondary revelation. The latter involves the formal representation of the mystical a priori in the symbols and myths of religion. Because the fundamental experience of primal Reality is irreducible, there is but one religion. But since the fallible human interpretations of the lived encounter with Being-itself vary widely, the forms of secondary revelation or religious symbolism prove to be quite diverse. The myths of secondary revelation ought not be excised from religion, for they provide faith with useful vehicles of religious expression.

We have seen that Tillich roundly rejects all classical forms of natural theology predicated on the distinciton between the natural and the supernatural. Nature reveals nothing about God. Nevertheless, Tillich himself developed an alternative natural theology based on a general and universal "revelation" in human religious experience. Through immediate participation in the divine Ground by the union of being with Being-itself, apprehension of God and the overcoming of existential estrangement and alienation become a live possibility for man. Not unjustly, Tillich's system could be designated a natural theology of ecstatic religious experience or mystical awareness.

Rejecting the biblical and theistic vision of reality, Tillich maintains that salvation is not deliverance from the realm of the natural to the realm of the supernatural. Rather, salvation should be viewed as the transcendental union of being with Being-itself, with the resultant overcoming of alienation and existential estrangement. When a person questions the meaning of Being, when he adopts an attitude of ultimate concern, when he encounters the Holy within the finite and the particular, that person is justified by faith. Whether an individual has heard of the Savior or not, he is through this existential process transformed by Christ, the new Being. Thus the man or woman who experiences ultimate concern is forgiven, accepted, and rendered at peace with the Unconditioned. He who has exercised ultimate concern can never be regarded as an atheist or an unbeliever.[28]

Tillich developed a lively interest in the history of religions through dialogue and interaction with Buddhist and Shinto scholars in the Far East. From these encounters with the non-Christian world, Tillich concluded that each of the world's faiths mediates a valid experience of the Unconditioned or the Holy. The symbols and myths of the concrete religions possess the power to induce authentic experiences of the infinity of Being. "There are revealing and saving powers in all religions,"[29] he insisted. The different religions are merely culturally bound expressions of man's fundamental experience of the ground and power of Being. The Ultimate, the Abyss, the Holy transcends each of its specific historical formulations. Since all religions are relative, no one religion may claim ultimacy. In Tillich's vision, the uniqueness of Jesus Christ and the normativeness of the Christian faith are set aside. "Liberal theology is right in denying that one religion can claim finality, or even superiority."[30] The goal of man's universal spiritual quest is "the religion of the concrete Spirit"[31]—i.e., the ecstatic experience of the Holy amid the flux of the finite and the particular. The history of religions attests the reality of an evolutionary advance pressing towards the actualization of the Religion of the Concrete Spirit. No extant religion—not even Christianity—can at present lay claim to this title. As Tillich would have it, Christianity should not seek the conversion of people of other faiths to Christ. The goal of the Christian mission is not the conquest of alien religions, but creative dialogue that will facilitate the recognition of new Being underlying all existence. On this showing, Christianity is latent in paganism, humanism, and the non-Christian faiths. The distinctively Christian task is to transform this latency into existential reality.

Tillich, who emerges as the direct heir of nineteenth-century liberalism, must be faulted at the level of his idealist vision of reality. His existential-ontological theism falters in its failure to differentiate God from the universe. In that God is continuous with nature, Tillich's theology is immanentistic and monistic, if not blatantly pantheistic. His assertion that the universe, with all that is in it, finds itself united with absolute Being allows room for no other judgment. But from a biblical perspective, neither the existence nor the operations of God can be equated with the dynamic processes of this-worldly existence. Moreover, since God is defined as Being-itself, and not a being, Tillich's deity lacks personality. The Ultimate or Unconditoned is far removed from the Creator-God who sovereignly upholds the universe and providentially guides the flow of history. Tillich, in fact, has substituted the god of a monistic philosophy (an abstract, unnamed cipher) for the warmly personal Deity who enters into I-Thou relationships with His people. Further, when Tillich refuses even to speak about the existence of God, we may question whether his God is truly *real*. The ultimately real is not the abstract cipher "Being-itself," but God the infinite, personal Spirit endowed with qualities of greatness and goodness. Tillich, in fact, is one with religious mystics and spiritualists who have searched for immediate participation in the ground or soul of the universe by absorption into its unity.

Tillich undoubtedly would respond to the preceding criticism by suggesting that the classical view that conceives of God as "a being" rather than "Being-itself," in fact, limits God and makes God finite. But in response to such a rejoinder, it needs to be said that only a distinct, personal being like the God of the Jewish-Christian tradition is properly free. In fact, it is precisely Tillich's god who is limited in terms of its passivity, inactivity, and inability to reverse the grave spiritual deprivation of the human condition. Contrary to Tillich's abstract and unrelated cipher, the biblical God lives, hears the cries of His people, answers prayers, and acts to correct the evils of a fallen world. Tillich's god is not self-determining, living, and active. God's unlimitedness does not mean God is diffused in space like a vapor or gas (C. S. Lewis), but that He is not prevented by space or time from accomplishing all that He has purposed. Granted, Tillich does claim that God, or Being-itself, although not a person, is "personal." But when he defines personal in terms of "the concreteness of man's ultimate concern,"[32] he clearly deviates from the customary definition of what it means to be a personal agent. Moreover, when he contemplates man as a personal being in his attempt to define what it means to be personal, Tillich fully begs the question. The same criticism could be levied against his faulty definition of the "freedom" of God.

With respect to the validity of Tillich's existential method, an anthropocentric theology from below falls far short of engaging the true God of the Bible. As we have seen, Tillich insists that through the universal light of the Logos man discovers in his own finite being a reflection of Being-itself. But the existential analysis of human existence yields more of what Heidegger called "the experience of nothingness" than the holy and majestic God of the Bible. Man's quest for Reality through the glass of his own self-consciousness discloses only the image of his finite personhood. When the apostle Paul said longingly, "I want to know Christ" (Phil. 3:10), a human subject sought to apprehend a divine, transcendent Person, not simply Being-itself. From the biblical perspective the knowledge of God involves personal acquaintance with the One who created, sustains, and reconciles man to Himself.

Moreover, the biblical concept of revelation differs substantially from Tillich's. Revelation is more than Reason in its depths, more than ontological shock, more than mystical, ecstatic union, more than the mysterious manifestation of man's ultimate concern. Whereas Tillich's definition of revelation leaves God unnamed and undefined, the divine self-disclosure through Jesus Christ and the Old and New Testament Scriptures brings to light the character and purposes of God the transcendent Person. Contrary to the awareness of a Mystery that remains mysterious, biblical revelation involves human reception of information about God's will and saving intentions. The problem with Tillich's theology of transcendent awareness is that it nullifies the substantive message confessed by the historic Christian church. And it is precisely this cognitive understanding of God and His saving purposes that establishes the uniqueness and finality of Christianity vis-à-vis every other religion and ideology.

Similarly, Tillich's understanding of salvation has little in common with the biblical perspective. Faith, at rock bottom, is the stuff of all human life. "There is no human being without an ultimate concern and, in this sense, without faith."[33] Salvation, for Tillich, is the finite being's participation in an encounter with Being-itself. As Hamilton observes, "Instead of the biblical question, 'What must I do to be saved?' Tillich substituted the question, 'How can man best pursue the quest for the New Being upon which he is universally engaged because he is man?' "[34] The whole world, in Tillich's scheme, is constituted the people of God. But again, on this showing, the finality of Jesus Christ is boldly set aside and the cross is evacuated of all meaning and relevance. Tillich's claim that all people have faith whether they know it or not stimulated Protestant and Roman Catholic theologians to develop the themes of "implicit faith" and "anonymous Christianity."

Robinson the Christian Humanist   J. A. T. Robinson (b. 1919), formerly bishop of Woolwich and latterly lecturer and dean of the chapel at Trinity College, Cambridge, has emerged as one of the most controversial figures on the contemporary religious scene. Robinson's provocative little book *Honest to God*[35] quickly sold well over a million copies to establish the bishop as a leading popular antagonist of evangelical Christianity. As Robinson personally testifies, "I am happy—with Erasmus and many others from the Renaissance onwards—to call myself a Christian humanist."[36] The theological task for Robinson involves far more than recasting time-honored biblical formulae in contemporary language. Today a more radical reinterpretation of God, the supernatural, and religion itself is mandated if Christianity is to make sense to contemporary scientific and secularized man. The gulf must be bridged between the orthodox supernaturalism in which traditional faith was framed and the monistic, evolutionary vision of the universe espoused by the enlightened twentieth-century mind.

Robinson is primarily an eclectic thinker who draws heavily on the insights of a great many twentieth-century philosophers and theologians. Yet he is particularly indebted to a triumvirate of thinkers—namely Tillich, Bultmann, and Bonhoeffer. In the first place, Robinson has popularized Tillich's thesis that God is not a supernatural Person but rather the ground or depth of Being. With Tillich, he adopts a position midway between naturalism and supernaturalism, between atheism and theism. Secondly, Robinson has recast for popular consumption Bultmann's radical program of demythologization. The British scholar follows the German in characterizing the biblical cosmology as patently prescientific and mythological. Both lament the fact that although science has demolished the old three-storied model of the universe, theology continues to uphold the antiquated cosmology with its crude literalism as the preferred frame of reference. Argues Robinson,

> There is no second storey to the universe, no realm of the divine over and above or behind the processes of nature and history which perforates this world or breaks into it by supernatural intervention. The traditional divisions with which theology has worked—body and soul, earth and heaven, this world and the other world, the secular and the sacred, the two natures human and divine—are decreasingly viable or useful.[37]

Finally, Bishop Robinson builds on Bonhoeffer's vision of a "religionless Christianity" for a "world come of age." Since rampant secularization pervades the modern world, theology must seek to rid itself of the traditional language and thought forms of the faith, or what Bonhoeffer called "the religious a priori." Just as Bonhoeffer wrestled in his prison cell with the question, "How do we speak . . . in a 'secular' way about 'God'?"[38] so Robinson struggled with the same issue of articulating Christian convictions in a world that has dispensed with the category of God.

A further word about Robinson's God-concept is in order. Following Tillich, Robinson rejects the notion of God as a discrete personal Being. "The simplistic representation of God as a Person is the source or at any rate the occasion of great stumbling."[39] The modern situation demands a recasting of the old anachronistic conception of Deity. God envisaged as a Person is a peculiar Western construct devised in the context of a bifurcated natural-supernatural cosmology. Both Oriental people and modern secularists in the West find it impossible to relate to the old dualistic vision of reality. For Robinson, the assertion that God is personal means that reality at its deepest level is personal. That is, reality is not abstract and coldly mathematical, but is characterized by love, trust, freedom, responsibility, and purpose. Indeed, Robinson argues, "I believe with Tillich, that we should give up speaking of the existence of God."[40] For all intents and purposes, the God of theism is dead.

Moreover, the bishop repudiates the classical concept of God as a tenant of a supernatural realm "up there" or "out there." To describe ultimate reality as a Being who dwells in another domain is to render God unreal and irrelevant to great numbers of modern people. Robinson identifies, on the one hand, with Tillich in asserting that God is not a Being beyond the blue, but the ultimate Ground or Depth of all being. And on the other, he sides with Bonhoeffer in asserting that God is "the Beyond in our midst." Robinson's revisionist concept of God shares much in common with Freud's recognition of the unknown depth of ultimacy within man. Since all language about the Ultimate is necessarily symbolical and relative, the cipher "God"

> points to the ultimate, incommunicable, ineffable mystery of reality—the divine Name of Judaism, the Tao that cannot be spoken, the Brahman of Hinduism, the *Urgrund* of Jacob Boehme, the Eternal Thou of Martin Buber. It is that which cannot be expressed yet which cannot be eliminated or translated without remainder into anything else. It is the Beyond in the midst, the Ground of all being. [41]

The proper world view from Robinson's perspective is panentheism. Simply put, panentheism affirms that God is in everything and everything is in God.[42] Man is a part of God and God is a part of man, analogous to the way in which a person or object relates to a magnetic field. We no longer can continue to talk, Robinson insists, of God and the world as if they were two separate entities. An important consequence of Robinson's panentheistic vision is that since God dwells at the heart of everything, "all things, all events, all persons are the faces, the incognitos of God."[43]

Since God resides not at the boundary but at the center of human existence, man as man meets the Ultimate or the Unconditional in the depths of everyday, nonreligious experience. Christian and non-Christian alike encounter primal reality, the *ens realissimum*, in an I-Thou confrontation of love at the heart of the human constitution. Thus in the depths of his personhood, man existentially encounters what Robinson describes as "depths of revelation, intimations of eternity, judgments of the holy and the sacred, awareness of the unconditioned, the numinous and the ecstatic."[44] Man fundamentally experiences God as nameless and ineffable Reality. God need not be proved since, as the ultimate Depth or Ground of Being, God is the inescapable datum of existence. Simply by being authentically human, man is claimed and held in a relationship of sustaining love. Robinson acknowledges that not all persons possess the same capacity for religious or mystical awareness. "Women, for instance, appear to be naturally more religious—and more psychic—than men."[45]

Since God in Robinson's scheme signifies "what you take seriously without any reservation,"[46] all human beings are, in fact, implicit believers. All good persons who demonstrate a serious attitude toward life, notwithstanding professions of atheism or agnosticism, are unconsciously Christians. In a relativistic and pluralistic world where the better part of mankind is not formally aligned with the church, it is harsh and unrealistic to affirm that adherents of other religions will be consigned to eternal punishment. Hence the church's missionary task should be conceived of not as "come *to* us" (proselytism), but "come *with* us" (dialogue and cooperation). In Robinson's scheme, the line of delineation between church and world has totally broken down.

The bishop's polemic against the supernaturalist conception of God "up there" or "out there" may be applied with equal force against his own position. When Robinson refers to God as "a Depth at the Center of Life," he employs the same kind of spatial imagery (depth) to unfold the mystery of God as does the traditionalist (height). His criticism of the supernaturalist model therefore lacks force. Moreover, Robinson overstates the case when he asserts that the classical metaphysic, or vision of reality, impedes faith in God. Myriads of Christians could testify that the chief factor hindering faith in God was their sinful desire for self-autonomy. Most believers have no problem with the biblical or classical Christian world view, but believe that it is well informed and sound.

Robinson's refusal to acknowledge that God *exists* points up the radicalness of his embargo on classical ontology. But is it faithful to the biblical record to insist that God cannot be objectified as an existent or a substantial Self? Is it unreasonable to demand that the God who acts and who may be experienced is the God who *is*? The bishop's denial of the personality of

God is equally specious. How can a God who is not a personal being impart love or institute a saving program or move to effect fellowship with people? As R. P. C. Hanson comments, "There is something slightly ludicrous in the Bishop's attempt to reduce God to 'the ground of existence' after the manner of Tillich, and then to insist that he is nothing but love."[47] If man, created in the image of God, is a personal being, we ought not stumble over the personal nature of God, the prototype (*Urbild*) of man. Consequently, Robinson's definition of God as that which man ultimately believes in (his ultimate concern) amounts to an anthropocentric reduction of the biblical representation of God. Alasdair MacIntyre, reflecting on *Honest to God*, boldly comments, "What is striking about Dr. Robinson's book is first and foremost that he is an atheist."[48] When Robinson, following Tillich, defines God as the mystery at the heart of all experience, he comes close to reducing Deity to a dimension of human existence. Clearly, our view of God ought to be shaped not by what modern secularity judges acceptable, but by the precepts of Scripture. It is contemporary humanistic man who needs to fall in step with God, not vice versa. If the Barthians erred in objectifying God as "Wholly Other," Robinson and his fellow panentheists err in the opposite extreme by merging the reality of God with everything else. Following Feuerbach, they have transformed theology into anthropology.

Since from the biblical perspective the reality of God is distinct from the reality of the world, it is false to assert that when one is in touch with anything whatsoever, he is in touch with God. To be sure, man qua man intuits the fact that God exists and that He bears certain defining characteristics. But what man gains from rational intuition goes beyond the panentheist's claims of union with the Ground and Depth of all reality. Robinson's transcendence, like that of Transcendental Meditation and Hinduism, is not transcendent enough.

It is difficult to resist the conclusion that Robinson, along with Tillich, Bultmann, and others, has propounded a system of atheistic naturalism clad in the garments of religious language. The bishop's program of radical secularization has confounded the city of God with the city of man. His attempt to lead people to God through the reality of the world leads nowhere. The gospel refuses to be rendered respectable to the mind-set of secular man. The Cross can never be anything but an offense to the autonomous, self-centered earth dweller. Mascal is not far from the truth when he suggests that Robinson has despaired of converting the world to Christianity and so has set out instead to convert Christianity to the world.[49]

A story is told of a Unitarian minister who years ago was preaching to an open-air audience in an impoverished section of Aberdeen, Scotland.[50] His humanistic message made no mention of the crucified Christ and His power to rescue hopeless sinners. A prostitute who listened to his talk in due course said to the preacher, "Your rope is not long enough for me." The same criticism might be levied against Robinson's humanistic gospel of openness to the ground of Being.

Process Theology: The "New" Challenge   One of the more significant movements in contemporary Christianity is the Anglo-American phenomenon known as process theology. The philosophical foundations of process thought were laid by A. N. Whitehead (1861–1947), the renowned English mathematician and philosopher. Whitehead's process vision of reality was developed and adapted to the Christian faith by Charles Hartshorne (b. 1897), the University of Chicago philosopher of religion. In recent decades, a host of process theologians have risen to prominence, including such thinkers as Wieman, Meland, Loomer, Williams, Ogden, Hamilton, Pittenger, Cobb, and Griffin. In general, process theology (alternatively known as neoclassical theism, or naturalistic theism) attempts to develop a post-modern theology based on a processive metaphysic. The movement has found considerable receptivity in the liberal wing of the church. As John B. Cobb, Jr., flatly asserts, "We are more attracted to the road to the left than to the theological right."[51]

Only the barest overview of process thought is possible in the present context.[52] Process theology supplants the classical Jewish and Christian metaphysical model based on being with a dynamic model based on becoming. At rock bottom, reality consists not of bits of substance but of subatomic moments of experience that process thinkers call "actual occasions" or "occasions of experience." Enduring entities, such as electrons, cells, or the human soul, are regarded as a series of events or actual occasions. In addition to being dynamic, reality is also said to be interrelational and societal; everything in the universe profoundly affects everything else. In a sequence of great rapidity, each actual occasion "prehends" (i.e., grasps or feels) prior actual occasions and incorporates the antecedent moments of experience into its own universe, thereby forming a creative and novel synthesis. The process by which antecedent thrusts, drives, and aims are brought together in the new synthesis is called "concrescense." The new occasion thus formed immediately serves as an experience to be prehended by later actual occasions. While each individual experience in turn perishes, it nevertheless is immortalized in the processive advance. In sum, then, the cosmos is a social process in which new occasions emerge from past syntheses of momentary experiences. The basic units of reality are not discrete entities that enter into relationships with other units; rather, the *relationship* itself (i.e., the moment of experience) represents the primary reality.

Since bottom-line reality in the universe is conceived of in terms of energy-events, God (the chief exemplification of reality) is defined by process theology as a very special kind of energy-event. Cobb, for example, argues that if we think of God as an energy-event, "as an occurrence of thinking, willing, feeling, and living, then we are close to the heart of Biblical faith."[53] As the exemplar energy-event, God is dependent, ever-changing, and thus relative. Envisaged as an actual entity or an exemplar moment of experience, God is viewed as transpersonal, not unlike Tillich's cipher

"Being-itself." The process conceptuality refuses to view God as a personal being distinct from other beings. Nevertheless, in the Whiteheadian scheme, the God that is in process functions as the "lure" that draws each occasion of experience toward novelty and fulfillment.

Neoclassical theism is totally committed to the formulation of a new type of natural theology based on man's general experience and thought. Natural theology, conceived of as that which is universal and recurrent in nature, must be conserved. But the old natural theology, defined as what can be known about God through the process of discursive reason, is of little value in the contemporary situation.

As has been noted, process theology focuses on the aesthetic dimension of life, namely, on feeling qualities, apprehensions, and intuitions. In the process metaphysic, reality is prehended or felt in a series of moments or drops of ecstatic experience. Hence God, the exemplar Reality, is immediately apprehended by man qua man in every moment of human experience. Each human being apprehends God via an immediate feeling of profound awareness. As Daniel Day Williams simply put it, "The God who is present to us can be known through our direct experience of him."[54] As a result of this ecstatic encounter, all people possess an elemental but ineradicable knowledge of sacred Reality. Man knows the energizing presence of God experientially in a series of moments of subjective immediacy. Cobb and Griffin articulate this fundamental truth in the jargon of process philosophy. "There are not actual entities that first are self-contained and then have accidental relations to God. God-relatedness is constitutive of every occasion of experience."[55] In sum, then, to be human, or to actualize oneself, is to experience the fundamental reality of God. Or as Hartshorne succinctly puts it, God is "a universal datum of experience."[56]

The Whiteheadian process schema parts ways with traditional empirical theology in its insistence that these prehensions of other actual occasions are nonsensory. What is prehended are not physical objects outside the body, but energy-events within the person. Process thinkers underscore that we are dealing with immediate apprehensions arising from the psychic life that are more primitive than sense data from the external world. As Cobb insists, "The foundation of all experience, certainly of the experience of God, lies in the non-sensuous prehension of individual entities."[57] ESP (extrasensory perception) and mental telepathy provide clues to the nonsensory character of the process experience of sacred reality.

But in addition to being nonsensory, the Whiteheadian prehensions are regarded as subconscious, prereflective, and unthematized. The elements of human experience lie below the level of human consciousness in unconceptualized form, much as the submerged hulk of an iceberg. Analogous to the tip of the iceberg, only a few prehensions of Deity rise to consciousness and to conceptual formulation. Here process thought follows Freud and depth psychology in the belief that the greater part of human experience lies repressed at the level of the subconscious. Consciousness, then, is viewed as an unusual and higher-grade form of experience. It follows that most process theologians view conscious beliefs as relatively unimportant. Propositions and doctrines must take second place to the unthematized elements of experience. The basic structure of reality inexorably imposes itself on man at the experiential level quite apart from what he consciously believes. All explicit beliefs and formal dogmas, Whiteheadians argue, are historically and culturally conditioned. As interpreters allow the data of nonsensory and subconscious experience to pass through their particular historical, cultural, and linguistic grid, the diverse doctrines of the world's ideologies and religions come into being. Process thinkers freely concede that their theology is relativistic. As Cobb insists, "Relativism in a very important sense is simply true."[58] Yet they insist that the goal of the movement is a healthy rather than a debilitating relativism.

It should be evident that process theology rejects the traditional distinction between general revelation and special revelation. The classical model involves a dualism that violates the fundamental Whiteheadian vision of reality. Revelation is viewed by process thinkers monistically in terms of man interpreting his experiences and attempting to grasp the significance of his own life. As R. C. Miller of Yale puts it, "Revelation is a form of experience in which a particularly sensitive mind grasps the significance of events which might be overlooked by the less appreciative or perceptive."[59] Revelation, then, is a single seamless garment. Understood as man's analysis of his own experience, revelation is intrinsically universal and general. And by virtue of the extensiveness of revelation, all people acquire a knowledge of God sufficient for their temporal and eternal destiny.

Plainly, process theology possesses an empirical rather than a rationalistic temperament, where empirical means a critical interpretation of human experience. The Whiteheadian school is more impressed by the evidence for God emerging from the consciousness of the experiencing subject than by formal arguments. In other words, God is known not indirectly and inferentially, but as the personal agent confronts, senses, feels, and interprets reality through a series of momentary drops of experience. Hence the formulation of rational arguments for the existence of God is not a dominant feature of the self-perceived task of process theology. Nevertheless, in order to fend off the challenges of nontheists successfully, process thinkers recognize the need to construct some sort of rational basis for belief in God. Thus Whiteheadians argue that process epistemology properly involves the correlation of the direct experience of sacred reality with an empirical analysis of the order, coherence, and intelligibility of the universe. In other words, philosophical arguments not only impart coherence and clarity to fundamental experience, but also highlight the reasonableness of belief in God. Thus we find Whiteheadians such as Hartshorne reformulating the onotological argument for God's existence. Others argue teleologically that the order, purpose, and beneficence of the universe points to the existence of something properly called God. Cobb, for example, maintains,

"The order of the world requires for its explanation some principle of order that cannot entirely be attributed to the entities that constitute the world."[60] Still others reason axiologically and insist that the presence of ostensible value in the universe argues for the existence of a Reality that embodies all value. The above pointers deduced from the realm of man and nature underscore the fact that there is something distinctly irrational about not believing in God.

We have noted that according to the Whiteheadian vision all people participate in a valid religious experience by virtue of their essential God-relatedness. A corollary to this assertion is that the ways to God and salvation are many rather than one. Christianity, in the mind of most process theologians, is one valid religion in a constellation of faiths. In spite of differing doctrinal structures, the great world faiths lead their adherents to authentic encounters with sacred Reality. Each religion, it is argued, mediates authentic subconscious prehensions of the processive reality that is God. Again, saving faith is a function of human self-consciousness rather than a matter of one's consciously held beliefs. Since the world's religions thematize man's fundamental experience of sacred reality in different ways, explicit doctrines overlap rather than precisely coincide. Thus Whiteheadians conclude that since all religions lead their adherents to a saving experience of God, Christianity ought to incorporate into its own system insights and emphases from other faiths. Indeed, the Christian faith should seek to undergo creative transformation by appropriating features from other religions, particularly from Buddhism. Cobb, for example, theorizes that as Buddhists internalize the God-consciousness granted by Christianity, and as Christians appropriate the God-consciousness afforded by Buddhism, a new unity will eventuate that will reverse the tragic fragmentation of religion.

Ostensibly, process philosophy bears many close affinities with Eastern thought, especially Buddhism. In its vision of reality as interdependent and interactive, its rejection of substance, its emphasis on awareness and intuition over reason, process thought shares many perspectives with the Buddhist system. Indeed, an influential process thinker such as Cobb insists that Whitehead's philosophy may be utilized to construct not only a Christian but also a Buddhist natural theology. Process thought, Whiteheadians argue, provides the framework for a universal and cosmic theology for people of every culture and nationality.

Process theology may be faulted fundamentally in its vision of God. The god of naturalistic theism, envisaged as the energy latent in the universe or the ceaseless flux of earthly becoming, is a finite, evolving, and relative deity. Not unlike the Stoic law of nature and reason, the Whiteheadian god is an impersonal power rather than a personal Being distinct from other beings. The god of process theology lacks not only personality but aseity, infinity, omnipotence, and timelessness. Since God is envisaged as eminent relativity, the world of process thought is a world without absolutes or unchanging principles. On this showing, the cosmos is no longer controlled by a supremely wise Mind. Hence process theology, which postulates an impersonal and becoming deity undifferentiated from the universe, is in fact a veiled form of evolutionary pantheism. Our primary criticism of process theology, simply stated, is that its god is not the God of the Bible.[61]

The neoclassical theism of Whitehead and company possesses, in fact, a long and checkered history. The central tenets of process thought are reflected in the pantheism of Greek philosophy, the immanency of Oriental religions (primarily Buddhism), the pantheism of Spinoza, the evolutionary monism of Hegel, and the subjective experientialism of Schleiermacher and nineteenth-century romantic liberalism. Process theology is thus thoroughly rooted in the liberal tradition.

Process theology's assertion that God is apprehended via ineffable aesthetic feeling establishes it as the true heir of Schleiermacher's teaching that God is known as the human agent instinctively senses or tastes sacred reality. The Whiteheadian emphasis on noncognitive feelings and intuitions unavoidably involves process theology in a mysticism of the *élan vital*. Clearly, process thought distances itself from Augustinian epistemology in that its intuitions of God are ineffable, noncognitive, and all-controlling. Moreover, as a scheme where revelation is monolithically defined as lived experience, process theology takes little account of the validity and centrality of objective special revelation. Its assertion that cognitively held beliefs are relatively unimportant contravenes the clear thrust of biblical teaching. And lastly, the uniqueness and finality of the gospel are compromised by the process insistence that the message of Christ must be exposed to radical transformation by the wisdom of the East, particularly Buddhist teaching. In short, the attempts of process theology to improve on the classical Augustinian explication of revelation and the knowability of God fall far short of the mark.

Hick the Universalist Philosopher

A contemporary scholar who has interacted extensively with the cluster of issues under consideration is John Hick (b. 1928), the English Presbyterian philosopher of religion. Educated at Edinburgh and Oxford, Hick served rural congregations in Northumberland, taught philosophy at Cornell, philosophy of religion at Princeton, and is presently H. G. Wood Professor of Theology at the University of Birmingham, England. From his own religious and theological perspective, Hick firmly opposes naturalistic humanism's attempt to interpret the world without reference to God. Moreover, Hick has little sympathy for what he regards as the literalistic biblicism and uncritical supernaturalism of the evangelical tradition. Although attracted to certain Barthian emphases, neither is he in full agreement with the sharp neoorthodox reaction to the liberal agenda. Thus, for instance, he rejects the neoorthodox assertion that sin has so incapacitated reason that all human formulations of God are falsehood and idolatry. Hick's own epistemological conclusions prove to be the antithesis of the Barthian assertion that there is no knowledge of God apart from the revelation of the Word. Drawing on the insights of modern empiricism, positivism, and the history-of-religion school, Hick attempts to break fresh trails within the broad expanse of modern liberal theology. Hick has attracted considerable attention in recent years for his involvement in the heated christological debates in Britain.[62]

Hick argues that the "Reformed" tradition to which he subscribes posits the locus of revelation not in language but in history, not in propositions but in events. With Baillie and other moderns, Hick says revelation consists of God's disclosure of *Himself*, rather than propositions about Himself. What Hick regards as the outmoded propositional theory of revelation, moreover, involves a distinction between natural theology (truths worked out by the human mind) and revealed theology (truths supernaturally disclosed by God). In place of the old dualistic model, Hick endorses a homogeneous, nonpropositional view of revelation conceived of as personal encounter and experience. Thus Hick views theology not as a divinely revealed body of knowledge, but as a set of speculative human interpretations of man's fundamental religious experience. The theological enterprise involves the endless process of reflection and theorizing by which man attempts to clarify the meaning of his religious experience. Since the cultural and intellectual framework within which man resides are parts of an ongoing stream, theology may undergo radical change. Hick personally is compelled to abandon many of the tenets of traditional theology. As a starter, the classical concept of God must be challenged in the light of impersonal and nontheistic visions championed by such Eastern traditions as Theravada Buddhism. Equally untenable or open to serious doubt are the traditional dogmas of the Trinity, the Fall of Adam and the human race, Christ's atoning work and bodily resurrection, and the eternal destiny of man either in heaven or in hell. Given the extent to which Hick has abandoned both the framework and the content of historic Christianity, he must be posited at the radical end of the theological spectrum.

The primary problem with which the English philosopher wrestles is the issue of the source and character of man's knowledge of God. Hick insists that the attempt to arrive at truths about God through the process of discursive reasoning has proved a dismal failure. "It is not possible to establish either the existence or the nonexistence of God by rational arguments proceeding from universally accepted premises."[63] Logic alone cannot establish any matters of fact and existence. Since none of the classical arguments are sufficiently cogent to compel belief in God on the part of the uncommitted, the traditional proofs are worthless and irrelevant. In addition, the method of Cartesian doubt, by which man seeks to prove the existence of the world in which he lives, is "perverse and irrational."[64]

God, if He exists, must reveal Himself somehow within the realm of human experience. People, both in biblical times and in the present, view God "as an experienced reality, rather than an inferred entity."[65] Thus from the empiricist perspective, Hick conceives of God as one with whom man already has to do in all the affairs of daily life. That is, God manifests Himself within the sphere of human life as a sheer given reality, as an inescapable datum of human existence. On the basis of man's innate tendency to recognize the divine behind the human, he directly perceives or apprehends God in his personal, social, and material environment. Natural experience is not to be distinguished from religious experience. Argues Hick, "It is not apart from the course of mundane life, but in it and through it, that the ordinary religious believer claims to experience, however imperfectly and fragmentarily, the divine presence and activity."[66] Man thus knows God as he is overwhelmed with a consciousness or awareness of the divine presence and demands. Moreover, this very act of perception or apprehension confers to the knowing agent total religious certitude. Again, it should be underscored that in Hick's scheme there is no revealed theology that one may differentiate from natural theology. Rather, "The divine Being and the divine self-communication are known in a single apprehension which is the awareness of God acting self-revealingly toward us."[67] Man possesses an ingrained propensity to recognize God behind the phenomena of life. But Hick does not specify exactly what constitutes the nature of the fundamental religious experience, although plainly it is suprarational if not mystical. Argues Hick, "The theistic believer cannot explain *how* he knows the divine presence to be mediated through his human experience. He just finds himself interpreting his experience in this way. He lives in the presence of God, although he is unable to prove by any dialectical process that God exists."[68]

On this showing, faith is not assent to propositions contained in Scripture, but it is the interpretive element that seeks to decipher the meaning behind religious experience. Faith has more to do with sense perception than with rational belief. Borrowing from the analytical philosopher Wittgenstein and his concept of puzzle pictures, Hick contemplates faith in terms of a "seeing-as," an "experiencing-as," and an "interpretation" of space-time realities that mediate the presence and activity of God. Faith is the recognition—indeed, the awareness or perception—that behind the visible world we have at all times to do with the invisible and transcendent God.

A second main concern to Hick is the relationship of Christianity to other religions. Hick's interest in this area is practical rather than strictly theoretical. In his native Birmingham, he has been exposed to large numbers of Muslims, Sikhs, and Hindus, who appear to be true worshipers of God. Hick concluded from his encounters with peoples of other faiths that religion involves consciousness of God and living on the basis of that consciousness. In this regard, Hick believes that the devout adherents of the world's great faiths authentically encounter the divine Presence in their religious experience. Islam in the Arabic world, Buddhism in Southeast Asia, Hinduism in India, and Christianity in Europe and North America all mediate a genuine awareness of the one eternal Reality. At rock bottom, the Christian's encounter with God through Christ is no different from the Buddhist's encounter with the Buddha or the Hindu's encounter with Krishna.

In Hick's view the world's religions represent *human* mappings of man's fundamental religious experiences in diverse historical, geographical, and cultural contexts. Thus the differences evident in Buddhism, Hinduism, Islam, and Christianity may be attributed to a number of environmental factors (broadly defined) that variously shape the ways in which the fundamental religious experience is understood and expressed. Eastern and Western minds, for example, express themselves in different conceptual, linguistic, social, and artistic forms. Instead of thinking of individual religions as true or false, it is preferable to think of the religious life of mankind as a dynamic continuum broad enough to include the full range of divine grace and truth on the one hand, and human faith and enlightenment on the other. On the basis of this model, one's own religious commitment is primarily a function of where one happens to have been born. Thus, argues Hick, "If I had been born in India I probably would be a Hindu; if in Egypt, probably a Muslim; if in Ceylon, probably a Buddhist; but I was born in England and am, predictably, a Christian."[69]

Hick boldly asserts that what is needed in the present hour is the courage to effect a full Copernican revolution in theology. Formerly prevailing was the Ptolemaic theory of the universe that posited the earth as the center of the solar system. But the old cosmology was overturned by the Copernican theory, which postulates the sun as the center of a system of orbiting bodies, one of which is the planet earth. Similarly, the old Ptolemaic theory of religion, which envisages Christianity as the center of a constellation of faiths, must give way to the Copernican model, which established God as the only proper center of the world's religions. According to the Copernican model, Christianity is no longer the norm and standard of religion, but rather one religion among many equals.[70] Hence Hick insists that one must

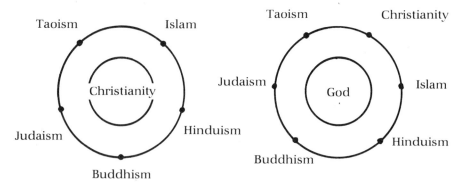

Ptolemaic Model of Religion   Copernican Model of Religion

desist from assertions such as "Christianity is the uniquely true religion," or "No one can come to God the Father except through His Son Jesus Christ." The claim that Christianity is the unique and final revelation of God has been rendered null and void.

In a profound sense, Hick is more radical than theologians who propose theories of "implicit faith" or "anonymous Christianity," for the latter continue to posit Christianity at the center of the constellation of world religions. Such theories, Hick insists, merely add various "epicycles" to the old and outmoded Ptolemaic model of religion.

Since God is authentically present and encountered in each of the great religions, Hick foresees a growing together—indeed, a gradual interpenetration—of world faiths. In a world that is rapidly drawing together because of far-reaching advances in transportation and communication, religious rivalries are being transcended and new bases of commonality and brotherhood are being forged. The process undoubtedly involves a growing religious ecumenism that may well terminate in a single global faith in which Christianity will be one of the prominent elements.

Since the various religious traditions mediate a genuine encounter with the one infinite Reality, the great religions of the world must be regarded as vehicles of salvation. From the very beginning, God has been pressing in on the human spirit through the world's faiths to draw all men savingly to Himself. Since God, the God of love and goodness, is the Father of all mankind, the whole world ultimately must be brought into harmony with the divine Ground of its being. Although in theory people are capable of damning themselves, in practice none in the end will do so.[71] Thus Hick postulates the ultimate salvation of all quite apart from a person's relationship to Christ. Whereas traditionally Christians proclaimed, "Outside the church there is no salvation," Hick sides with the modern spirit of nondogmatism and tolerance in making the opposite assertion, "Outside Christianity there is salvation."[72] Indeed, Hick the universalist argues that the non-Christian religions have been the principal means of salvation for the great majority of people who have lived outside the church's sphere of influence.

The biblical Christian will find much fault with Hick's assertion that the main tenets of the Christian faith are mythological and therefore not to be taken seriously. Moreover, his universalistic theology is built around a fuzzy concept of God. Whether Hick's God is a personal being distinct from man or an impersonal, pantheistic reality similar to the vision of Hinduism is not made clear. Furthermore, Hick's epistemology concedes too much to ineffable religious experience. Even if man should perceive God at the subjective level, there is no guarantee from man's side that the terms for his acceptance with God have been met. Needed is an objective understanding of God and His purposes that transcends the subjective religious affections. Equally unbiblical is Hick's insistence that God is so remote and ineffable that no cognitive knowledge of God and His ways is attainable by man. The Augustinian tradition teaches that all men know God via the innate sense of Deity, but it goes beyond the religious a priori to insist that man must press on to learn what God has willed concerning his sinful condition.

Hick, moreover, has falsely argued that the differences between Christianity and other religions should be attributed solely to historical-cultural factors. But is it not more accurate to argue that the distinctives of the Christian faith came into existence through the life and teachings of Jesus, much as the distinctives of Buddhism arose through the influence of the Buddha? In his assessment of the Christian faith, Hick has failed to take account of the extraordinary significance of the historical person Jesus Christ. Hick undoubtedly senses the import of Jesus when he states that the only permanent and unchanging factor in Christianity is "the Christ event." However, he fails to develop the full implications of this statement for faith, indeed, for the Christian faith to which he claims to adhere. The fact is, Christianity is far more than a human creation that arises naturally out of the history and culture of the race. Far from being a human invention, the Christian gospel conveys the radical announcement of God's saving initiatives toward lost mankind. Insofar as the gospel concerns God's saving action directed manward and religion concerns man's groping quest Godward, the relationship between Christianity and the other religions is more discontinuous than Hick is willing to concede. Finally, Hick merely offers a stale restatement of an old deist argument (one that was examined and critiqued in chapter 5) when he claims that if Christianity is the only way to God, then God has made no reasonable provision for the salvation of the greater part of humankind. The sentimental view that a loving Father could not possibly condemn the majority of mankind loses sight of the awesome holiness of God and the radical sinfulness and rebellion of the creature.

IMPLICIT FAITH AND
X ANONYMOUS CHRISTIANITY: VATICAN II CATHOLICISM

In the face of great odds, Alexander Pope's aphorism, "Time . . . changes all," has come true in the Roman Catholic church. The old scholastic theology of Aquinas, Anselm, and Abelard has undergone wrenching changes in the modern world of critical, free-thinking scholarship. The totally new situation in church and theology is outlined in David Wells' helpful survey *Revolution in Rome.*[1] In the present chapter we will discover that Roman Catholicism's current position on the issues of the knowability of God and the validity of the non-Christian religions represents a marked if not a radical shift from traditional perspectives and commitments. But in order to appreciate the revolution that has occurred in Vatican II Catholicism, a brief overview of the relevant teachings of Vatican I must be presented.

Vatican I — The Historical Datum   The First Vatican Council (1869–1870), convened by Pope Pius IX, reaffirmed and consolidated the classical Thomistic position vis-à-vis natural theology and the knowability of God. Vatican I—by Rome's reckoning the twentieth Ecumenical Council—promulgated two important doctrinal constitutions on theology and the church. The first, the Dogmatic Constitution on the Catholic Faith, dealt with the interrelationship of the natural and supernatural knowledge of God. The second, the Dogmatic Constitution on the Church of Christ, asserted the primacy and infallibility of the Roman pontiff. The papacy, founded by Christ Himself, represents the final and absolute authority in the Roman Catholic church.

The more important doctrinal constitution for our purposes, the Dogmatic Constitution on the Catholic Faith, plainly distinguishes two orders of knowledge—namely, natural knowledge of God (*ratio*) and supernatural knowledge of God (*fides*). At one level, the mind draws conclusions from the rational evidences and thus arrives at a valid elemental knowledge of God's existence and character. On a higher level, faith assent to the teachings of

181

Scripture and tradition yields a more complete and salvific knowledge of God. In this traditional scheme, rational knowledge is propaedeutic to the higher, faith knowledge afforded by grace. Moreover, the judgments of faith can never contradict knowledge gained by the right use of reason.

The Constitution on the Catholic Faith reiterated the traditional Thomistic position by insisting that the human mind is capable of knowing God by rational reflection on the data of the created order. In its assertion that God could be known through the natural light of reason, Vatican I polemicized, on the one hand, against philosophical atheists who insisted that there is no possibility for the attainment of a valid natural knowledge of God. On the other hand, it disputed against certain fideists and traditionalists who argued, respectively, that God is known only by a faith reception of supernatural revelation or by the teachings of church tradition. Thus chapter two of the Constitution on the Catholic Faith upholds a natural knowledge of God in the following words: "The same Holy Mother Church holds and teaches that God, the beginning and end of all things, can be known with certitude by the natural light of human reason from created things; 'for the invisible things of Him, from the creation of the world, are clearly seen, being understood by the things that are made.'"[2] Moreover, the corresponding canon asserts: "If anyone shall have said that the one true God, our Creator and our Lord, cannot be known with certitude by those things which have been made, by the natural light of human reason: let him be anathema."[3] Man created in the *imago Dei* is endowed with sufficient light to discern from the visible Creation God's existence and divine attributes.

The Antimodernist Oath of the Council spelled out this same conviction in somewhat greater detail. "God, the beginning and end of all things, can be known for certain and proved by the natural light of reason, through the things which he has made, that is to say, through the visible works of His creation, just as the cause is made known to us by its effects."[4] The Oath suggested several important conclusions: (1) the object known is the true God Himself—His existence and such attributes as His infinity, omniscience, immortality, freedom, and goodness; (2) the efficient cause of this knowledge is not religious awareness or experience but human ratiocination; (3) the means by which this knowledge is acquired are the objective evidences of the visible Creation over which causal reasoning operates; (4) the kind of knowledge thus afforded is a knowledge that can be demonstrated with certainty. Consequently, since the natural man who follows his reason must conclude that God exists, atheism no longer represents a credible option. We should observe that whereas Thomas Aquinas postulated the demonstrability of God, Vatican I affirmed only the knowability of God through natural means.

But Vatican I in its Constitution on the Catholic Faith upheld the reasonableness of a further knowledge of God mediated by a faith reception of special revelation deposited in Scripture and tradition. To the rudimentary knowledge gained via reason, one must add the richer knowledge afforded by faith. As chapter two of the document teaches, "Nevertheless it has pleased His wisdom and goodness to reveal Himself and the eternal decrees of His will to the human race in another and supernatural way, as the Apostle says: 'God, who at sundry times and in diverse manners, spoke in times past to the fathers by the prophets, last of all, in these days hath spoken to us by His Son' (Heb. 1:1ff.)"[5] Moreover, the corresponding canon to the dogma of supernatural revelation states, "If anyone shall have said that man cannot be drawn by divine power to a knowledge and perfection which is above the natural, but that he of himself can and ought to reach the possession of all truth and good by a continual process: let him be anathema."[6]

Vatican I asserted that supernatural revelation is not an absolute necessity by virtue of reason's ability to apprehend God from the visible Creation. Yet because of humanity's present sinful condition, special revelation must be seen as a "moral or relative" necessity. As a practical matter, only by the divine revelation is a full and certain knowledge of God attained. Thus while positing an adequate natural knowledge of God in principle, Vatican I conceded that in a sinful world saving knowledge of God is dependent on a supernatural self-disclosure. Only through faith can God be known with certainty by the common man, who thinks and wills in a state of sin.

Vatican I also upheld the traditional view that salvation is mediated exclusively through the church. The Roman see, founded by Christ, is sole custodian of the saving grace of God. The council thus allowed no room for the mediation of a saving knowledge of God either through the separated bodies of Christendom or through the world's non-Christian religions. It upheld without any reservation the dictum of Cyprian and the Fourth Lateran Council (1215): "Outside the Church there is no salvation" (*extra ecclesiam nulla salus*).

Vatican II—A Daring Departure   From the preceding overview of the teachings of the First Vatican Council, it is clear that the traditional Thomistic perspective prevailed in the church of Rome through the nineteenth century. In fact, only during the last three or four decades of the twentieth century has the monolithic hegemony of scholastic Catholicism been seriously challenged. Free-thinking Catholic scholars, weaned on the results of radical Protestant biblical criticism, have increasingly distanced themselves from the traditional convictions of the church. Indeed, the breakup of the old theological order within Catholicism has occurred with astonishing rapidity. Whereas liberal Protestantism slowly evolved over a period of two hundred years, the radical wing of Catholicism has transformed the church's teachings within the span of only a few decades. Nowhere is the revolutionary realignment within the Roman Catholic church more plainly displayed than in the deliberations of the Second Vatican Council (1962–65). Summoned by Pope John XXIII, Vatican II represents the most significant assembly of the Roman Catholic church in the last four hundred years. The sheer volume of its written constitutions, decrees, and declarations exceeds the body of literature produced by any of the church's councils, including the Council of Trent, which deliberated for nearly twenty years. The stated purpose of Vatican II was to affirm and to order church discipline. However, when the Roman church promulgates a constitution, a redefinition of Catholic doctrine is signaled. By examining the relevant documents of the Council, we intend to delineate the marked shifts that have occurred within contemporary Catholicism on the issues of the knowledge of God and the validity of the non-Christian religions. It should be added, as an aside, that Vatican II became in a real sense a battleground where radical and conservative churchmen struggled to assert their perspectives. If the documents of the Second Council appear to present divergent viewpoints (and they do), this merely confirms the thesis that Vatican II reflects the divided mind of a church in the throes of change.

Vatican II, indeed, made significant modifications in the church's historic understanding of divine revelation. Faithful to the Thomistic tradition, Vatican I had posited two distinct orders of knowledge—one natural and the other supernatural. Nature and supernature independently lead the inquirer to divine knowledge. Discursive reason working on the data of nature and the faith reception of special revelation yield two levels of divine knowledge. Vatican II, however, abandoned the two-source scheme of revelation and postulated rather the gradual unfolding of the divine self-disclosure in the flow of salvation history. Instead of setting the revelation of God in Christ over against the divine display in nature, Vatican II, through the Dogmatic Constitution on Divine Revelation, identified Jesus Christ as the culmination of the long line of God's revelatory acts in the world. Thus at Creation God provided man with ample evidence of His existence and character through the natural order (Rom. 1:19–20). Thereafter God disclosed Himself to Adam and Eve in the Garden and favored them with the promise of salvation (Gen. 3:15). In due course, God called Abraham and made of him a great nation (12:2). Subsequently, God revealed Himself through Moses and later through the prophets of Israel. Finally, after numerous preliminary revelations, God sent His Son to dwell among men and to proclaim His Word. In the total reality of His existence—His teachings, miracles, death, and resurrection—Christ represents the ultimate sign or sacrament of God's presence in and for the world.[7] In this emergent, salvation-history approach to revelation, word and deed are bound up in an inner unity.[8] The goal of revelation—encounter with God—is mediated by redemptive-historical events, the significance of which is grasped by natural insight abetted by the fallible witness of Scripture. The Council's reluctance to differentiate general revelation from special revelation is reflected in a statement asserting that God's "providence, evident goodness, and saving designs extend to all men."[9] Revelation, viewed organically and holistically, spans the entire spectrum from the witness of nature to the historical manifestation of the Christ. It should be clear that the difference between traditional scholastic and the Vatican II perspectives is that the old philosophical quest for intellectual knowledge gives way to the mediation of knowledge at the personal, subjective level. Through His acts in history, God enters the orbit of man's experience and elicits the creature's response of faith.

Vatican II thus moves in the direction of liberal Protestantism when it claims that man finds God experientially in the religious dimension of life. In this respect, the Council's view of revelation involves a marked shift from the objective to the subjective, from doctrine to life, from formal propositions to the mystical relationship that exists between God and man. In contemporary Catholicism, faith assent to the Magesterium's dogmas gives way to religious insights that arise out of a person's religious experience. Vatican II defined this apprehension of the Ultimate, common to all men, as "implicit faith." In the contemporary existential climate, man is viewed as a feeling, rather than a thinking, being. The new datum for knowledge thus lies in man's direct awareness, intuition, and apprehension of the hidden power behind the universe. In the new situation, revelation and faith focus on man's prereflective experience of transcendent reality. As the Council asserts:

> Throughout history even to the present day, there is found among different peoples a certain awareness of a hidden power, which lies behind the course of nature and events of human life. At times there is present even a recognition of a supreme being, or still more of a Father. This awareness and recognition results in a way of life that is imbued with a deep religious sense.[10]

In sum, then, the Second Vatican Council committed itself to the view that "what revelation makes known to us is confirmed by our own experience."[11]

Any discussion of Vatican II's views on revelation and salvation would be remiss if it overlooked certain key pronouncements on the nature of the church. Since the Catholic church is identical with the body of Christ and is custodian of the gospel, the Council viewed the church as a universal sign or sacrament of communion with God.[12] In the words of the Council, "The Lord . . . founded his Church as the sacrament of salvation."[13] Several conciliar documents teach that the fullness of salvation is obtained through the church alone.[14] Yet these remnants of particularism are offset by more frequent assertions of universality; namely, that God is at work through the Roman church to unite savingly all humankind in Christ. In the plan of God, Vatican II asserts, the church functions as the instrument by which the unity and salvation of the race shall be effected.[15] The Council thus has advanced a broad ecclesiological Christomonism. Christ, through the church, is a sign of God's presence *in* the world *for* the world.

Within the continuum of God's manifold modes of self-disclosure from Creation to the present, man fundamentally experiences the reality of God and responds with "implicit faith." The Council thus points to the riches of truth, light, and life that the bountiful God has distributed among the nations of earth.[16] On the basis of man's profound interior experience of the Ultimate, Vatican II insists that "many elements of sanctification and truth"[17] are found outside the confines of the Roman church. In the new scheme of things, the world's religions and ideologies may be envisaged as a set of concentric circles whose common center is Christ.[18] The innermost circle, closest to Christ, is the Roman church, the very body of Christ and custodian of the keys to the kingdom. The next larger circle represents non-Roman Christians, whom the Council concludes are genuinely enlivened by the Spirit of Christ. Thereafter, one finds the circle representing non-Christian religions, which embody a considerable store of spiritual and moral truths. Finally, the outermost circle represents unbelievers and atheists, who likewise are not untouched by the grace of God.

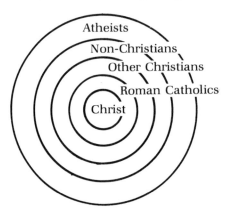

Turning attention to the world's non-Christian religions, Vatican II, not unlike liberal Protestantism, views them as culturally and historically thematized expressions of man's innate religious consciousness. The Council was remarkably optimistic about the spiritual potential of the world's non-Christian religions. Indeed, it went to great lengths to exalt the spiritual light and moral good present in Hinduism, Buddhism, Judaism, and Islam.[19] For example, regarding the latter, the Council could say:

> The Church has also a high regard for the Muslims. They worship God, who is one, living and subsistent, merciful and almighty, the Creator of heaven and earth, who has also spoken to men. They strive to submit themselves without reserve to the hidden decrees of God, just as Abraham submitted himself to God's plan, to whose faith Muslims eagerly link their own. Although not acknowledging him as God, they worship Jesus as a prophet, his virgin Mother they also honor, and even at times devoutly invoke. Further, they await the day of judgment and the reward of God following the resurrection of the dead. For this reason they highly esteem an upright life and worship God, especially by way of prayer, alms-deeds and fasting.[20]

Thus God is not far from adherents of the great non-Christian religions who implicitly yet unconsciously lay hold of the grace of God. Wherefore, the

Council concludes, "The Catholic Church rejects nothing of what is true and holy in these religions. She has a high regard for the manner of life and conduct, the precepts and doctrines which, although differing in many ways from her own teaching, nevertheless often reflect a ray of that truth which enlightens all men."[21] Given this new spirit of openness, Pope Paul VII in 1965 established a Secretariat for Non-Believers, in order to promote new ways of understanding and cooperating with the non-Christian religions.

The Council's attitude to atheists—those ostensibly farthest from the church—was no less benevolent. "Nor shall divine providence deny the assistance necessary for salvation to those who, without any fault of theirs, have not yet arrived at an explicit knowledge of God, and who, not without grace, strive to lead a good life. Whatever truth or good is found amongst them is considered by the Church to be a preparation for the Gospel."[22] On the one hand, the Council points up the fallacies of atheism. But on the other, it maintains that the professing atheist unconsciously has been renewed by divine grace.

Clearly then, Vatican II believes that the church, which constitutes less than 18 percent of the world's population, holds no monopoly on the saving knowledge of God. Since non-Christian religions and ideologies mediate valid encounters with God, these systems should be regarded as salvific and their adherents as implicit believers. Indeed, the Council maintains that all who live up to the light of a good conscience are united to Christ, filled with the Holy Spirit, and made members of His mystical body.[23] No teaching is set forth more clearly in the documents of Vatican II than the assertion of universal salvation.[24] The Council maintains that mankind as a whole has been called by God's grace through implicit faith to eternal life. "The Church awaits the day, known to God alone, when all people will call on God with one voice and 'serve him shoulder to shoulder.' "[25] The goal of God's striving with men is that humankind should become one people of God, thereby fulfilling the divine purpose for man's creation. Thus, "The Church was founded to spread the kingdom of Christ over all the earth for the glory of God the Father, to make all men partakers in redemption and salvation, and through them to establish the right relationship of the entire world to Christ."[26] The reality of eternal punishment in hell has been a traditional dogma of the church. Yet Vatican II would have the world believe that the chambers of hell are forever empty.

Since on the basis of mystical apprehension of God the entire world is implicitly Christian, the church's missionary task is envisaged as that of leading the human race to a full and explicit realization of its spiritual standing. This the church seeks to accomplish through a program of dialogue, collaboration, and mutual understanding *vis-à-vis* the non-Christian world.[27] There is no place in missions for a call to renounce one's cultural or religious heritage that only robs a person of his dignity. Indeed, in its missionary activity, the church should "uncover with gladness and respect those seeds of the Word which lie hidden" in the world's religions and "through sincere and patient dialogue" bring to light "the riches which a generous God has distributed among the nations."[28] Through such efforts, the Council insists, the whole world in due course will attain a Christian faith that is fully explicit.

As mentioned earlier, Vatican II reflects the divided mind of contemporary Catholicism. It pays lip service to traditional views on revelation, the knowability of God, and salvation, but in the end sides with the naturalistic and relativistic perspectives of modern humanism. It is difficult to avoid the conclusion that the Second Council speaks with a forked tongue. From its universalistic perspective, Vatican II overlooked the Pauline teaching that mankind's uniform response to the divine self-disclosure in Creation and conscience is one of resistance to and distortion of the truth. In addition, its congenial attitude toward non-Christian religions and ideologies fails to take into account the fanatical hostility of many systems (e.g., Islam, Marxism, nationalism) toward Christ and His church. The New Testament, moreover, distances itself from the Council's vision of the missionary task as a mere program of peaceful coexistence with competitive ideologies. Liberal Protestantism scarcely could have written a script more in tune with the accommodating mood of the modern world.

Rahner's Transcendental Thomism   From Vatican II we now pass to a consideration of two leading spokesmen for the new-shape Catholicism. One of the most penetrating Roman Catholic thinkers in modern times is Karl Rahner (b. 1904), the German-born Jesuit scholar. Rahner, who studied under Heidegger at Freiburg in Briesgau, spent most of his career lecturing in theology and philosophy of religion at Innsbruck and Munich. A powerful thinker and prolific writer, Rahner stands in the vanguard of the Catholic renewal movement, whose concerns were incorporated in the documents of the Second Vatican Council. In the tradition of German scholarship, Rahner's writings are philosophical in substance and ponderous in style. The leadership in theology, which once was safely ensconced in Protestant hands, may well have shifted to creative, *avant-garde* thinkers such as Rahner, Küng, and Schillebeeckx on the Roman Catholic side. George Lindbeck pays tribute to Rahner with the observation that here is a "man who in comprehensiveness and sheer intellectual quality can, alone among contemporary Catholics, be ranged alongside of Barth and Tillich, and who in terms of balance is perhaps the greatest of the three."[29]

In opposition to the neoscholastic Thomism of Jacques Maritain and Etienne Gilson, Rahner attempts a modern reinterpretation of Aquinas, guided by insights from Kant, Heidegger, and Joseph Maréchal, the Belgian Jesuit proponent of transcendantal Thomism. Rahner's point of departure is the Aristotelian-Thomistic thesis that all knowledge is grounded in sensation. Intellectual knowledge (metaphysics) "is possible only in an encounter with the material world through sensibility."[30] Rahner imparts a new twist to the Thomistic epistemology by maintaining that human knowledge, structured to the objects of immediate sense experience, transcends the space-time world to gain a partial knowledge of absolute Being-itself. Moreover, Kant's transcendental philosophy stimulated Rahner to search for those a priori conditions in the knowing subject that underlie all human knowledge. Rahner explicates his fundamental Thomistic vision with the language and conceptuality of his teacher Heidegger relative to the meaning and significance of Being (*Sein*). From Heidegger's assertion of the unity of being and knowing, Rahner postulates the knowability of all being, including the infinite Being, God, through an immediate illuminating preapprehension. Man knows ultimate Being, not extrinsically as a subject in relation to an object, but intrinsically as an instance of spirit in the world. Rahner, in other words, attempts to work a Heideggerian exposition of Thomas Aquinas.

Rahner's interpretation of Thomas follows in large measure the transcendental Thomism of the Louvain Jesuit philosopher Joseph Maréchal (d. 1944). Maréchal adopted Kant's transcendental method in his attempt to analyze the a priori conditions for the possibility of knowing and the power of the intellect to apprehend Being-itself. From Maréchal's principle of the primordial unity of being and knowing, Rahner concluded that analysis of the knowing subject constitutes the starting point for an understanding of Being. Moreover, the human spirit possesses not only openness to the whole of Being, but a natural desire or longing for God, the ultimate Being. In sum, then, Rahner appropriated from the philosopher Maréchal the idea that the medium for apprehending absolute Being is the human consciousness. Man need not go beyond his own inner self to lay hold of God, for he is a being fundamentally orientated toward the Absolute.

Building on the base of Kant, Heidegger, and Maréchal, Rahner develops in detail his scheme of transcendental philosophy or theological anthropology. The German scholar postulates that a transcendental a priori relationship exists between God and the human person. Man blessed by grace is a being orientated toward the life of God. Man is endowed with a transcendentalism that instinctively causes his spirit to rise to the divine Reality. As Rahner puts it, "The spiritual movement of man in his transcendental knowledge and freedom is orientated towards the absolute immediacy of God, towards his absolute closeness, towards that immediate possession of God's very self which finds its full actuality in the beatific vision of God face to face."[31] Every pulse of human consciousness, Rahner insists, involves a preconceptual apprehension of God the ultimate Mystery.

The dynamic impulse in man that impels him toward the immediate presence of God is called the "supernatural existential." This a priori openness of the human person to the Infinite is an abiding ingredient in man's spiritual mode of being. It necessarily belongs to graced human nature always and everywhere. "This 'supernatural existential,' considered as God's act of self-bestowal which he offers to men, is universally grafted into the very roots of human existence."[32] Rahner's supernatural existential means that man is totally open to the mystery of ultimate Reality. It involves a "subjective, non-objective luminosity of the subject in its transcendence . . . always oriented towards the holy mystery."[33] By virtue of the supernatural existential, man already dwells in a graced state existentially, even though he may be quite unaware of it. He possesses a consciously experienced but unthematic knowledge of the infinity of reality. Thus Rahner concludes that the being of man (menschlichen Seins) is able to perceive a revelation from God because he already knows God in the depths of his spirit.

Rahner's transcendental philosophy clearly emphasizes the human experience of receptivity to God's self-communication. Because God gives Himself transcendentally in personal self-revelation, knowledge of God is strictly a function of human subjectivity. Knowledge of God, in fact, is equivalent to the original and unthematic experience of God. The two realities are identical. Clearly, Rahner's emphasis on subjective experience marks a radical shift in the Roman Catholic approach to the problem of the knowability of God. Indeed, it signals a marked "turn to the subject" inaugurated three hundred years earlier by Descartes. The proper focus of theology is now man, viewed as transcendental consciousness.

It follows, moreover, that Rahner's transcendentalism involves a radical revision of the Thomistic ordering of nature and grace. The old extrinsicism, by which nature and grace were viewed as two contiguous layers that interpenetrate as little as possible, represents a faulty model. No neat horizontal line can be drawn that cleanly separates nature from supernature. Man "can never find the nature he wants in a 'chemically pure' state separated from its supernatural existential."[34] Grace, in fact, interpenetrates nature and divinizes it; i.e., supernaturally imparts to it divine life and power. Man thus finds grace where he finds himself—in the everyday life of his finite spirit. Man, as transcendental consciousness, discovers that he is energized by the élan of grace, as the inescapable condition of his existence. On this showing, the existence even of the unbeliever is constantly being shaped by the supernatural grace that inexorably is being offered to it. Even secular experience in a profound sense is an experience of grace.

Rahner's transcendentalism likewise involves a new understanding of revelation. The traditional concept of revelation as an intrusion ab extra, which conveys truths in the form of propositions, must be abandoned. In lieu of the familiar categories of general and special revelation, Rahner postulates a transcendental revelation and a predicamental historical revelation. The first mode of revelation, which replaces universal general revelation, occurs within the depths of the individual as a supernatural experience. It involves a heightening of human awareness and an orientation of the person to the incomparable and ineffable Mystery. In Rahner's words:

> The divine self-bestowal . . . penetrates to the ultimate roots of man's being, to the innermost depths of his spiritual nature, and takes effect upon him from

there, radically re-orientating this nature of his towards the immediate presence of God. It imparts to this nature an inward dynamism and an ultimate tendency towards God himself that is a grace.[35]

In its God-given dynamism, transcendental revelation produces no new knowledge, but only a new consciousness. It is a preconceptual, unobjectified, and non-reflexive meeting between God and the finite human spirit. Transcendental revelation, in fact, is equivalent to the supernatural existential that effects the divinization of man's fundamental subjective disposition. It is "God's personal gift of himself to man in absolute, forgiving intimacy."[36] And it is received in faith whenever an individual follows his conscience and willingly accepts his supernaturally elevated self-awareness. "It is *ipso facto* present, albeit unconsciously and, in a certain sense 'anonymously,' everywhere where the transcendentality of the spirit and moral freedom are exercised."[37] Transcendental revelation is a profound reality even in the experience of the atheist who manifests no overt interest in the things of God.

But following the a priori experience of awareness, there occurs the process of thematization, which Rahner denotes as predicamental historical revelation. This involves the conceptual objectification of the ecstatic transcendental experience in a specific historical and cultural context. Here Rahner argues that if the transcendental revelation is to serve as the principle of man's concrete behavior, it must be translated into formal objective propositions. Nevertheless, the historical categorical revelation, which roughly corresponds to special revelation in the traditional scheme, necessarily involves errors, misinterpretations, and numerous abuses.

It should be clear that the supernatural elevation of human transcendence (general revelation) is universal in scope. By virtue of God's will to save, the transcendental revelation is potentially available to all and is effectively actualized whenever a person lives authentically within the new horizons proffered to him. Thus Rahner insists that the history of the self-communication of ineffable mystery is coextensive with the history of religion and, indeed, with the history of mankind.

One must underscore Rahner's conviction that the knowledge afforded by general revelation is an unthematic and nonobjective consciousness, rather than a knowledge that can be objectified in words and propositions. The knowledge Rahner envisages is an ordered drive to the Absolute, or a nonobjective luminosity of the subject in its transcendence. It is exemplified in history by the ecstatic experiences of sensitive mystics and visionaries. Since the ever-present transcendental experience is an a priori datum of human experience, there is no person who does not actually know God. "Man is and remains a transcendent being, that is, he is that existent to whom the silent and uncontestable infinity of reality is always present as mystery. This makes man totally open to this mystery."[38] Even if man is unable formally to articulate his religious convictions, he nevertheless knows God in the depths of personal self-realization. It goes without saying that since the knowledge of God is universally impressed upon human consciousness, the theoretical a posteriori proofs are quite superfluous. Ultimately, there exists but one proof for the existence of God, namely, the individual's own transcendental experience of the Absolute and the significance of that experience for life.

Any study of Rahner must come to grips with the application of his transcendental theology to the validity of the world's religions. From his Roman Catholic perspective, Rahner regards Christianity as the highest religion. The Christian faith represents the fullest embodiment of God's supernatural grace. The way of Christ is the God-ordained way of salvation. Thus it is mandatory that the Christian gospel be proclaimed to the world. Nevertheless, in the spirit of Aquinas, Rahner presupposes that God wills the salvation of all men. This implies the possibility, if not the probability, of a divine revelation over the whole length and breadth of history, even outside the bounds of institutional Christianity. In fact, God confronts all people with the reality of grace that imparts divine life and power through the universal supernatural existential. It is foolish, Rahner continues, to believe that those outside the bounds of official Christendom are so evil and blind as to reject the supernatural grace offered in the transcendental experience. Hence God's gracious self-communication to man must prove effectual, even within the context of non-Christian religious experience. Thus in spite of the presence of falsehood and errors, the world's non-Christian faiths authentically mediate saving grace, which Rahner holds to be the grace of Christ. That is, Christ is present and operative in Buddhism, Hinduism, Islam, and other non-Christian religions in and through his Spirit. In spite of some appearances to the contrary, the non-Christian faiths are lawful and salvific religions, whose adherents stand under grace. Thus Rahner concludes:

> Every way by which a man travels from genuine motives of conscience is a way leading to the infinitude of God. The ways are of various lengths, and not every one, not every age in history, and not every people either, progress at the same rate or arrive at the same point in their journey when these are compared with one another. But everyone who genuinely embarks upon such a way does arrive.[39]

In a 1961 essay entitled "Christianity and the Non-Christian Religions," Rahner introduced the revolutionary concept of "anonymous Christianity."[40] By an anonymous Christian, Rahner means "the pagan after the beginning of the Christian mission, who lives in the state of Christ's grace through faith, hope and love, yet who has no explicit knowledge of the fact that his life is orientated in grace-given salvation to Jesus Christ."[41] As a result of God's universal will to save and the supernatural existential (i.e., the transcendental self-communication of God as an offer to man's freedom), every human being is unavoidably confronted with the grace of

Christ. In experiencing transcendence, man experiences God's offer of justifying grace. Argues Rahner:

> The grace of Christ is at work in a man who never expressly asked for it, but who already desired it in the unspeaking, nameless longing of his heart. Here is a man in whom the unspeaking sighing of the Spirit has invoked and petitioned for that silent but all pervading mystery of existence which we Christians know as the Father of our Lord Jesus Christ.[42]

The person who believes in holy mystery and who allows such a belief to shape his existence, the person who does not reject his orientation to the Absolute, even though outwardly he be an atheist, such a one may be a true Christian without knowing it. In fact, an individual may be a recipient of sanctifying grace and thus be formally justified before God quite apart from any cognitive understanding of Christian truth. Authentic Christian experience may be a reality in a life when it is not explicitly recognized, or even when Christ is overtly rejected. Thus Rahner postulates that the Buddhist, Hindu, Muslim, or dogmatic atheist unwittingly are partakers of the redeeming grace of Christ. Consequently, "God's little flock does not live surrounded by ravening wolves but among sheep who may have gone astray and not yet found their way home, who may look like wolves from the outside but who may already have been or could be transformed inwardly, through God's grace into gentle creatures of God."[43] In other words, the non-Christian world properly ought to be regarded as an anonymous Christendom. Humankind is truly Christian without knowing it. Rahner's thesis of anonymous Christianity was warmly welcomed by Vatican II and incorporated into its official documents.[44]

But if the adherent of a non-Christian religion who accepts his own existence without reservation is already an anonymous Christian, what remains of the church's missionary task? The program of Christian preaching and teaching should be regarded not as a process of recovering the blind and ignorant from eternal perdition, but as the means whereby the anonymous Christian is enabled to confess explicitly what he believes implicitly and unthematically. As Rahner insists:

> The proclamation of the Gospel does not simply turn someone absolutely abandoned by God and Christ into a Christian, but turns an anonymous Christian into someone who now also knows about his Christian belief in the depths of his grace-endowed being by objective reflection and in the profession of faith which is given a social form in the Church.[45]

In short, the church in mission proclaims to pagans the good news that they have already been freely accepted by God in Christ.

On the basis of universal general revelation, envisaged as God's transcendental self-communication of mankind, Rahner postulates the salvation of the entire race. People who have had no contact with the concrete, historical revelation in Old or New Testaments nevertheless have been confronted with the self-communication of God through the supernatural existential. And all who accept their supernaturally elevated transcendence, in fact, exercise saving faith. Thus as Rahner sees it, mankind *in toto* has been accepted in Christ for salvation. Not only the knowledge of God but the history of salvation is coextensive with the history of religion and, indeed, with the history of the whole world. As Rahner himself argues, "The history of the world, then, means the history of salvation. God's offer of himself, in which God communicates himself absolutely to the whole of mankind, is by definition man's salvation. For it is the fulfillment of man's transcendence in which he transcends towards the absolute God Himself."[46]

What are we to make of Rahner's new-shape theology? His transcendental theism, first of all, must be faulted for its thoroughgoing anthropocentrism. In Rahner's scheme, the human agent becomes the measure of the Word of God, indeed, the measure of God Himself. But surely it is erroneous to argue, as Rahner does, that an anthropocentric orientation is necessarily theocentric. It is a fundamental mistake to insist that God is redemptively known by an exhaustive analysis of the human subject. Whereas conscience is one valid modality of general revelation, knowledge of God is not exclusively or even primarily a function of subjective human consciousness. Man is not the primary locus of divine revelation; otherwise God would not have been compelled to give a categorical revelation of His saving purposes in Holy Scripture. More likely, what man perceives in the depths of his being, or in the heights of accentuated luminosity, is not the saving reality of God, but his own finite psyche.

Second, Rahner's concepts of the supernatural existential and transcendental revelation destroy the proper biblical relation between nature and grace. While acknowledging that Thomas Aquinas created too severe a tension between nature and grace, we judge that Rahner has swung to the opposite extreme by merging the two realities. One must reject the Rahnerian notion that the entire realm of nature (man included) is uniformly made divine by the infusion of supernatural grace. Moreover, Rahner confuses the postulates of common and special grace. Whereas Scripture indicates that the human mind is enabled by common grace to intuit eternal, changeless principles, including fundamental truths about God, only special grace enables the sinner to perceive redemptive verities. There is no scriptural basis for the assumption that sinful humanity via the supernatural existential is unavoidably enveloped by the grace that justifies and saves. From the biblical perspective, special saving grace is not a fundamental and universal datum of human experience. Or to put it otherwise, in the biblical scheme, man's a priori knowledge of God as an unthematic given falls short of the encounter with God that redeems.

It is also clear that Rahner's transcendental theology empties the Cross of its biblical significance. One searches in vain for assertions that the Cross of Christ effects the sinner's transfer from darkness to light, from despair to hope, or from death to life. Conspicuously absent from Rahner's theology are such fundamental New Testament emphases as a radical summons to a decision for Christ, the need for an explicit act of repentance, and the cognitive character of faith. Rahner's transcendentalism flies in the face of the biblical insistence that specific truths about God and Christ must be believed before one can be saved. Postulates such as man's openness to the Absolute, orientation to the Infinite, or experience of holy Mystery lack the specificity of the biblical teaching on repentance, reconciliation, and justification.

Moreover, Rahner naively glosses over the determined hostility of atheism and unbelief toward the gospel of Christ. Scripture represents the non-Christian world not as friends of God, but as rebels and haters of the Most High. The assumption that the opponents of the Cross, who leave no stone unturned in their efforts to destroy Christianity, are implicit believers in Christ is too absurd to seriously entertain. How many fanatical Muslim nationalists, for example, would for a moment concede that they are, in fact, anonymous Christians? How many atheistic Marxists would welcome such an honorary title? Just as a practicing Christian would be offended by being called an anonymous Buddhist, so a practicing Buddhist likewise would be offended by being called an anonymous Christian. In his raging fury against the church, Saul the Jew never thought of himself as an anonymous Christian. Rather, he freely acknowledged that prior to his Damascus conversion experience he lacked a life-changing knowledge of the Lord Jesus. It is naive to suppose that God's desire for man's eternal welfare should override the stubborn and persistent rejection of Jesus Christ. We conclude that Rahner's theology has been shaped less by the normative teachings of Scripture than by the perspectives of philosophical idealism, existentialism, and modern religious humanism. And as such, it must be set aside in favor of a theology more faithful to the Word of God.

Küng, the Tübingen Rebel   Hans Küng (b. 1928), the Swiss-born Catholic theologian, also reflects extensively on the themes of revelation, the knowability of God, and the validity of the non-Christian religions. At age thirty-two Küng was appointed to the Chair of Fundamental Theology at the Catholic Theological Faculty of the University of Tübingen. More recently, he has served as Professor of Dogmatic and Ecumenical Theology as well as Director of the Institute for Ecumenical Studies of the same university. In 1979, amid a storm of controversy, Küng was banned by Pope John Paul II from teaching theology under the auspices of the church. Küng's *avant garde* stance has earned him the reputation of being a highly controversial catalyst for change in Catholicism. He has become a legend for his attacks on papal infallibility and the church hierarchy and for his activism in the areas of Christian unity, revision of the Mass, and birth control. Among church traditionalists, Küng is viewed as an extreme radical, if not a heretic. He has been accused by Catholic conservatives of watering down his theology to render it palatable to modern radical Protestants. *On Being a Christian*,[47] which Küng himself describes as "a kind of small 'Summa' of the Christian faith,"[48] represents one of two of his monumental works to date, the other being *Does God Exist?* (1980).

Küng writes in a less philosophical and more readable style than does Rahner. But this does not mean that he fails to interact with the contemporary thought-world. With Marcuse, Küng views modern man as locked into a "one-dimensional," secularized world. Contemporary humanistic man is agnostic, disillusioned, disconsolate, and isolated. Against this backdrop Küng seeks to formulate the Christian faith so as to enable it to enter into serious dialogue with modern man who has no faith.[49] Unconcerned with traditional church dogmas and religious formulae, Küng seeks to demonstrate that Christian faith may be harmonized with modern philosophical views, scientific achievements, and social concerns. His theology, not unfairly, could be described as a synthesis of religious and secular consciousness, of faith and reason, and of revelation and enlightenment. Moreover, Küng's approach is broadly anthropological insofar as his point of departure is man and the human situation. Religion begins with man's own concrete experience of reality. Limitations of space prevent us from showing that Küng's theological system has been shaped by Hegelian logic, existential concerns, and insights from contemporary depth psychology.

Brief attention must be given to Küng's theology proper. The personhood of God, for the Catholic scholar, is problematic. God is not a person "up there" or "out there." Following Tillich and Rahner, Küng sees God as the immanent Power that underlies the whole of man's life experience. God is the primordial and ultimate Mystery that refuses to be grasped by human conceptualization. Since man is in God and God is in man, a constant intercommunication occurs between the two. Man does not encounter God through supernatural intervention from above or from without. Rather, it is only in the dialogical experience of listening to and speaking with God that man realizes his destiny. This meeting between God and man may be regarded as secular, since it occurs immanently in and through the world. Put in other terms, God's love and grace are not transmitted through sacred channels, but are experientially discovered in every dimension of human life in the world. For Küng, as for Rahner, the experience of God is a universal human datum.

Pursuing further the problem of the knowability of God, Küng rejects what he regards as two extreme historical positions. The first is the fideistic and authoritative appeal to the biblical revelation, and the second, Thomistic natural theology based on discursive reason. For Küng the scholastic way of Aquinas is far too rational to have any bearing on man's existential situation. The Catholic scholar prefers a middle way—not unlike Kant's scheme of practical reason—that involves what he calls a "meditative reflection"[50] on the concrete experience of the whole reality of the world. On the road to God one does not look outward or upward, but backward or inward to the transcendental in human experience. Since God is that which underlies man's total experience of life, an inductive elucidation of experienced reality eventually leads to God. A risk-orientated venture of decision and trust seals man's apprehension of God. As Küng puts it, "Belief in God is nourished by an ultimately substantiated basic trust: When he assents to God, man opts for an ultimate reason, support, meaning of reality. In belief in God assent to reality turns out to be ultimately substantiated and consistent: a basic trust anchored in the ultimate depth, in the reason of reasons."[51] Those who have made this kind of trusting commitment to the primal reality underlying human experience are rightly called "believers in God."

Küng links this prehension of the Ultimate in the depth of life with the work of the divine Logos, whose rays enlighten all men. The illumination of the Logos serves as the constant, relentless, and richly diverse self-presentation of the real in the reality of the world. Knowledge of God ensues as the human agent through the Logos perceives the "ultimate identity, significance and value of reality."[52] As man in the totality of his reason reflects on the phenomena of human experience and then commits himself to the meaning of primal reality, God is authentically yet subconsciously known. Clearly what Küng, like Rahner, has done is to construct a natural theology founded on experience—but an experience that involves no necessary assent to cognitive truths. When man attempts to objectify his empirical intuition of reality, a diversity of conceptual formulations results. Hence there are the formal differences that exist among the world's ideologies and religions.

Since all religions accept the underlying reality of the world and attempt to answer the basic questions of existence, their adherents enjoy a valid spiritual experience of God. The Hindu who worships the Brahman, the Buddhist, the Absolute; the Chinese, the Tao; and the Muslim, Allah; all engage the same mystery of ultimate Reality. Even amid the darkness of paganism, God is graciously near His creatures. Küng thus affirms that salvation is a reality among the unbaptized outside the church. Religions other than Catholic Christianity, in fact, represent the "normal" and "ordinary" means of salvation. In the plan of God, all people are saved by divine grace through the practice of their non-Christian religion.

> The other religions were regarded formerly as lies, works of the devil and—at best—vestigal truth. Now they count as a kind of ("relative") revelation through which innumerable individuals of ancient times and of the present have experienced and now experience the mystery of God. Formerly they seemed to be ways of damnation. Now they are recognized as ways of salvation—whether "extraordinary" or "ordinary" is a matter of dispute among scholars—for innumerable persons, perhaps indeed for the majority of mankind.[53]

The fact that pagans and other non-Christians find salvation in the practice of their own religions is, for Küng, a matter of thanksgiving.

> We can be glad that God's grace, as it is revealed to us in Christ, is so vast and wide that it embraces the whole world; all men are within his good pleasure. We can be glad that we do not need to condemn any of these pagans in Asia or Africa or in the middle of Europe. As witnesses to the faith and apostles of Jesus Christ we may and should proclaim the Gospel to them, in the knowledge that God's grace in Jesus Christ has already reached out to embrace them.[54]

In propounding the above views, Küng sides with the judgment of Vatican II that all men of good will—in spite of idolatry, magic, and superstition—are enveloped by the saving grace of God. Incontestably, Küng sees the religions of the world as authentic vehicles of salvation.

If the non-Christian religions represent the "ordinary" means of access to God, the Roman Catholic church represents the "extraordinary" or "special" vehicle of salvation. Even though the non-Christian religions authentically mediate salvation, Küng insists that Christianity's loyalty to Jesus endows it with a certain plus. While not the exclusive vehicle of salvation, Christianity is unique in the sense that it is the paradigm of true religion for mankind. As Küng argues, Jesus of Nazareth is "ultimately decisive, definitive, archetypical, for man's relations with God, with his fellow man, with society."[55] While people of all religions are truly saved, not all religions are equally true.

Christianity, in fact, represents the fulfillment and crystallization point for all other religions. The non-Christian is duty bound to seek God within his own religion *until* such time as he is personally confronted with the message of Christ. Whereas Rahner holds that the church rightfully exists among the saved in other religions, Küng calls for the saved in other faiths to unite with the community of baptized Christians who celebrate the Lord's Supper. Küng thus rejects Rahner's notion of "anonymous Christians," choosing rather to describe people in other faiths who embrace the primordial Mystery as "pre-Christians." In other words, adherents of the non-Christian religions are delivered from condemnation as they follow the light within their own systems. Yet sooner or later these "pre-Christians" must formally align themselves with the Christian church. The church's missionary task involves not arrogant proselytism, which takes too restricted a view of other religions, but the inviting of "pre-Christians" to Christ, their true spiritual center.

In Küng and the new Catholicism, the Thomistic emphasis on discursive reason working on the data of nature has been largely supplanted. The objective cosmos is now regarded as an ambiguous witness, and the formal proofs for God's existence are judged too abstract and remote from life to be of any practical value. In any case, Kant's demolition of the traditional proofs has put an end to the rational approach to God. In lieu of the scholastic method of logical reasoning, post-Vatican II Catholic theology posits an inner, formless, and mystical experience of the Absolute. God unveils Himself to man through the exigencies of human experience. Man's experience of the world and himself is viewed as religious, supernatural, and grace-mediating. Revelation, conceived of as mystical address or existential experience, is intrinsic to the human soul rather than extrinsic, and its focus is anthropocentric rather than theocentric. The universal general revelation postulated by the new Catholicism takes the form of a thoroughgoing immanence, if not a kind of mystical pantheism.

Contemporary *avant garde* Catholicism thus replaces classical Thomism with a subjective, empirical, natural theology. The old rational scheme of theology based on the objective cosmos has given way to a new natural theology grounded in human experience and self-understanding. What has transpired in the new situation is the enlargement of the scope of general revelation to include a knowledge content traditionally ascribed to special revelation. In this respect, modern Catholicism postulates a new form of natural theology that far outdistances traditional Thomism in its claims of saving efficacy. With the ascendency of a universal self-disclosure of God in the human psyche, revelation through Scripture and tradition takes on diminished importance. In the existential climate of post-Vatican II Catholicism, the Bible is no longer viewed as the primary datum for knowledge of God.

Contemporary Catholicism regretably has adopted a syncretistic stance relative to other religious traditions. That non-Christians as well as Christians are heirs of salvation no longer is a novel thesis but a generally accepted conclusion. The longstanding Augustinian model, which views humankind as divided in two cities—the city of God and the city of mammon—is set aside in favor of the universalist model where every human being and every world religion is an heir of God's grace. The world's non-Christian faiths represent the providential means of salvation for the majority of the human race. Buddhism, Hinduism, Islam, and other living religions are part of God's plan for the redemption of the world.

The church is thus enjoined to recognize that the adherents of the world's leading religions already have been embraced by grace. The calling and mission of the people of God is to dialogue with other faiths so as to render implicit faith explicit. Their task is to strengthen the non-Christians' encounter with God in the context of their indigenous religious traditions. Some Roman Catholic missiologists unfortunately argue that the goal of missions is to make the recipients of Christian preaching better Buddhists, better Hindus, or better Muslims.

At the metaphysical level, the new Catholicism errs in supplanting biblical dualism with an Eastern form of monism. In its rejection of the twofold order of knowledge, Catholicism has blurred the distinction between nature and grace and compromised the antithesis between light and darkness, truth and falsehood. Modern Catholic theologians, moreover, hold an inflated estimate of the reliability of subjective experience as interpreted by sinful man. More accurate surely is the estimate of the great preacher, C. H. Spurgeon, who said, "Man's nature is not an organized lie, yet his inner consciousness has been warped by sin, and though once it was an infallible guide to truth and duty, sin has made it very deceptive. The standard of infallibility is not in man's consciousness, but in the Scriptures."[56] Faith is more than man's intrinsic experience of reality. Biblical belief involves cognitive assent to God, His revealed purposes, and His righteous demands.

Finally, the new Catholic claim that all religions mediate a saving encounter with God flies in the face of the biblical assertion that Jesus Christ is "the way and the truth and the life" (John 14:6). If the modern Catholic claim that all people are savingly enlightened were true, then the costliness of Christ's death would be undermined and the rationale of the Incarnation itself would be subverted. In such a case, it would be difficult to find sufficient justification either for the church's existence or for its mission in the world.

CHRIST AND INDIGENOUS DEITIES: THEOLOGY MADE IN THE THIRD WORLD

XI

The conviction is growing among younger churches in the developing world that the classical theology bequeathed to them by the established churches in Europe and America is inadequate for the present situation. Voices are being raised that question whether theology, polity, and worship must continue to be structured along traditional Western lines. "How can we sing the foreigners' songs and pray the foreigners' prayers in our own land?" many Christians in the third world ask. A question frequently heard today is whether theology always need have a European stamp on it.

The dissolution of Western colonial domination has brought about a spirit of theological independence on the part of many younger churches in the third world. The achievement of political freedom in recent decades has stimulated a corresponding interest in theological and ecclesiastical freedom. There is also the concern that, in addition to the text of Scripture, theology needs to consider the particular cultural context in which churches find themselves. And so it is argued that the classical theology of Augustine or Aquinas is largely irrelevant to the cultural situation of modern Argentina or Angola. Many argue, in addition, that traditional Western theology has not addressed itself to the phenomena of injustice, oppression, and poverty that exist on a large scale in today's world. A theology must be shaped that is relevant to the social, economic, and political realities of the developing nations at the present moment of history. Finally, the surge of interest in non-Christian religions in our century has prompted theologians to search out areas of agreement among the world's leading faiths. Armed with the conviction that God has never left Himself without a witness in the world, specialists have set out to construct regional or national theologies that purportedly do justice to the divine working in traditional indigenous religions.

Thus many churchmen, particularly in the third world, are persuaded that the received theology needs reshaping if it is to speak relevantly to the needs of the emergent churches. Somehow the pure essence of Christianity must be separated from the Western philosophical and cultural baggage. Somehow a theology faithful to the African, Asian, or Latin American cultural situation must be developed. As one African sociologist-theologian puts it, "Our attempt is to rescue theology from the shelves of the universities and the sanctuaries of the churches and to make it a living, dynamic, and active reality in our societies."[1]

An Indigenous African Theology   A spokesman representative of theological trends on the African continent is E. Bọlaji Idowu, professor of religious studies at Nigeria's premier institution of higher learning, the University of Ibadan. An ordained Methodist minister, Idowu did his doctoral thesis at Cambridge under Dr. E. Geoffrey Parrinder on the Yoruba concept of Deity. His study has subsequently been expanded into a book entitled *Olódùmarè: God in Yoruba Belief.*[2] As the leading West African Christian theologian, Idowu has wrestled with the problem of the relationship between Christianity and the traditional religions indigenous to African soil. During the past quarter-century, Idowu's convictions on this crucial issue have changed dramatically. In his little book *Towards an Indigenous Church,*[3] which outlined his perspective in the 1960s, Idowu challenged the church of Jesus Christ in Nigeria to become a truly national church independent of Western influences. However, in his substantial study *African Traditional Religion,*[4] which represents his revised perspective for the 1970s and beyond, Idowu argues that the African's experience of the reality of God is most faithfully mediated by the various forms of traditional religion native to the African cultural situation. This shift in Idowu's thinking involves a number of considerations that warrant closer attention.

Professor Idowu's early theological outlook, shaped during the 1950s and 1960s, was broadly evangelical.[5] The Nigerian churchman insisted that Christianity is the definitive religion and as such demands the allegiance of the entire world. The Christian faith owes its existence to the loving God who, in a stupendous act of self-revelation, became flesh in Christ to redeem a fallen race. Assurance of heaven is predicated on a person's acceptance of Jesus Christ as Savior and Lord. But in addition to this evangelical theological focus, Idowu's earlier writings also reflect a wider cultural concern; namely, to rid the Nigerian church of alien colonial elements and to bring it to full indigenous status. Idowu laments the fact that after more than a century of evangelical activity, Christianity in Nigeria remains "a white man's cult, a kind of imperialistic witchcraft which has been employed to fetter the souls of Nigerians for the sinister purpose of colonial exploitation."[6] The Nigerian theologian likens the church in Africa to "a marionette with its strings in the hands of some foreign manipulators."[7] Christian people in Nigeria must seize the initiative and break the fetters of a foreign structure and foreign traditions arbitrarily imposed on them. The church in Nigeria must rid itself of its European complexion and strive to realize its unique African personality and destiny. In order to break out of the pattern of European domination and become truly African, the church must develop its own Bible translations, theology, hymnody, liturgy, and language of evangelism. Idowu's overriding concern during these earlier years was to create an indigenous African church that would be truly free to acknowledge the lordship of the eternal Christ, who alone is preeminent. At all costs, "The Church should bear the unmistakable stamp of the fact that she is *the Church of God in Nigeria.*"[8]

But even during this early, orthodox stage, Idowu toyed with the opposite notion that perhaps Christianity, as a Western religion, could not fully or even adequately penetrate the depths of the African soul. If religion is to strike a resonant chord on the African's heart, Christian teaching must be supplemented by traditional beliefs. Perhaps the imported Christian religion needs to be enriched with the age-old wisdom of indigenous tribal faith. With this in mind, Idowu makes this statement about the church: "It is time for her to realize that in order to be effective in her life and mission in Nigeria, she must respect, preserve and dedicate to the glory of God *anything that is of value in the culture and institutions of the country*"[9] (italics added). What lay buried in Idowu's mind was the tantalizing thought that God may, after all, speak to African people through the ancient traditions of African life and culture.

However, it was Idowu's 1975 work, *African Traditional Relgion*, that made a clean break with his earlier exclusivist Christian stance. Now in lieu of the assumption that God's normative mode of addressing man is the incarnate Christ, Idowu asserts that God bares His heart to the African soul in the midst of her time-honored forms of worship. If in the new scheme Christianity has any place at all, it is in a syncretistic fusion with indigenous modes of belief and worship. Idowu seeks to justify his new hypothesis that the African discovers God through traditional religion by appeal to the following theological considerations.

In the first place, Idowu insists that the God of heaven, who creatively works in the world to accomplish His purposes, has never left Himself without a witness in any generation or nation. Moreover, he asserts that all human beings possess the inborn capacity to receive a revelation from God. "It is this God, therefore, who reveals Himself to every people on earth and whom they have apprehended according to the degree of their spiritual perception, expressing their knowledge of Him, if not as trained philosophers or educated theologians, certainly as those who have had some practical experience of Him."[10] This ability of the human soul directly to engage God is as much a reality for the simple African tribesman as for the cultured European city dweller. "It would be looking at facts through the spectacles of cultural pride and affected superiority to deny this; it would be blasphemous to say that while the loving God cared for a particular section of His world, He had nothing in a clear, unmistakable way, to say to, or do with the rest."[11]

The African scholar follows Brunner, Baillie, and DeWolf to argue that revelation, or "theophany," consists of a personal encounter between God and the human soul. On the divine side, God, who dwells in unapproachable light, has disclosed Himself to the creature in two ways: first, through the natural phenomena of the visible cosmos; and second, through man's inner link with Deity. In asserting this, Idowu appropriates from Otto and Eliade the notion that the "Wholly Other" manifests itself in and through the created order. This twofold revelatory initiative of the Deity is fully universal in extent. Argues Idowu, "If revelation indeed means God's self-disclosure, if he has left his mark upon the created order and his witness within man—every man—then it follows that revelation cannot be limited in scope and that it is meant for all mankind, all rational beings, irrespective of race or colour."[12] On the human side of the equation, revelation involves man's subjective apprehension of and response to the divine initiative. In concert with neoorthodox theology, Idowu insists that apart from the participation of the receiving agent there would be *no* revelation at all. Again, borrowing from Otto and Eliade, Idowu argues that through the instrumentality of the external and internal worlds, man achieves a profound experience of the "Wholly Other." Through a universe that is transparent to the Sacred, the creature engages Ultimate Reality, which evokes within him feelings of awe, eeriness, self-abasement, and irresistibly attractive power. In short, through the universal divine disclosure, every person, regardless of circumstances, is overwhelmed with a sense of "numinous uneasiness."[13]

Idowu further insists that one must differentiate between the *experience* of living Power and the *expression* of that experience. The expression of man's experience of noumenal Reality predictably varies from culture to culture and from age to age. For example, African tribal people in their primitive setting express the experience of the Sacred in the familiar forms of traditional tribal religion. People in Europe or North America inevitably express their experience of the Holy in quite different Christian forms of creed and worship. But Idowu's main point is that African traditional religion constitutes a true expression of the tribesman's experience of God. It is totally false to affirm that Christians in the West worship a "High God," whereas African tribal people blindly render obeisence to a perverted deity. Both Christianity in the West and traditional religion in Africa are valid expressions of the human experience of noumenal Reality. In their primitive situation, Africans may create a picture of God that is incomplete or perhaps even faded or blurred. But the God that Africans have worshiped for generations is the same God that Christians worship. Certainly, Idowu argues, it is a mistake for Westerners to boast that Christianity affords an exclusive knowledge of God. The tribal African possesses an awareness of the true God—an awareness that at rock bottom is no less authentic than that achieved by the sophisticated European or American worshiper.

Since African traditional religion represents the sweet fruit of divine revelation to the heart of the African people, Idowu insists that one does native religiosity a serious disservice by referring to it in derogatory terms. For example, the pejorative word *pagan* greatly misrepresents the sincere character of African spirituality. Pagan is really a sociological term that denotes a rustic country dweller, as opposed to one who is enlightened. There is no justification, save narrow-minded prejudice, for its use in a religious sense. Similarly, the word *heathen* betrays the pure religion handed down by tribal people from generation to generation. In its original sociological context, heathen signified a heath dweller. The term is a complete misnomer when applied to the sphere of religion. By the same reasoning, those who follow the worship of their ancestors ought not be called "idolaters." True, idols are widely employed as cult objects in African traditional religion. But according to Idowu, the visual and material object (idol) serves only as a symbol to facilitate the worshiper's perception and awareness of the divine Presence. Since, in Idowu's mind, the idol enhances the quality of the worship experience, it performs a positive service in religion.

In like manner, Idowu argues, other elements of African traditional religion ought not be disparaged and dismissed as demonic perversions. African religion is predominantly animistic, which means that all nature is believed to be crowded with spiritual agents that impact people's lives for good or ill. Hosts of spirits are said to reside in sacred animals, trees, rocks, watercourses, and mountains. Animism, or spiritualism, is a legitimate feature of African traditional religion "if it is understood in the sense of the recognition of the fact that man's spirit is in communication and communion with the Divine Spirit. In this sense, it refers all worship ultimately to the Divine Spirit, often through ministering spirits."[14] Idowu maintains that Western religion has failed to take sufficient account of the spiritualist or occult character of the divine due to the smothering weight of its arid intellectualism.

Traditional religion, in addition, gives significant place to fetishism or juju, where various charms or amulets, viewed as the habitation of a spirit, are regarded as having magical potency. But fetishism, in Idowu's mind, is a symbolic expression of the tribal African's finely attuned sensitivity to the spiritual world. The indigenous practice of ancestor worship likewise ought not be regarded as an expression of darkened and confused minds. Idowu acknowledges that African religion involves the veneration of ancestors, which admittedly comes close to worship. "Our conclusion is that while technically Africans do not put their ancestors, as ancestors, on the same footing with Deity or the divinities, there is no doubt that the ancestors receive veneration that may become so intense as to verge on worship or even become worship."[15] Furthermore, the practice of magic, wherein African tribal people attempt to tap the supernatural forces of the universe, is a symbolic expression of the existence of a power wholly other to the creature. The point Idowu seeks to make is that spiritualism, fetishism, ancestor worship, magic, ritual medicine, and other practices are all appropriate responses of the African soul on African soil to the *mysterium tremendum et fascinans*. And as authentic responses to the divine revelation, they ought not be disparaged or ridiculed by those outside the African context.

African traditional religion plainly posits the existence of a whole host of lesser deities. Idowu's own Yoruba tribe, for example, recognizes up to 1,700 divinities in its pantheon. In view of this situation, it would appear that African traditional religion is polytheistic. Proof of polytheism, of course, would cast a fatal blow to Idowu's thesis that African indigenous religion constitutes a valid expression of the person's experience of the one true God. Inasmuch as African tradition teaches that the host of lesser divinities emanated from the supreme God, Idowu prefers to describe traditional religion not as polytheism, but as "diffused monotheism."[16] The black African concept of God, then, would be similar to that of the ancient Egyptians, who combined belief in one supreme God with assent to a multitude of subordinate deities that assist in the ordering of the universe.

Thus Idowu concludes his apologetic for the existence of a valid, life-giving revelation of God in African traditional religion. Those who argue that religion can be divided into two categories—the first based on God's climactic revelation in Christ, and the second embracing all other forms of perverted religion—fly in the face of the facts. Idowu insists that God has revealed Himself redemptively to the African soul, and thus the tribal African ought not repudiate the rich spiritual heritage God has granted his ancestors in traditional religion. Indeed, the Nigerian professor argues that Africans today are coming to the pleasant realization that

> the foreigners who brought their own religions and cultures to displace African religious ones have only come to cheat them of their God-given heritage. They often, therefore, expressed cheerful surprise in their discovery that Africa is blessed with so many indigenous spiritual and cultural treasures. And an oft-repeated question is, "Since we have such a wealth of indigenous spiritual and moral values, why should we have abandoned them for imported ones?"[17]

The great need of the hour is for Africa to recover her soul, to attend to her God-given spiritual heritage, and to adhere to the wisdom of her divinely appointed teachers and prophets. It is proper that African traditional religion should claim the loyalty of the majority of the African people. Yet in the course of adapting to the modern world, Idowu envisions that the future of religion in Africa lies in a syncretistic union of traditional tribal worship, Islam, and Christianity, with the former being the predominant element in the mixture. Thus Idowu concludes, "It appears that those who outwardly profess faith in other religions but are constantly resorting to the traditional religion for succor may not decrease substantially in numbers for a long time to come. It appears also that there will always be the 'faithful remnant' whose loyalty to the religion of their forebears will continue steadfast."[18]

It is apparent from our discussion thus far that Idowu has made a remarkable turnaround from a Methodist clergyman concerned to build an

IDOWU'S SCHEME

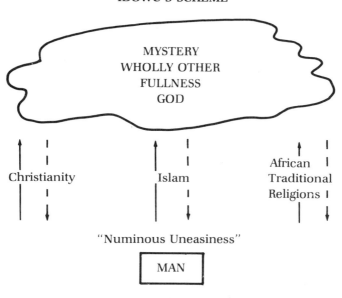

indigenous church under "the absolute Lordship of Jesus Christ"[19] to an African nationalist determined to preserve at any cost Africa's religious and cultural values. Idowu is right in condemning those who ignorantly or perhaps arrogantly depreciate everything African as barbarous, base, or worse. He is justified in exposing the fallacy that the "Dark Continent" is devoid of intellectual, cultural, and moral values. But in the process of defending the merits of African culture, he has erred in extolling natural religion as a true expression of the will of God. Every culture, whether African, Asian, European, or American, is a mixture of noble and ignoble elements. But every form of natural religion, whatever label it bears, is an expression of sinful man's refusal to honor the God who has plainly revealed Himself through the several modalities of general revelation. In truth, the citizen of the first world or the second world who rejects the light of God and who asserts his own autonomy is no less culpable than the citizen of the third world who fails to embrace God on *His* own terms. The Christ-rejecting European or American is fully as much a pagan and an idolater as the non-Christian African or Asian. Indeed, by virtue of the sheer intensity of available light, the Western man is exposed to the greater condemnation. It would be arrogant for the present writer to justify the sincerity and commitment of the unbelieving, pagan American because of his own identity as an American citizen. Similarly, when Idowu extols the virtues of non-Christian African religion, it would appear that he has done so on nationalistic grounds. Christ's followers need the courage to expose blind unbelief wherever it is found, even when it is in one's own backyard.

A further criticism of Idowu is that in constructing his system of religion he violates one of his own first principles. We recall that Idowu has scolded Africans for allowing themselves to be dominated by Western thought. The African expression of the faith must be shorn of all traces of Western colonial influence. The tragedy of Africa is that it has sold its soul to alien European traditions. But ironically, Idowu's own theology builds on the foundation laid by Kant, Schleiermacher, and Tillich. Moreover, his views on revelation are heavily indebted to insights from Brunner, Baillie, and De-Wolf. And his conception of religion as ineffable experience has been borrowed point for point from the Europeans Otto and Eliade. Indeed, if the European elements were excised from Idowu's theology, it would collapse and come to naught.

Idowu also must be faulted for his belief that all religions represent a valid expression of ineffable religious experience. Scripture gives no warrant for the supposition that the full reality of God is apprehended through an individual's naked experience. In holding this, Idowu has bought into the subjective empiricism of Schleiermacher, Tillich, and the neoliberal tradition. It is more accurate to argue that by rational reflection on the data of general revelation a person gains a rudimentary knowledge of God's existence, character, and moral demands. However, Scripture plainly teaches that in the darkness of his mind and stubbornness of his will, natural man refuses to treasure this knowledge, but perverts it into false worship (Rom. 1:22-23). Whereas the African theologian insists that the majority of people respond positively to the consciousness of God that wells up from within, Scripture concludes, "There is no one righteous, not even one; there is no one who understands, no one who seeks God. All have turned away, they have together become worthless; there is no one who does good, not even one" (Rom. 3:11-12). My point is that the revelation all perceive in nature and in conscience is from God and is representative of Him, but natural man tragically spurns that knowledge rather than allowing it to lead him to a saving experience of the Redeemer-God.

As suggested above, Western society is replete with its own destructive idols: affluence, ease, moral license, etc. But as we reflect on the beliefs and practices of African traditional religion, it too proves to be a false system whose roots lie in ignorance and rebellion against God. With respect to its idols carved out of wood and hewed out of stone, Scripture replies, "We should not think that the divine being is like gold or silver or stone—an image made by man's design and skill" (Acts 17:29). Concerning the ubiquitous African shrines where the deities are worshiped, Scripture replies, "The God who made the world and everything in it is the Lord of heaven and earth and does not live in temples built by hands" (Acts 17:24). With respect to libations, incantations, taboos, oracles, omens, blood sacrifices and human sacrifices, and superstitious practices such as taking the life of an infant because it was a twin or taking the life of a child because an upper tooth came in first, Scripture replies, "Turn from these worthless things to the living God" (Acts 14:15). The only conclusion that fits the facts is that

African traditional religion is not the effectual way to God Idowu supposes it is.

Finally, Idowu has made a fundamental mistake in confusing God's universal revelation in nature and conscience with special, redemptive revelation. Not the former, but the latter possesses saving potency. The fact that the tribal African conceives of God as immortal, all-powerful, holy, righteous in judgment, and the cause of all that comes to pass must be attributed to God's universal general revelation. The idea of the God of the Bible is universally impressed upon the human heart and mind. But the knowledge that leads to a saving relationship with God comes only from a higher disclosure of the divine will. The central message of the Bible, as Idowu formerly believed, is that a person comes to God redemptively by a faith appropriation of the atoning work of Jesus Christ. All other ways, however earnest and attractive, are ultimately in vain. One empathizes with Idowu's concern for the many generations of tribal people who have had neither Bible nor Christian proclamation. God, however, has given an adequate display of His character and demands in His works. If in the end a person is lost, the reason will not be that he has never heard the gospel, but that he has spurned the light of God that brightly shines on every hand. In the following chapter I will argue that in rare cases the sovereign God may choose to reveal Christ in some extraordinary way to the pagan who, without the Bible or gospel preaching, through the enabling of the Holy Spirit casts himself on the mercy of God in an act of total contrition.

Latin American Liberation Theology   One of the most significant developments in the Christian world today is liberation theology. The movement was born in Latin America between 1968 and 1970 through a series of international conferences of theologians and biblical scholars concerned with social and political conditions on the continent. With Roman Catholic theologians and churchmen in the vanguard, the theology of liberation has sought to root out poverty, injustice, and oppression in Latin American society by radical political action. Impetus was given to liberation theology by left-wing pronouncements from the World Council of Churches and by the radical stance adopted by the Second Vatican Council. This largely Latin American movement bears affinities to the political theology of J. B. Metz and Dorothy Sölle, to the theology of hope articulated by Jürgen Moltmann, and to black and feminist theologies in the U.S.A. Roman Catholic theologians of liberation, who comprise the largest block within the movement, include such figures as Gustavo Gutiérrez, J. A. Hernandez, Peres Ramirez, and Juan Luis Segundo. On the Protestant side, the liberation standard is borne by Rubem Alves, José Míguez Bonino, and Richard Shaull.

The acknowledged father of liberation theology is the Peruvian-born Catholic theologian Gustavo Gutiérrez (b. 1928). Gutiérrez studied philosophy and psychology at the University of Louvain and theology at Lyons, France. Currently he is professor of theology at the Catholic University in

Lima, Peru. His chief work to date, *A Theology of Liberation*,[20] has been acclaimed the Bible of the liberation movement. Since Gutiérrez is generally regarded as the leading spokesman for liberation theology, and since his writings are representative of the movement as a whole, we shall focus attention on his understanding of revelation and the knowability of God.

Gutiérrez argues that the church historically has seriously misunderstood the nature of the theological enterprise. During the early centuries of its life, the church concentrated on the spiritual function of the discipline—defining theology as "wisdom." From this perspective, the theological task focused on withdrawal from worldly concerns, meditation on the Bible, and the mystical quest for spiritual perfection. However, from the eleventh or twelfth century on, theology increasingly came to be viewed as a body of formal knowledge. Here emphasis was placed on the rationality of the Christian faith, the systematization of faith into a body of truths, and the defense of a doctrinal position. The high-water mark of this latter approach to theology was achieved during the time of Thomas Aquinas, who firmly established theology as a rational science. Gutiérrez adamantly insists that these two traditional models—theology as wisdom and theology as science—must give way to the twentieth-century vision of theology as *praxis*. In a world whose horizons are dominated by masses of poor, oppressed, and despoiled people, a radically new way of doing theology is mandated.

Gutiérrez thus envisions theology not as pietistic spirituality, nor as reflection on doctrine, but as *act*, or practical *involvement* in the plight of the poor and the powerless of the world. The supreme need of the hour is for the church "to recognize the work and importance of concrete behavior, of deeds, of action, of praxis in the Christian life."[21] To believe is not to seek a mystical experience or to give assent to abstract truths. To believe is to act to abolish poverty and misery among the masses, to eliminate the injustices and exploitation caused by unequal distribution of wealth. To believe is to overcome the repressive character of an economic system where the means of production are controlled by the privileged few. To exercise faith is to free society from the bondage of an alienating religion that deliberately seeks to preserve the status quo. To believe is to restructure the bases of the Latin American social and economic system, and to immerse oneself in the process of social, cultural, and political revolution. Thus Gutiérrez insists, "To believe is . . . to be united with the poor and exploited of this world from within the very heart of the social confrontations and 'popular' struggles for liberation."[22]

In defining theology as a critical reflection on the historical praxis of liberation,[23] Gutiérrez and other liberation theologians have freely appropriated the Marxist socioeconomic analysis of the human situation. The theological task and the church's mission is thus prosecuted along the revolutionary guidelines set down by Marx, Lenin, and Che Guevara. Marxism enables Gutiérrez not only to identify the cancer in society but also to prescribe the treatment needed for a cure. Gutiérrez thus argues that if the church seeks the creation of a just and compassionate society, it must be prepared to participate in the world-wide class struggle on behalf of the poor and exploited. Moreover, it must be willing to engage in conflict and violence, if necessary, to eliminate domination and repression. "The Church must place itself squarely within the process of revolution, amid the violence which is present in different ways. The Church's *mission* is defined practically and theoretically, pastorally and theologically in relation to this revolutionary process."[24] In short, the church must work to replace the anti-Christian capitalist system with a socialist type of society in which greed, exploitation, and oppression will be eliminated. In pursuing such a path to a just society, Gutiérrez urges those involved not to be intimidated by accusations of being "communist."[25] From the standpoint of the theology of liberation Gutiérrez concludes:

> It is becoming more evident that the Latin American peoples will not emerge from their present status except by means of a profound transformation, a *social revolution*, which will qualitatively change the conditions in which they now live. The oppressed sectors within each country are becoming aware—slowly, it is true—of their class interests and of the painful road which must be followed to accomplish the breakup of the status quo.[26]

In support of his thesis that the heart of theology is liberation praxis, Gutiérrez discovers a model for the political mission of the church in Israel's Exodus deliverance from Egyptian bondage. Liberationists point out that in Egypt Israel languished in a condition of misery and alienation. In an hour of great social crisis, Moses was raised up by God to serve the people as a political liberator. Israel's revolt against the Egyptian pharaohs and their long march to the Promised Land is viewed as a supreme instance of political liberation from oppression and servitude. As Gutiérrez notes, "The liberation of Israel is a political action. It is the breaking away from a situation of despoilation and misery and the beginning of the construction of a just and fraternal society."[27] Turning to the New Testament, Gutiérrez and other liberationists view the mission of Jesus primarily in political terms. While not Himself a Zealot, Jesus had considerable sympathy for the Zealot party and their popular revolutionary program. In His own ministry He launched a frontal attack against the roots of an unjust order. Jesus challenged the rich and powerful minority on behalf of the oppressed majority. Even Jesus' death at the hands of the Jewish and Roman authorities was supremely a political event. Thus liberationists allege that both Old and New Testaments encourage and support a political interpretation of the Christian message.

From this brief overview of the agenda of liberation theology, we pass to a consideration of its theological interaction with the subject at hand. Consistent with their definition of theology as praxis rather than wisdom, liberationists maintain that God does not communicate "truths" from some heavenly, supra-historical realm. There are no such things as preexistent, eternal propositions that wait to be discovered. Rather, truth is constituted at the level of personal engagement through concrete acts of charity and compassion. Moreover, since man is the living temple of the Divine, God is met and known through our encounters with people, particularly the poor and exploited of this world. From the liberationist perspective, God is on the side of the oppressed. As Gutiérrez insists, "Our encounter with the Lord occurs in our encounter with men, especially with those whose human features have been disfigured by oppression, despoilation, and alienation."[28] Gutiérrez follows Congar and other "advanced" Catholic thinkers in affirming "the sacrament of our neighbor."[29] Through profound involvement in the plight of one's neighbor, God Himself is engaged and known. Truth is actualized and God is encountered whenever a person strives on behalf of his neighbor to construct a more just and less oppressive society. As Gutiérrez succinctly puts it, "To know God is to do justice."[30] In other words, God is known as an individual commits himself to the revolutionary transformation of his economic, social, political, and cultural worlds. The knowledge of God is achieved through the process of liberation on behalf of "the neighbor, the oppressed person, the exploited social class, the despised race, the dominated country."[31] Gutiérrez sums up his position as follows:

> The encounter with Christ in the poor man constitutes an authentic spiritual experience. It is a living in the Spirit, the bond of love between Father and Son, God and man, man and man. Christians committed to an historical praxis of liberation try to live this kind of profound communion. They find the love of Christ in their encounter with the poor and in solidarity with them.[32]

Clearly, then, Gutiérrez's foundational epistemological principle is that involvement with one's neighbor constitutes involvement (encounter and knowledge) with God Himself. Man apprehends God through the process of interhuman justice. Man knows God as he strives to build a just and brotherly world. Gutiérrez attempts to support this line of reasoning by appealing to the parable of the sheep and the goats (esp. Matt. 25:45), the parable of the good Samaritan (Luke 10:30–37), and other texts such as James 2:20 and 1 John 3:24; 4:7-8, 20.

Liberation theology likewise distances itself from the traditional Christian way of thinking about salvation. In the liberation scheme, salvation is not a matter of the faith reception of Christ in an experience of spiritual crisis. Rather, salvation is a process in which a person moves outside of himself in an attitude of openness and concern for others. As Gutiérrez puts it, "Man is saved if he opens himself to God and to others, even if he is not clearly aware that he is doing so."[33] Concern for one's neighbor and efforts to build a just social order free from oppression and despoilation, in a profound sense, is a salvific work. According to Gutiérrez, when the fetters of political, economic, and social injustice are broken, then men and women will be free to live and express themselves as the people of God. The liberationist vision thus coincides with that of Angela Davis, who in the

1960s uttered the following slogan: "Remove these bonds and I will be free!" The goal in the struggle against misery, injustice, and exploitation is the creation of a new person. Indeed, the aspiration to create a new person lies at the very heart of the liberation struggle in Latin America. As Gutiérrez insists, "By working, transforming the world, breaking out of servitude, building a just society, and assuming his destiny in history man forges himself."[34] Via the dialectical process of world-wide liberation, salvation lies within the reach of all peoples.

Through political, economic, and cultural revolution man, in fact, forges the kingdom of God. Gutiérrez argues that through the popular struggle for liberation, evils such as hatred, greed, and repression will give way to a society characterized by brotherhood, justice, and love. To participate in the struggle for the liberation of the oppressed is to place oneself squarely within the perspective of the kingdom. In fact, the restructuring of the world by human effort is the principal way in which the kingdom of God will be inaugurated in history. As Gutiérrez argues, "The historical, political liberating event *is* the growth of the Kingdom."[35] Liberationists maintain that the process of historical liberation represents the chief sign of the eschatological salvation to come. By this means, "the political is grafted into the eternal."[36] Yet it is clear that liberation theology emphasizes the *realized* character of the kingdom of God. Through human achievement, man creates his own future and is responsible for his own destiny. Through political action, man transforms the world from a hellish to a redeemed state, which the liberationists define as the kingdom of God.

According to liberation theology, salvation and participation in the kingdom of God represent the inalienable birthright of all people everywhere; that is, a strong universalist strain permeates the literature of liberation theology. On the basis of the universal salvific will of God and the universal lordship of Christ, Gutiérrez insists that "all men are in Christ efficaciously called to communion with God."[37] In other words, "the salvific action of God underlies all human existence."[38] Not only individual Christians, but humanity as a whole will become the temple of the living God. As Gutiérrez expresses it, "Salvation is not something otherworldly, in regard to which the present life is merely a test. Salvation—the communion of men with God and the communion of men among themselves—is something which embraces all human reality, transforms it, and leads it to its fulness in Christ."[39] Since salvation is coextensive with humankind, Gutiérrez cautions against compartmentalizing the divine activity, as for example, into church and world, or the sacred order and the secular. Liberationists, in fact, argue that the boundary between the church and the world has become more fluid. Following Schillebeeckx, Metz, and others, Gutiérrez reasons that the church may be identical with the world. And, of course, if the church and the world should be one, there would be no need to evangelize the great masses of peoples who make no Christian profession.

By way of critique, there are several features of liberation theology to

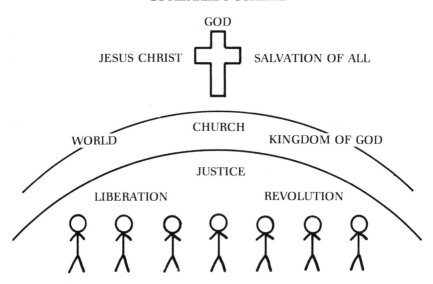

GUTIÉRREZ'S SCHEME

GOD

JESUS CHRIST   SALVATION OF ALL

CHURCH
WORLD   KINGDOM OF GOD

JUSTICE

LIBERATION   REVOLUTION

Knowledge of God: Implementation of Social Justice

which we can and should respond positively. In the main, liberationists sensitively attend to the cries of the poor and downtrodden of the world. They properly insist that it is not sufficient merely to believe rightly; Christians must implement their beliefs with practical deeds of mercy and compassion (James 2:14–17). Orthodoxy without orthopraxis is only half the truth. Moreover, liberation theology performs a valuable service when it points out that sin is not only personal and individual, but also societal and institutional, as the Old Testament, the minor prophets especially, implicitly teaches. Conservative Christianity as a whole has yet to learn that the judgment of God must be brought to bear on sinful structures. The work of Christ ought to touch the individual heart and the existing social order. Too frequently, Christian missions and the churches enter into unholy alliances with the privileged sectors of society at the expense of the legitimate interests of the masses. Liberationists are also correct in their judgment that society's basic need is not quantity of goods, but quality of life; not unlimited wealth, but unmeasured well-being (Luke 12:15). With remorse, we must agree with the following judgment of Gutiérrez: "The Christian has not done enough in this area of conversion to the neighbor, to social justice, to history. He has not perceived clearly enough that to know God is to do justice."[40]

But on the other side of the ledger, Gutiérrez and liberation theology must be faulted for reaching the Bible through the spectacles of Karl Marx. The Marxist-socialist critique of capitalistic society wrongly forms the basis for the liberationist's interpretation of the Word of God. Instead of allowing its vision of the world to be shaped by the teachings of Scripture, liberation theology permits its understanding of Scripture to be shaped by analysis of the existing social order. The Christian's text must be the Word of God rather than the historical situation (Deut. 4:1-2, 5-6). Moreover, liberation theologians are notably deficient in the area of exegesis. Biblical texts are commonly used as pretexts to justify pet economic and political theories. Gutiérrez and other liberationists often do little more than hang biblical window dressing on the framework of a sociological theory.

In addition, liberationists reverse the biblical ordering by upholding the priority of doing over knowing, or praxis over revealed truth. From the biblical perspective, action represents the appropriate and necessary *response* to the truth that God has revealed (2 Tim. 3:16-17). Truth sets the agenda and provides the motivation for praxis. In other words, theology properly constitutes ethics rather than ethics constituting theology. It simply is not so that acts, especially acts of liberation, possess their own intrinsic legitimacy. In terms of its monolithic emphasis on action, liberation theology illustrates the operation of the pendulum syndrome. In reacting against what they perceive to be an inordinate emphasis on truth to the neglect of action, liberationists focus on action to the sore neglect of truth. The Christian need not buy into the Marxist scheme to legitimize praxis. The assertion that theology and praxis must be done together is thoroughly biblical, Pauline, and evangelical.

Liberation theology likewise errs in its assertion that man comes to know God savingly by identification with the poor and oppressed. Since Christ is the neighbor, involvement with one's neighbor amounts to involvement with Christ. But this claim of the liberationists appears to buy into the panentheistic vision whereby all reality (here the neighbor) is included in the reality of God. Moreover, by following this line of reasoning, liberation theology has shifted the question of revelation from a matter of knowing God to acting in accordance with His purposes. It is true that participation in the plight of one's fellow-man does heighten one's concern and compassion for that person (Luke 10:33-35). But from a biblical perspective, God is known only as one enters into a personal relationship with Him through the mediation of Christ (Eph. 2:13-18). God is redemptively known not in the neighbor but through the divine Savior whose teachings, claims, and works are set forth in Holy Scripture. In truth, participation in the plight of the poor and oppressed represents the *fruit* rather than the *root* of one's knowledge of God. The Christian loves his neighbor, not that he might thereby come to know God, but vice versa. Indeed, apart from the prior love of God in the heart, it is doubtful whether a person can truly relate to his neighbor on the basis of *agape* love (1 John 4:19). Thus it is the Christian's knowledge of God in Christ that impels him on the path of genuine love and sacrificial service for his neighbor. God calls His people to a personal relationship with Himself to the end that they might glorify Him by deeds of compassion and mercy (1 Peter 2:9).

Furthermore, liberationists are flatly unbiblical in their insistence that the seat of sin is less in the human heart than in oppressive social and political structures. Believing that man is essentially good, Gutiérrez rejects the idea that sin is "an individual, private, or merely interior reality."[41] But Jesus Christ taught very clearly that sin originates in the human heart (Mark 7:20-23). Fundamentally, sin is lack of conformity to the moral law of God in act, thought, and disposition. Hence the underlying cause of unjust and repressive social structures is the fundamental sinfulness of man's heart. Gutiérrez and liberation theology thus are mistaken not only in their prescription of the cure for society, but also in their analysis of the basic problem.

Similarly, liberation theology misses the mark when it regards salvation as a this-worldly, intrahistorical reality. Just as sin is something more fundamental than institutional evil, so salvation involves more than the transformation of social and economic structures. Liberation theologians adopt an impoverished view of salvation when they regard it as a process of social betterment rather than the radical transformation of the entire person, both in this life and in the life to come. Moreover, liberationists fundamentally misinterpret the nature of the kingdom of God. The rule of God over history is inaugurated by the power of God rather than by human programs of political and social transformation (Col. 2:15; Rev. 11:15). The liberationist agenda focuses more on the formation of the city of man than on the city of God. Yet this humanistic utopian vision serves an idol that cannot be realized and a program that can only end in despair and frustration. Indeed, the new humanism embodied in liberation theology is as empty as older forms of humanism because it relegates God to the sidelines. A system that identifies Christ as my neighbor and redemption as participation in the revolutionary process, in fact, involves commitment to an idol—an idol that is as empty as more blatant forms of idol worship.

The sovereign God reserves to Himself the prerogative of judging the intents and motives of the human heart. But Scripture leads us to the conclusion that deeds of mercy in themselves do not merit acceptance and fellowship with God. Jesus Himself taught that in the day of judgment many religionists who plead deeds of compassion as a basis for salvation will be turned away: "Many will say to me on that day, 'Lord, Lord, did we not prophesy in your name, and in your name drive out demons and perform many miracles?' Then I will tell them plainly, 'I never knew you. Away from me, you evildoers!'" (Matt. 7:22-23). In sum, liberation theology's "re-reading of the Gospel"[42] based on solidarity with the poor and oppressed suffers from serious deficiencies that must be redressed before it can serve as a viable model for the people of God in the modern world.

An Asian "Christian" Theology   A theologian who seeks to shape the Christian faith in the light of the wisdom of the East is Raimundo Panikkar (b. 1918). The son of a Hindu father and Spanish Catholic mother, the

Barcelona-born scholar learned the Hindu scriptures along with the Bible. After earning the doctorate in philosophy from Madrid, Panikkar lectured at the universities of Mysore and Benares and at Harvard; he is currently lecturing at the University of California at Santa Barbara. Beginning with his seminal study, *The Unknown Christ of Hinduism*,[43] Panikkar has explored the relationship between Christianity and Eastern religions, particularly Hinduism. Persuaded that Eastern philosophy is more congruent with Christianity than with Greek thought, Panikkar has labored to construct a "Christian" existentialism based on Hindu precepts. In the same way that the Scholastics, especially Thomas Aquinas, grounded Christianity in Aristotle, so Panikkar attempts to explicate Christianity by using the framework of Hindu thought. There are, however, two main strands in Hindu philosophy, the dualist and the nondualist. The dualist (theistic) tradition, espoused by Ramanuja and the Bhakti movement, postulates a personal God or gods that sustain and rule the world. On the other hand, the nondualist or advaitist tradition of Hinduism, upheld by Shankara and Ramakrishnan, affirms a thoroughly pantheistic philosophy. God in the latter, more dominant strand of Hinduism is the one, all-pervading impersonal Reality. It is with the latter advaitist or monistic branch of Hinduism that Panikkar aligns himself.

In his attempt to synthesize Eastern and Western religious traditions, Panikkar strives to reconcile the abstract and impersonal Brahman with the concrete and living God of Christianity. Whereas the Jewish, Christian, and Islamic traditions emphasize the radical transcendence of God, Panikkar follows Hinduism and Buddhism in broadly stressing the immanent side of the divine transcendence. But as Panikkar adds, "The divine immanence is not simply a negative transcendence; it is quite a different thing from the divine welling in the depths of the soul. Essentially, it signifies the ultimate innerness of every being, the final foundation, the *Ground* of Being as well as of beings."[44] Guided by monistic advaitist Hinduism, Panikkar envisages God as the impersonal and formless world-Ground, the All, the Real, or absolute Being.[45] That is, God, the ultimate Reality, or Brahman, transcends the limiting category of personality. Panikkar regards the leading personal deities, such as Yahweh, Allah, or Krishna, as images created for the benefit of the majority of people whose understanding of the Absolute is enhanced by anthropomorphic figures.

But Panikkar insists that God, the Ultimate, or Reality, at bottom is trinitarian in character. Indeed, the central thesis of his book, *The Trinity and the Religous Experience of Man*, is that the principle of triunity permeates all levels of being, consciousness, and spirituality. That is, the trinitarian conception of the Ultimate (and with it the whole of reality) is not an exclusive Christian insight; all religions, in truth, perceive the trinitarian character of things. Thus Panikkar argues that the Trinity represents the junction or the focal point where the spiritual dimension of all religions meet. Whereas the christological model possesses a domineering and imperialist ring, the trinitarian model allows for genuine openness and pluralism. For example, the Hindu concept of Braham (Absolute, Imperishable, Real), Ishvara (nonhistoric Logos, Revealer of Brahman), and Atman (the Soul or Self) are said to correspond to the Trinity of Christianity. Panikkar thus argues that when the Hindu contemplates Ishvara, the personal agent of Brahman and the source of grace, he in fact is acknowledging the hidden Christ of Christianity. For Panikkar, then, any real contact with God or the Ultimate is always consciously or unconsciously trinitarian in character.

Panikkar prefers to use the term theandric rather than trinitarian to describe man's religious consciousness or spirituality for the reason that theandrism possesses no explicit Christian connotations. Theandrism, then, is the fundamental attitude through which we are able to understand and share the common religious insights of mankind. According to Panikkar:

> The fundamental insight of theandrism consists in the realization that man possesses an infinite capacity which links him up to the asymptotic limit called God; or to put it the other way round, that God is the end, the limit of man. In other words, theandrism is in a paradoxical fashion . . . the infinitude of man for he is tending towards God, the infinite, and the finitude of God, for he is the end of man.[46]

In short, theandrism provides a most adequate explanation for the universal phenomenon of mystical and religious experience.

From this brief overview of Panikkar's theological vision we pass to the issue of chief interest, namely, the divine knowability. Panikkar rejects the personalist approach to the knowledge of God, which involves discovery of and dialogue with Another, with a divine Thou. Knowledge of God is mediated not through the intellect or through the senses; rather, God is fundamentally known through the existential theandric experience. Panikkar appeals to the nondualistic advaitist school of Hinduism, which postulates the existence of an *anubhava*, namely, a vital intuitional experience of grace and faith. The ineffable and ambiguous advaitist experience involves an intuitional grasping of total Reality through the absorption of the experiencing agent. It is not a matter of a subject knowingly apprehending an object. Rather, the soul's contact with God is an experience of pure consciousness, which Panikkar defines as "an awareness that it is not aware that it is aware, an infinite experience."[47] Through union with transcendent Reality, the embodied soul in some way becomes part of the All-Soul or the ultimate Ground of everything. In Panikkar's own words, the advaitist experience may be regarded as "the supra-rational experience of a 'Reality' which in some way 'inhales' us into himself. The God of the Upanishads does not speak; he is not Word. He 'inspires'; he is Spirit."[48] The nondualistic Hindu experience, according to Panikkar, is "the ultimate experience,"[49] because it involves immediate contact with the absolutely Real. The authentic advaitist experience of God as All-in-All resists objectification in thoughts or words. Through the ego-transcending vision of total Reality, ignorance gives way to mystical enlightenment. The only fitting response of those who have experienced *"the in-stacy of union"* is "silence, abandonment, total conformity, [and] absolute non-attachment."[50] No objective validation is needed, for the advaitist experience itself brings total and incontrovertible assurance of truth.

In the language of traditional Christianity, the unutterable and transcendent God has never left man without an objective witness to Himself in the visible universe. But it is not the existence of extrinsic modes of revelation with which Panikkar is chiefly concerned. The divine self-unveiling is an intrinsic reality that is inherent in human nature as such. Man qua man is the locus of "revelation." What Christian theology specifies by the myth of "revelation" is the fundamental unveiling of the veils of existence, the upward thrust of the human ego toward discovery of the Absolute Spirit. It is precisely from this immediate, existential, and nonrational contact that the Real is known. In the categories of Christian theology, God is known in the depths of the mystical or spiritual life. In following this line of reasoning, Panikkar has exchanged the Western emphasis on the rationality of truth for the Eastern focus on the ineffable experience of the Spirit. More pointedly, he has adopted the monistic Hindu perspective of man's essential identity with transcendent Reality. Just as one must distinguish an experience from its expression, so one must differentiate underlying existential faith from conceptualized beliefs. Panikkar defines faith as existential openness toward transcedence, as a vital questioning, as a deep longing and desire for the Absolute. Analogous to the awakening of reason, faith is a primal anthropological act that every person performs in one way or another. This is to say that faith is constitutive of human nature; faith is necessary to *be*. Indeed, Panikkar replaces the classical Christian axiom "Believe that you might understand" (*crede ut intelligas*) with the alternative thesis "Believe that you might be" (*crede ut sis*). Faith, moreover, places man at the heart of the theandric (trinitarian) relationship and thus opens to him the possibility of spiritual perfection.

Religious faith, since it is rooted neither in the intellect nor in the will but in man's very existence, resists conceptual and verbal formulation. Nevertheless, man in his given cultural and intellectual context haltingly shapes his existential faith into formulas of belief, or dogmas. However, the formulations of the underlying faith are necessarily multifarious and pluralistic. "Due to the influence of time, a primordial and original form takes on an almost infinite number of possible transformations through the twisting of men, the stretching of history, the bending by natural forces and so on."[51] Hence Panikkar's theological vision allows for a genuine doctrinal pluralism. One must bear in mind when confronted with divergent and even contradictory doctrines that faith, not belief, saves. Indeed, beliefs tend to divide people, whereas the common existential faith unites. But faith expresses itself not only in different beliefs, but also in divergent forms of ethical behavior. Even though the behavioral norms of other religions may appear immoral to Christians, nevertheless genuine faith underlies their conduct. Of course, given the monistic presupposition, there is no basis in advaitist Hinduism for an ethical system. God is not moral but amoral, hence good and evil are equal. Panikkar, in other words, subscribes to both a doctrinal and an ethical pluralism. But "just as doctrinal pluralism does not mean conceptual chaos, so ethical pluralism does not imply anarchy."[52]

Earlier I pointed out briefly that in Panikkar's judgment the focus of the universal theandric experience is Christ. Since the Christian claim is true that there is no redemption apart from Christ, the Logos or the Christ must be present in one form or another in every person's approach to God. In his earlier work, *The Unknown Christ of Hinduism*, Panikkar appealed to Acts 17:23 in support of his claim that there is a living presence of Christ in Hinduism. In his missionary preaching, the apostle proclaimed to the Athenians the very God whom they unknowingly worshiped. Paul did not point the pagans to another God, but unveiled the true face of the God they were accustomed to worship. As in the case of the pagan Greeks, so it is with the Hindu worshiper. "In the footsteps of Saint Paul, we may believe that we may speak not only of the unknown God of the Greeks but also the Hidden Christ of Hinduism. Hidden and unknown indeed! Yet present there, for he also is not far from any one of us."[53] Christ is not only present in Hinduism, but He is at work in Hindu piety, prayer, and worship for the purpose of completing His redemptive mission there. As Panikkar himself put it, "Christ is not only the ontological goal of Hinduism but also its true inspirer, and His grace is the leading though hidden force pushing it towards its full disclosure."[54] Christ's presence and operation in Hinduism is incognito, for He has not yet unveiled His face and allowed Himself to be fully recognized.

It needs to be added against Panikkar that Paul in his Athens address refers only to the "unknown God" of the Athenians. There is no basis in the apostle's remarks to construe the presence of the hidden Christ in Greek polytheism or any other religion. Indeed, Paul directs the attention of his audience to Jesus, "the man he [God] has appointed" (Acts 17:31). Whereas in Hinduism Christ is at best the nonhistoric Logos, and the avatars are more mythological than historical, in Christianity Christ is at the same time *the Man*, Jesus of Nazareth. Lacking a sense of history, Panikkar's Hindu Christ is far removed from Jesus Christ of the Christian faith.

Panikkar continues by claiming that Christ is savingly at work in other religions and ideologies regardless of their name and form. "What Christ claims to be and to perform is valid for the Animist, Hindu, Muslim, etc., as well as for the Aztec, the Mongol, Greek, European, etc., as also for the Cro-Magnon man, for those who lived 15,000 years ago or for the man of our time."[55] Indeed, it is Christ, recognized or unrecognized, who makes religion possible. Without Christ there would be no religion. Panikkar insists that the Christ hidden and operative in the world's religions is not identical with Jesus, the son of Mary. "Christ is Lord, but the Lord is not only Jesus."[56] Panikkar's Christ represents the ontological link or mediator between God and the world. Christ is the non-historic Logos, confessed by Christians as Jesus but known in other religions by different names. However, in his most recent books, Panikkar is less explicit about the role of the hidden Christ in world religions. Instead, he elects to focus more broadly on man's immediate existential contact with the transcendental Reality, similar to Tillich and Rahner on the Christian side and to Hinduism and Buddhism on the other.

Although formal differences exist between religions both in belief and practice, Panikkar's monistic vision of reality permits him to postulate that all the world's faiths mediate the same existential experience of the Absolute and that this experience leads to fullness and perfection. Panikkar's Hindu perfection, however, is not a matter of moral maturity, but involves a state of realization through absorption into the Absolute. According to Panikkar, the theandric or trinitarian character of all religions ensures that none are excluded from the ineffable intuitional grasping of total Reality. That is, there exists in Christianity, Hinduism, Buddhism, and Islam genuine supernatural grace-bearing moments. All religions are equally viable, since "one can have an authentic internal religious experience in more than one religious tradition without betraying any of them."[57] Panikkar, in typically Hindu fashion, finds the analogy of the spectrum of light useful in illustrating the thesis that there are many paths to the realization of God. "Through any particular color, viz., religion, one can reach the source of the white light. Any follower of a human tradition is given the possibility of reaching his or her destination, fulness, salvation provided there is a beam of light and not sheer darkness."[58] Another analogy he employs is the vehicle of language. Each individual expresses himself in his own language; yet no language is superior to any other—all are valid means of communication. Panikkar believes that the contemporary religious situation is like a vast supermarket where the shopper is free to pick and choose whatever product pleases him.

Given the transcendental unity of human religious experience, Panikkar suggests that the boundaries that separate religions are beginning to dissolve. Through the attraction of an inner dynamic, the religions of the world are slowly but steadily converging toward a higher unity. In the opening pages of his book *Intrareligious Dialogue*, Panikkar tells a tale of three sages whose quest for a synthesis of world religions represents his own personal vision. The sages remark, "Our discussion should continue as long as necessary until we arrive at one faith and one religion so that we will have a form of harmony honoring each other and serving each other."[59] Panikkar's religious syncretism is an inevitable result of his monistic advaitist world and life view.

Panikkar believes that to fully understand a particular religion one must enter into the heart of it; i.e., one must be "converted" to it. By conversion,

Panikkar does not mean the same thing signified in Christian theology, namely, a volitional turning away from sin to God. Rather, Panikkar's conversion means the Hindu or the Buddhist experience of realization, which one *has* but which cannot be meaningfully described. Early on in his pilgrimage, without losing his identity as a Christian, Panikkar "converted" to Hinduism, which he described as "a kind of Christianity in potency,"[60] and "a vestibule of Christianity."[61] Hinduism relates to Christianity as promise to fulfillment, as seed to fruit, as symbol to reality, and as desire to the thing-in-itself. By virtue of the presence of the hidden Christ in the sacraments of Hinduism, the sincere Hindu who worships God through the sacraments of his religion is actually worshiping God through Jesus Christ, even though he is ignorant of this fact. Thus Panikkar maintains:

> The good and *bona fide* Hindu is saved by Christ and not by Hinduism, but it is through the Sacraments of Hinduism, through the message of morality and good life, through the *Mysterion* that comes down to him through Hinduism, that Christ saves the Hindu normally. This amounts to saying that Hinduism has also a place in the universal saving providence of God.[62]

If earlier Panikkar's primary loyalty was to Hinduism, in recent years he has shown great interest and affinity to the Buddhist religion. In fact, Panikkar leads us to believe that he "converted" to Buddhism without having ceased to be either a Hindu or a Christian. As he himself responded to a European inquirer, "I 'left' [Europe] as a Christian, I 'found' myself a Hindu, and I 'return' a Buddhist without having ceased to be a Christian."[63] Plainly, Panikkar personally practices the pluralistic harmony of religions he commends to others.

We have noted Panikkar's conviction that salvation is mediated through the sacraments of the world's religions. Hinduism, Buddhism, Islam, and other faiths lead their adherents to fullness and perfection in the Absolute. Given this situation, the Christian church no longer ought to conceive of its task as that of evangelism or conversion. "The Christian attitude does not regard Christians as members of what we could call the 'exclusive bourgeois club of truth,' who are sitting comfortably on the true way, and condescending to point out to others the path of salvation."[64] No, the proper task of the Christian mission—persuaded that neither it nor any other religion has an exclusive corner on the truth of God—is to engage in creative dialogue with other faiths. Through the process of dialogue, the Christian and the non-Christian open themselves to each other, share their insights to reality, and thus embark together in the search for truth. Since according to the Hindu vision all roads lead to God, conversion is regarded as a betrayal of one's cultural heritage and as a renunciation of allegiance to the community in which one was born. The Christian convert from Hinduism is thus viewed as a traitor to his people. The stated goal of the Christian mission is to deepen and transform each religion and ideology it encounters. According to Panikkar, the Christian mission is successful if it makes those it

TRANSCENDENT REALITY

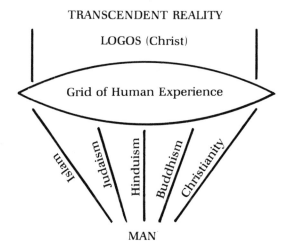

encounters better Hindus, better Buddhists, or better Marxists. Through the dialogical process even the church itself will be transformed into a more authentic institution.

Panikkar's supreme passion, as we have noted, is to effect a marriage between the Christian faith and the spirituality of the East, particularly advaitist Hinduism. Unfortunately, the product of this unholy union bears little resemblance to the gospel of Jesus, Paul, Luther, or Wesley. Panikkar's vision, in fact, falters at the level of its philosophical foundations. His scheme of pantheistic monism, by which all reality including the self is an aspect of Brahman, radically diverges from the Christian postulate of a Creator-God who is distinct from the universe. Moreover, Panikkar's god is not a discrete personal agent with whom one is able to enter into a mutual relationship of love. The god of advaitist Hinduism, which Panikkar commends, is viewed as abstract, impersonal, all-pervading Reality and is far removed from the loving, free, and personal God of the Jewish-Christian faith.

When Panikkar defines knowledge of God exclusively in terms of the ineffable experience of the human self with the divine Soul, he fails to do justice to the cognitive dimension of biblical knowledge. In Scripture, knowledge of God is both practical (experiential) and theoretical (cognitive). From the biblical perspective, knowledge involves an intelligent ordering in the mind of what has been perceived from the world of experience. Scripture enjoins man to know that God is one (Deut. 6:4). Moreover, man can know that God is immortal (1 Tim. 1:17), powerful (Dan. 2:20), righteous (1 Chron. 29:17), and wise (Jer. 32:19). God's will (Col. 1:9), works (Job 37:16), and revealed truths (Amos 3:7) are eminently knowable by man. Whereas Panikkar affirms that to be human is, by definition, to possess a (saving) knowledge of God, Scripture plainly suggests otherwise. In His encounter with religious Jews, Jesus repeatedly stated that they were devoid of the knowledge of God (John 8:19, 55; cf. 15:21). Even those who fervently practiced religious exercises were not of God (John 8:47) but were of the flesh (John 8:15). The prophet Isaiah said of pagan religionists in his own day, "Ignorant are those who carry about idols of wood, who pray to gods that cannot save" (Isa. 45:20). From the New Testament perspective, only through a conscious experience of conversion to Christ does one pass from darkness to light (John 8:12), from ignorance to knowledge (1 Tim. 2:4), from falsehood to the truth, indeed, from death to life (John 11:25). Scripture then, against Panikkar, inextricably links faith not so much to mystical enlightenment as to knowledge.

Moreover, Panikkar's monistic Hindu vision of salvation likewise shares little common ground with Christian theology. In the biblical scheme, as the human soul enters into a real, vital, and spiritual union with the personal God through Christ, his individuality and personality are raised to higher levels of authenticity. However, in Panikkar's system, the consciousness of the human self is transcended, as the soul is absorbed into the nothingness of the universe. "I am Brahman"—the cry of the redeemed in Panikkar's theology—is a pantheistic rather than a Christian utterance.

Panikkar, in fact, displays similarities to the neo-Vedanta philosopher S. Radhakrishnan (d. 1975). We see Panikkar in Radhakrishnan's claim that the mystical experience of union with the Absolute, whereby man's soul merges into the soul of God, is common to all religions. Moreover, Panikkar, like the Hindu scholar, rejects all exclusivist claims for sole possession of the truth and argues for a pantheon of religions based on freedom and mutual respect. Like Radhakrishnan and Mahatma Gandhi, Panikkar highly esteems the ideal Christ—the Christ of faith—but pays little attention to the Jesus of history. But the fact is that Panikkar's ideal Christ, isolated as it is from the Jesus of history, has no basis in Scripture. Consequently, the Hindu christology is little more than a figment of the imagination.

On the Christian side, Panikkar's system bears similarities to the transcendental theology of Karl Rahner. Like Rahner, Panikkar postulates an a priori orientation of the human soul toward the divine Soul. Man as transcendental consciousness immediately knows all Being by virtue of the supernatural existential that lies at the heart of human existence. Rahner and Panikkar agree that what derives from the supernatural existential is not a fund of knowledge, but a heightened consciousness—a preconceptual ineffable awareness of transcendent Reality. Both, moreover, affirm the speciality of Christ, who lies hidden in all faiths and who thus is the true object of all religious worship. The criticisms that were directed to Rahner's theology in chapter 10 are equally relevant to Panikkar's system of thought.

In their drift toward pantheism, mystical apprehension of the Divine, and vision of truth as an endless circle, recent Protestant and Roman Catholic theologians slowly but steadily have been moving toward the East.

On the other hand, the classical religions of the East are boldly venturing Westward. In this crucial juncture of history, Panikkar has undertaken to construct a bridge between Christianity in the West and Hinduism and Buddhism in the East. Insofar as Panikkar's god is not the God of the Bible but the world-Ground of monistic Hinduism, we may safely conclude that Panikkar accommodates Christianity to the framework of advaitist Hindu philosophy. In his views of man, faith, and salvation, Panikkar's explication of Christianity is guided by insights from the East. As an eclectic syncretistic thinker, Panikkar likely will provide strong impetus to the increasing convergence of Eastern and Western religious traditions. As mankind seeks solutions to humanly insurmountable social and political problems, he is likely to turn to a synthetic world religion similar to the East-West model proposed by Panikkar.

SCRIPTURE SPEAKS:
XII THE BIBLICAL TEACHING AND CONCLUSIONS

Our broad overview of the history of theology has pointed up a multiplicity of proposals in response to the overarching question, How is God known? Scholastic Roman Catholic theology has followed the a posteriori approach, insisting that from the data of general revelation the existence, character, and moral demands of God can be formally established. In the liberal tradition, both Protestant and Roman Catholic, immanence swallows up transcendence, and general revelation supplants special revelation as the primary means by which God is known. God, in the liberal scheme, is envisaged as the reality that naturally wells up from the depths of the human psyche. Consequently, in the new theology experience of God is an inescapable datum of human existence. Reacting against this radical have-ability of God, the Barthian movement not only denied natural man's ability to perceive general revelation, but it repudiated the idea of general revelation altogether.

In the light of the history of doctrine, but especially from the biblical testimony, our purpose will be to explicate the character and content of general revelation, to set forth the sources of man's knowledge of God, and to evaluate the competing truth claims of leading non-Christian religions. We now take up these crucial issues in turn. We begin by asserting that God, the infinite personal Spirit, could never be known by finite man save as He took the initiative to reveal Himself. Because God is neither totally other than man nor identical with him but analogous in being to man, He is capable of communicating with man by word and deed.

In the first place, natural man may possess, albeit dimly and vaguely, what could be called a reminiscent knowledge of God. With senses, sight, and mind unclouded by sin, Adam and Eve in Eden knew God and communed with Him as in the clear light of the noonday sun. Not only did the unspoiled cosmos plainly portray the Creator's perfections (Gen. 1:31), but God spoke directly to the progenitors of the race in their garden environment (Gen. 2-3). Consequently, Adam and Eve knew God in an unblemished relationship of intimacy and friendship. But tragically, after the spiritual rebellion and fall of our first parents, fellowship between Creator and creature was broken, and the original bright light that once illumined the human soul was reduced to a faint reminiscence of the glorious original. With the passing of time, Adam's descendents may not have completely unlearned this primal or Edenic knowledge of God. Natural man thus may retain a dim and distorted memory of the progenitors' Edenic concourse with the Creator. Calvin advances this view when he suggests that "there, no doubt, still survives in us some small remains of the first creation."[1] Perhaps, then, all men by reminiscence vaguely know that God exists, that He is all-powerful, just, and good, and that He is to be worshiped. Although we tentatively postulate the possibility of a vague knowledge of God by reminiscence, clearer and fuller knowledge of God is secured by other means. The fact is, however, that all the subsequent means *remind* people of a God previously known. Hence they do not need to prove a transcendent Being wholly unknown or unexperienced.

Intuitional Knowledge of God   In the second place, man, created in the image of God and universally illumined by the Logos, effably intuits the reality of God as a first truth. Scripture appears to support the aprioristic form of knowing enunciated fifteen hundred years ago by Augustine. John, in the fourth Gospel, describes the Logos as "the true light that gives light to every man who comes into the world" (John 1:9 NIV margin). The Logos, who is "the truth" (John 14:6), may be regarded as the principle of reason that enables the sinner to function as the rational creature God intended him to be. Through the common operation of the Logos, man qua man is endowed with the capability to think God's thoughts after Him. The psalmist may have had this truth in mind when, speaking of the Lord, he wrote, "With you is the fountain of life; in your light we see light" (Ps. 36:9). Effable intuition, as one aspect of reason, may be regarded as the eye of the soul that perceives first principles with immediacy. Upon reflection before the self, the mind enabled by a general illumination intuits eternal, changeless truths, including the reality of God, from the first moment of mental and moral self-consciousness. The mind does not learn from observation or experience that the whole equals the sum of its parts or that "a" and "non-a" are not equivalent. This and other first principles are acquired spontaneously and independently of the will by the mind abetted by general light from God. Some scholars such as Carnell, Hackett, and Clark include in these first principles something akin to the Kantian set of categories so that the noumenal world is not unknown to man.

Descartes rightly observed that knowledge exists in the soul prior to sense experience: "One certainly ought not to find it strange that God, in creating me, placed this idea [i.e., God] within me to be like the mark of the workman imprinted on his work; and it is likewise not essential that the mark shall be something different from the work itself.'[2] On the same note, Pascal viewed the heart as the instrument of intuition: "We know the truth through our reason but also through our heart. It is through the latter that we know first principles, and reason, which has nothing to do with it, tries in vain to refute them." Continues Pascal, "Knowledge of first principles, like space, time, motion, number, is as solid as any derived through reason, and it is on such knowledge, coming from the heart and instinct, that reason has to depend and base all its arguments.'[3] Without divorcing the mind from the heart, one can appreciate the point Pascal is making.

Thus against the classical empirical tradition, we assert that the mind is not a *tabula rasa*. Apart from observation and sense experience, the human mind, abetted by a general illumination, effably intuits timeless truths, including the first truth, God. Indeed, the mind's intuitive consciousness of God logically precedes and grounds all reasoning about God from the observable world. For unless the term *God* is invested with meaning through the religious a priori, all God-talk is not only meaningless, but impossible. Unless man acknowledges God in and of Himself in his mind, all predication about God on the basis of causation or order lacks signification. Carnell underscored this point with compelling cogency:

> How can we possibly know *that* a thing exists when we do not know *what* it is? What *is it* that we are talking about? What is the *Him* in the proposition, "We know *Him* not as He is in Himself, but as He appears in His works"? If we do not first know *Him*, how can we possibly establish any relation between the *Him* and the as-He-appears to us God?[4]

Our thesis is that the human mind intuitively grasps the existence of a Power, a Perfection, and a Personality[5] who is primal, uncaused, and infinite. Man at large has no need to be introduced to God, for he intuitively acknowledges the existence of a supreme spiritual Being on whom he is dependent. Missionaries and anthropologists relate from experience that prior to hearing the Christian message, primitive tribespeople appear to possess a rational consciousness of a supreme Power to whom they are accountable and whom they feel obliged to placate. The universal fear of God and man's incurable religiosity are evidence of the fact that the reality of God is universally impressed upon the human mind. More than a hundred years ago David Livingstone testifed that "the existence of God and of a future life is everywhere recognized in Africa."[6] A specialist in African traditional religions comes to the same conclusion:

> I am convinced that the conception, in the Ashanti mind, of the Supreme Being has nothing whatever to do with missionary influence, contact with Christians or even, I believe, with Mohammedans. . . . In a sense, therefore, it is true that the Supreme Being, the conception of whom has been innate in the minds of the Ashanti, is the Jehovah of the Israelites.[7]

A. H. Strong observes that "the lowest tribes have conscience, fear death, believe in witches, propitiate or frighten away evil fates. Even the fetish-worshipper, who calls the stone or the tree a god, shows that he has already the idea of God."[8] We now turn to the biblical data to test our hypothesis that a rudimentary knowledge of God is naturally implanted in the human mind.

The very first statement of the Bible assumes the reality of God: "In the beginning God created the heavens and the earth" (Gen. 1:1). In the opening chapter of Genesis, the writer offers no definition or explanation of God, neither does he present a demonstration of God's existence.[9] Since the author refers to God thirty-two times in the first chapter of the Bible without defining Him, we may assume that the idea of God was the common property of all people. As he enumerated God's creative works, the writer fully assumed that the idea of God was universally understood. Further support for the a priori postulate might be found in a saying by Bildad in the book of Job, where he asks concerning God, "Upon whom does his light not rise?" (Job. 25:3). Calvin maintained that as partakers of His light men and women perceive in their minds the existence and glory of God. "Man cannot move unless he experiences that God dwells in him; it is from Him that we have life, and it is also to Him that we have to render thanks that He has made us reasonable creatures rather than brute beasts."[10] But the most explicit support for religious apriorism is found in the New Testament, particularly in the teachings of the apostle Paul, to which we now turn.

In his response to the Greek philosophers at Athens, Paul recited two pieces of Stoic wisdom: "In him we live and move and have our being" and "We are his offspring" (Acts 17:28). The latter saying Paul intended anthropologically to mean that man by creation bears the image and likeness of God. Whereas the Stoics understood the first saying pantheistically, the apostle envisaged the truth that man's physical and intellectual life is totally grounded in God. As man made in the image of God perceives truth, he in fact perceives God, for God is truth. This, of course, is equivalent to asserting that man qua man effably intuits God as a first principle.

Following the order of ascending plainness, we turn to Paul's extended discussion of Gentile responsibility before God as set forth in chapters 1 and 2 of the Romans letter. In Romans 1:18ff. Paul argues that the human race is guilty and exposed to God's punishment, for although all men know God, they have deliberately chosen the path of godlessness and wickedness. Thus the apostle declares concerning the Gentiles, "What may be known about God is plain to them, because God has made it plain to them" (Rom. 1:19). In the first place, we observe that God has made certain things perspicuous "to them" (en autois), that is, to the Gentiles' minds or consciousness. And second, that which has been disclosed to their minds apart from supernatural revelation is properly knowledge of God (to gnōston theou). Does the apostle in this Romans text contemplate intuited knowledge of God as a first truth, or (with the immediately following context) knowledge acquired by rational reflection on the visible Creation? Most interpreters of Romans (Godet, Hodge, Hughes, Litton, et al.) believe that

Paul in verse 20 offers a summary statement inclusive of both an a priori knowledge stamped on man's mind and an inferential knowledge acquired from the created order. Hodge, for example, comments,

> It is not a mere external revelation of which the apostle is speaking, but of that evidence of the being and perfections of God which every man has in the constitution of his own nature, and in virtue of which he is competent to apprehend the manifestations of God in his works.... This knowledge is a revelation; it is the manifestation of God in his works, and in the constitution of our nature.[11]

We conclude, therefore, on the authority of Romans 1:19, that God in common grace grants man a knowledge of Himself that, in the first instance, is ingrained in human nature as such.

Intuitional knowledge of God, in the second place, involves consciousness of God's moral law written on the heart. Kant's interest in the moral dimension of knowledge is well known. The German philosopher insisted that the man who wishes to find God must look not only to "the starry heavens above," but also to "the moral law within." Man qua man is intuitively aware of the categories of good and evil, of right and wrong. Man the creature is attuned to a voice that commands him to do his duty, or to put it otherwise, to the categorical imperative that is not learned or otherwise acquired. Calvin rightly points out that natural man shudders at the flash of lightning and at the roaring clap of thunder not because of physical discomfort, but because these phenomena strikingly remind him of the God of justice whose holy law he has violated.[12] Man intuitively knows not only that God values goodness and abhors evil but also that he is ultimately accountable to such a righteous Power. Origen sums up the matter with the observation that "men would not be guilty, if they did not carry in their minds common notions of morality, innate and written in divine letters."[13]

Paul acknowledges the reality of an innate moral consciousness when in Romans 1:32 he says of mankind, "They know God's righteous decree that those who do such things deserve death." The apostle's verb for know, epiginōskō, denotes knowledge that is thorough and complete. "In Romans 1:32 'knowing the ordinance of God' (epiginōskō) means 'knowing full well,' whereas in verse 21 'knowing God' (ginōskō) simply suggests that they could not avoid the perception."[14] In 1 Corinthians 13:12, the word epiginōskō is used of the complete knowledge of the saint in glory and of God's perfect knowledge of man: "Now I know (ginōskō) in part; then I shall know fully (epiginōskō), even as I am fully known" (epiginōskō). Thus in this Romans text, Paul claims that all people possess a highly developed intuitive knowledge of God's moral laws and further that contempt for God's laws will incur the penalty of death. This realization of God's righteous decrees was not learned but was implanted in the human soul by God Himself.

The apostle's most explicit teaching regarding intuitional knowledge of God's moral law is found in Romans 2:14-15. Paul argues that all people are inexcusable and stand condemned before God because all have violated

God's holy statutes. Jews are guilty because they have transgressed the written law given by special revelation. Likewise, Gentiles are guilty because they have transgressed the unwritten law divinely implanted in their hearts. Moreover, the Gentiles will be judged by the standard of the moral law that the soul intuits in the first moment of self-consciousness. Thus in Romans 2:14, Paul argues that those who have not the Mosaic law by nature not only know many of its prescriptions, but also *do* them. The demands of God's moral law (*ta tou nomou*) are implanted in the human constitution and are responded to (although not fulfilled) by man's inner moral instinct (*physai*). By virtue of the innate knowledge of God's moral demands, Paul declares that the Gentiles are "a law for themselves."

Lest there be any mistaking of his teaching, the apostle repeats his main point in the next verse: "They [the Gentiles] show that the requirements of the law are written on their hearts" (Rom. 2:15). Here again the point is that Gentiles (lacking the written law) possess an a priori knowledge of basic moral principles. In Calvin's words, "There never was a nation so barbarous or inhuman that it did not regulate life by some form of law. . . . We see clearly from that that there are certain original conceptions of right which are imprinted on the hearts of men by nature."[15] Berkouwer argues that Romans 2:15 has nothing to do with the moral law inscribed on the hearts of natural man. So antinatural theology is the Dutch scholar that he rejects any suggestion of a natural morality in man as man. *To ergon tou nomou grapton en tais kardiais autōn*, which Berkouwer translates as "the work of the law written in their hearts," refers to the norms, ideas and ideals—the affects of the law—that the sinner learns from his social and religious environment. The law of God works on the human heart, but in no way is it implanted in the heart as an innate endowment.[16] But the apostle, in the preceding context, draws a precise parallelism between the moral law of God given to the Jews through Moses and the moral law that is a no less valid possession of the Gentiles. The Gentiles are obliged to perform their duties before God because they have in their hearts what the Jews have in writing. Although one is outward and the other inward, both Jews and Gentiles will be judged by the same moral law of God. Thus against Berkouwer, *to ergon tou nomou* designates the statutory dimension of the law that is indelibly engraved on the hearts of all people, by virtue of which all know the difference between right and wrong, good and evil.

Next the apostle introduces the function of conscience in the human being's inner moral apparatus: "their consciences also bearing witness, and their thoughts now accusing, now even defending them" (Rom. 2:15). Conscience (*suneidēsis*, "co-knowing") represents a second voice or witness that testifies to the individual's compliance or noncompliance with the implanted moral law. As Godet expresses it, "Conscience joins its testimony to that of the heart which dictated the virtuous action by commanding it, and proves truly, as a *second* witness, the existence of the moral law in the Gentile."[17] Conscience may be regarded as an inner monitor, or the voice of

God in the soul, that passes judgment on man's response to the moral law within. Although conscience may be weakened and blunted, the accusations of conscience convey the realization that there exists a supreme Lawgiver and Judge, who rewards good and punishes evil. Thus man's inner moral instinct and the testimony of conscience provide further a demonstration that all people know God as a supreme moral Being. It follows, then, that there are no true atheists. A person may outwardly profess disbelief in God, but inwardly he is endowed with the compelling consciousness that God exists.

Acquired General Knowledge of God   Man by common grace not only intuits the reality of a supreme Being on whom he is dependent, but man, created in the image of God and illumined by the Logos, also infers the existence and character of God by rational reflection on the data of the created universe. The first mode of knowing is knowledge by effable intuition; the second is knowledge by rational inference. Or to put it otherwise, man's knowledge of God is first innate and then acquired. We have argued that there can be no acquired knowledge of God unless the fundamental idea of God be settled in the soul as a first truth; otherwise, the term *God* would lack all signification. Effable intuition provides man with the rules for right thinking, on which all further knowing is grounded. On the other hand, being entirely subjective, intuitional knowledge alone is not adequate for constructing a broadly verifiable metaphysical system. Knowledge by intuition must be supplemented with cognitive knowledge acquired from the *indicia* of the space-time universe.

It is true that the Bible sets forth no explicit and clearly defined theory of knowledge; hence one finds a wide range of religious epistemologies held by Christian philosophers. Nevertheless, the implicit evidence seems to point us in the following direction. Although man is a sinner, he uniquely bears the image of God. The crippling effects of sin on the human mind are overcome in part by a general illumination of the Logos (John 1:4, 9). God wills that man, the pinnacle of His Creation, should use his reason to secure truth, including elementary truths about Himself. Equipped with an intuitional knowledge of God, including the light of conscience, and enabled by common grace, man by rational reflection on the data of the natural and historical order draws inferences about God's character and operations. By inspection of the created order that surrounds him and by the discursive workings of the mind by which one thing is inferred from another, man reaches conclusions that confirm the fact of God's existence and enlarge his understanding of the character of the Creator, Preserver, and Judge who stands over him.

Carnell suggests that "the process that man follows when learning is called 'discursion,' the running to and fro of the mind between facts until a coherent pattern of meaning is achieved; as opposed to God's changeless knowledge by an eternal intuition."[18] Thus man, created a rational creature and touched by general illumination, formulates judgments about God to varying degrees of probability on the basis of the evidence from his surrounding environment. As man reflects on the phenomena of nature and history as the loci of God's working, his intuitive knowledge of God is enlarged. When man confronts the *indicia* of the intelligibly ordered cosmos with an open mind, his innate idea of God is supplied with further characteristics that augment his overall understanding of God. Carnell agrees with this judgment, adding, "Paul truly taught that God is known through sense perception; but that does not involve us in empiricism. May it not equally be that, *knowing* God (by innate knowledge, which Paul teaches) we are reminded of Him in His works?"[19] According to Berkhof, man obtains an acquired knowledge of God as follows: "It does not arise spontaneously in the human mind, but results from the conscious and sustained pursuit of knowledge. It can be acquired only by the wearisome process of perception and reflection, reasoning and argumentation."[20] In sum, then, all people who know God innately, now by observation and reflection are reminded of Him *in* nature, and through the process of discursive reasoning form a cognitive representation of God that is empirically coherent and logically noncontradictory. What natural man actually does with this elementary knowledge of God gained by general revelation is another matter that will be considered later.

Scripture supports our thesis that further truth content about God is acquired by rational reflection on God's general revelation in nature and history. As Strong insists, "The universe is a source of theology. The Scriptures assert that God has revealed himself in nature."[21] It comes as no surprise to us that the God who created and now sustains the universe should be discerned in His works. Attention first of all will be directed to the book of Job. Even a casual reading of this ancient document reveals that Job paid great attention to the order of nature. When faced with the grim reality of suffering and the gnawing suspicion that God may be neither omnipotent nor just in His government of the world, Job was directed to the natural world where the power, majesty, and beneficence of the Creator are plainly displayed. Elihu, in his speech to Job (esp. 36:24-37:24), relates that men look on God's operations in nature with wonder and awe. The variegation and order of the natural world attest God's wisdom and goodness; the dark clouds laden with rain, which water the earth, witness to His greatness and kindness; the brilliant flash of lightning and the roaring clap of thunder point to God's anger and righteous judgment; the snow and ice remind man of God's power in nature either to bless or to curse; the delicate balance of sunlight, cloud, and wind allude to the perfection of His knowledge; and the vast expanse of the heavens attest God's infinity and eternity. After his brief survey of the natural world, Elihu concludes, "God comes in awesome majesty. The Almighty is beyond our reach and exalted in power; in his justice and great righteousness, he does not oppress" (Job 37:22-23).

In chapters 38 and 39, God Himself answers Job out of a whirlwind and turns Job's attention to the vast panorama of the created order. The magnificent nature poems that constitute the record portray a universe pulsating with the life of God. The earth, the dawn that daily overspreads the earth, and the great expanse of the sea (Job 38:4-18) all reflect the timeless might of a wise Creator. Light and darkness, snow and hail, stormy wind, rain and ice, and the precise movements of the heavenly bodies (38:19-38) highlight not only man's smallness and helplessness but also the wisdom, power, and beneficence of God. Finally, the incredible diversity, complexity, and harmonious interrelationship of the animal world (38:39-39:30)—the lion, raven, wild goat, ox, ostrich, horse, hawk, eagle—display the wisdom and goodness of the divine Mind that created and that provides for all these creatures. Each of these vignettes from the "wild kingdom" portrays a world luminous with God. Inanimate and animate worlds, with their mind-boggling vastness and intricacy, reflect the power, wisdom, goodness, and justice of God. Job's response, after he learned these lessons in the school-room of God's Creation, is instructive. Through the medium of a magnificent Creation, Job perceived the reality of God. Awe-struck, abased, and filled with reverence at the contemplation of God in His works, Job opened his mouth and said, "My ears had heard of you but now my eyes have seen you. Therefore I despise myself and repent in dust and ashes" (Job 42:5-6).

The Scriptures teach that God is revealed in His works not only by frequent reference to the data of nature as manifestations of the divine perfections (as in Job above), but also by direct, unqualified assertions. In the former case, it could be argued that God is beheld in nature by eyes that have been opened by His grace. But the latter category of biblical teaching assures us that nature is revelatory for all persons of sound mind. Psalm 19 provides precisely this kind of direct teaching. The psalmist declares that divine revelation is analogous to a two-volume book. The first volume concerns God's self-revelation in nature (Ps. 19:1-6), the second, His revelation through the law (vv. 7-13). The first volume deals with that which is the common property of all; the second, with that which is the special property of the chosen people of God. The names for God used in the psalm confirm the validity of this twofold division. The personal name *El* in the first section draws attention to the all-powerful and majestic God of Creation who engages the nations. The name *Yahweh* in the second section of the Psalm directs us to the eternal, self-existent One who entered into a covenant relationship with His chosen people. Spurgeon once remarked that "man walking erect was evidently made to scan the skies, and he who begins to read Creation by studying the stars begins the book in the right place."[22]

We turn now to the first volume of Psalm 19 to discover what can be learned about God from the realm of nature. The psalm starts by drawing attention to two cosmic realities: the starry heavens (vv. 1-4a) and the sun (vv. 4b-6). The first section opens with two unqualified assertions that of themselves ought to establish the validity of natural revelation: "The heavens declare the glory of God; the skies proclaim the work of his hands."

The verbs "declare" and "proclaim" are participles, suggesting that the action has been continuous, i.e., since the beginning of Creation. That which the heavens "recount" or "reiterate" is the divine "glory"—the sum total of God's revealed perfections, and that which the heavens "proclaim" or "declare," is His exquisite workmanship. The psalmist makes three statements about the divine witness in nature. First (v. 2), through the symbolism of day and night succeeding each other, God's witness to Himself is *perpetual*. Each bright day and each starry night pours forth knowledge of God as water bubbles forth from a copious spring. Second (v. 3), the witness is *wordless*. Although the grand display of God in the heavens is silent, it is capable of universal comprehension, for it is cast in the silent langauge of common experience. And third (v. 4a), the witness is *universal*. The wordless message of God's glory extends to all the earth. The reflection of God in the vast array of heavenly bodies pulsating with light is viewed by a worldwide audience.

During the French revolution a group of atheistic soldiers in the revolutionary army angrily announced to peasant Christians across the countryside, "We will pull down all your steeples, then you will no longer be reminded of your old superstitions." The wise Christians replied, "That you may do, but you can never take from us the stars." Radio waves may be jammed to render a transmission unintelligible, but the starry heavens can never be prevented from lucidly displaying to the eyes of all the glory of the Creator-God.

In the second section of the volume of nature, the psalmist draws attention to the sun (vv. 4b-6). No person of sound mind can behold the size, energy, heat, and luminosity of the sun without being reminded of the great Creator-God. Earth's sun is but an inconspicuous star in a spiral arm near the outer edge of the Milky Way galaxy. Our sun, which orbits the Milky Way at one hundred sixty miles per second, is 330,000 times more massive than the earth. It possesses fuel to sustain its vast energy output for ten billion years. The temperature at the sun's surface is 10,000 degrees Fahrenheit, but at its core, more than 18,000,000 degrees. All the power in earth's winds, rivers, lakes, wood, coal, oil, gas, and uranium is stored up sunlight. And yet only 2.2 billionths of the sun's generated power is received by planet earth. In spite of such evident power, the sun is but a tiny speck in the universe. Our sun is only one of one hundred billion suns in the Milky Way galaxy alone. And the Milky Way galaxy is but one of billions of galaxies in the universe. Appropriately, then, it is said, "He who has never read a book in his life can see God in the world which God's hands have made."[23] While the vast created order does not disclose God as *Yahweh*, it does present Him as *Elohim*—the eternal, omnipotent, wise, and good Creator and Sustainer of all that is, as the originators of modern science also attest.

Psalm 29 deals not with the peaceful display of sun, moon, and stars in orbit, but with the violent thrashing of a Palestinian thunderstorm. Accompanied by flashes of lightning and sharp claps of thunder, the tempest moves across the sea with the water boiling in its path (vv. 3-4). As the storm moves inland, its fury bends the tall trees of the forest and causes the hillsides to quake (vv. 5-6, 9). Finally, making its way out into the desert, the powerful storm picks up sand and dust and whirls the debris around in a furious cloud. In the furor of the thunderstorm, the psalmist declares that the awesome majesty, power, and judgment of God are displayed. Calvin made reference to the special revelatory value of this song about a Palestinian thunderstorm:

> The Psalmist invites our attention to those instances which strike the rude and insensible with some sense of the existence of God, and rouse them to action, however sluggish and regardless they are. He says not that the sun rises from day to day, and sheds abroad its life-giving beams, nor that the rain gently descends to gently fertilize the earth with its moisture; but he brings forth thunder, violent tempests and such things as smite the hearts of men with dread of their violence.[24]

Other psalms such as 8, 93, and 104 celebrate the glory of God in the natural world. But since it could be argued that they represent songs from the perspective of faith, we will move on to a consideration of two crucial New Testament texts. Still, it should be clear from this brief study of selections from Job and the Psalms that only the fool could utter the sentence, "There is no God" (Ps. 14:1). In this text, David did not say that the fool has *thought* in his heart, "There is no God," for the knowledge of God is innate in all and is strengthened by daily contemplation of the natural world. But the psalmist rightly acknowledges that the fool merely speaks the *words* "God does not exist," perhaps with the hope that he might convince himself of this opinion. Thus, on the authority of Scripture, the sinner who stifles the light within and the light without is the eminent fool. We agree, then, with William Barclay, who said, "Fifteen hundred years before Jesus came into the world men were stretching upwards catching however distantly some glimpse of God."[25]

The apostle Paul dealt with general revelation and the knowability of God in his Areopagus speech to the Athenians (Acts 17:22-31). In the first century, Athens continued as the center of Hellenistic philosophy, art, and science. Yet in Paul's day the religious condition of the city was one of blatant idolatry. Lifeless idols abounded on every hand, and, lest one deity should be overlooked, an altar was erected with the inscription "TO AN UNKNOWN GOD" (Acts 17:23). When preaching to Jews and God-fearers, for example, at Pisidian Antioch (Acts 13:16ff.), it was Paul's custom to address his hearers from the Scriptures. But when speaking to a largely pagan audience, as was the case at Athens, the apostle wisely sought meaningful points of contact with his hearers. The common ground Paul chose focused on truths about God that the Athenians possessed on the basis of common grace and general revelation. The knowledge that the Greeks had of God was partial and distorted, but they did possess a modicum of truth, which the apostle used to establish rapport and introduce his sermon. From the record of Paul's speech in Acts 17, we learn that the pagan Athenians, especially the Stoics, believed more or less the following about God from general revelation: (1) that the universe was created by God (v. 24a); (2) that God is sovereign over heaven and earth (v. 24b); (3) that God is self-sufficient and dependent on man for nothing (v. 25a); (4) that God is the source of life and the provider of all that man values good (v. 25b); (5) that God is a person possessing intelligence, for so God has designated the seasons and set the bounds of man's habitation (v. 26); (6) that God is omnipresent and thus immanent in the world: "He is not far from each one of us" (v. 27); and (7) that man is totally dependent on God for life and existence (v. 28). All the above Paul believed should be evident to man from an honest inspection of the world about him. Or as Gärtner put it in his definitive study of the Acts 17 text, "Creation and history provide a revelation of God apprehensible by man and imparting to him a certain knowledge of what God is."[26] Indeed, when the apostle said, "God did this so that men would seek him and perhaps reach out for him and find him, though he is not far from each one of us" (v. 27), he believed that God was near mankind in His general revelation. Hence, if the hearts of the Athenians were favorably inclined, they could know God in a relationship of personal acquaintance. But tragically people did not welcome the light, and even though they knew of God's self-sufficiency, creativity, power, and beneficence, their spiritual condition was one of "ignorance" (v. 30). Thus since natural man was not able to find God redemptively in nature, God made a special self-disclosure through His Son. And so in his speech to the Athenians, Paul moved from that common knowledge afforded by general revelation to the specifically Christian message conveyed by special revelation, namely, that God would judge the world by Jesus Christ, whom He certified by raising Him from the dead (v. 31). Implicit in Paul's message of judgment is the truth that by virtue of their failure to live up to the light of general revelation, the Athenians were not only inexcusable but, indeed, guilty before the bar of God's justice.

Surely the *locus classicus* for God's self-disclosure in nature is Paul's discussion in Romans 1:18-21. Here the apostle explicates most completely the relationship between natural revelation and man's knowledge of God. In this key text, Paul makes at least three important assertions. The first is that *mankind properly perceives truth about God from nature* (vv. 19-21). I have suggested above that when Paul wrote, "What may be known about God is plain to them, because God has made it plain to them" (v. 19), he had in mind both the knowledge that man effably intuits (the *sensus divinitatis*) and the additional knowledge that man acquires by rational reflection on the created order. Thus we believe Godet has accurately explained the words "what may be known about God" (*to gnōston tou theou*): "'What can be known of God without the help of an extraordinary revelation is clearly manifest in them.' A light was given in their conscience and understanding, and this light bore on the existence and character of the Divine Being."[27]

Rudimentary knowledge of God resides "in them" (*en autois*), that is, in their minds and hearts, because God has granted such knowledge through a process of self-revelation.[28] Moreover, in verse 20 Paul reiterates by way of elaboration that God is authentically known: "Since the creation of the world God's invisible qualities—his eternal power and divine nature—have been clearly seen." The apostle defines God's "invisible qualities" (*ta aorata autou*) as his "eternal power and divine nature." The first divine quality, *aidios dynamis*, is the most prominent aspect of the divine nature, or the characteristic of God that the creature initially confronts. Here the apostle undoubtedly implies the eternity of God's person and of His power. But in addition God's "divine nature" is clearly perceived. *Theiotēs* (Lat., *divinitas*) signifies the sum of the invisible perfections that characterize the reality of God; or as Meyer put it, "the totality of that which God is as a Being possessed of divine attributes."[29] Insofar as *theiotēs* focuses on the divine attributes or perfections, it must be differentiated from *theotēs* (Lat., *deitas*, Col. 2:9), which specifies the divine personality. The apostle has drawn attention to God's eternity and power as the objects of man's knowledge, but obviously other perfections such as God's wisdom, goodness, justice, and anger (clearly enunciated in the Old Testament nature texts examined) are implicit in the term "divine nature." The point that needs to be reinforced is that it is not the essence of God that is said to be known, but only His divine qualities or perfections. In Romans 1:21 Paul asserts for the third time that man possesses an actual knowledge of God: "although they knew God" (*gnontes ton theon*). The verb *ginōskō* in both verses 19 and 21 involves the idea of perceiving with the senses and grasping with the mind the object beheld. *Ginōskō* thus includes both a seeing with the physical eyes and a knowing with the eye of the soul.[30] Hence it should be clear from the Romans 1 text that natural knowledge of God cannot be denied. Man qua man knows that God the Creator and Sustainer of the universe exists and that He bears certain defining characteristics.

The second important assertion Paul makes in this Romans 1 text is that *knowledge of God is mediated by natural revelation* (v. 20). From the beginning of the world God's invisible attributes "have been clearly seen, being understood from what has been made." Paul here teaches that God has disclosed to man His invisible perfections through His works in the visible Creation. It bears repeating that the knowledge of which Paul speaks is a gift of God, for all human knowing is totally dependent on His self-revelation. Examining the text more closely, Paul asserts that God's invisible perfections "have been clearly seen" (*kathoratai*). The verb denotes perception by the senses and implies that eyes, ears, and other faculties fasten on "what has been made," namely, the *indicia* of the visible space-time universe. Through the process of inspection utilizing the senses, the observer beholds the immensity, variegation, order, and beauty of the created universe. But Paul goes on to say that God's invisible qualities are also "understood" (*nooumena*, present passive participle of *noeō*, "to perceive, apprehend, understand, gain an insight into'[31]). This second verb signifies the fact that by reflecting on the visible data of the cosmos man rationally infers further features of God's character. Biblical teaching such as that of the apostle leads us to conclude that endowed with intuitive knowledge of God, man's mind, as it beholds the *indicia* of the magnificent Creation, reaches rational conclusions concerning the great Cause of all observable effects. By the process of observation and rational perception, man's a priori understanding of God is reinforced and enlarged.

As an aside, the intellectual process Paul envisaged does not involve a set of truths that is strictly formal in the sense of logical deduction from first principles. Neither Paul nor any other biblical writer attempted to prove God's existence by means of formal demonstration. By reason of the religious a priori, the existence of God needs no proof. It is true that the latter chapters of Job, the nature Psalms, Acts 14 and 17, and Romans 1 and 2 advance arguments that are broadly cosmological, teleological, and moral. But these take the form of arguments in support of the reasonableness of belief in the God of biblical revelation. As asserted in chapter 2, while not formally demonstrative, the arguments corroborate to a high degree of probability the validity of the theistic hypothesis. In practice, however, most people live and make decisions on the basis of probabilities rather than certainties. In this regard Barclay makes the following valuable and helpful observation:

> If you saw a splendid house, Cicero says, you surely would not assume that it was built by mice or weasels. A splendid house implies a splendid architect; and a wonderful world implies a divine Creator. There is still a place for natural theology, for argument from the here and now to the there and then, for arguing from the seen to the unseen, for arguing from the world to God.[32]

Although the arguments for God's existence have fallen on hard times at the hands of modern liberal and neoorthodox theologians, they undoubtedly are useful apologetic tools by which a rationally significant case for biblical theism can be advanced.[33]

Returning to the process by which man learns about God, I suggest that the *indicia* of the external world mediated by sight pass through the mind and strike the chords of the knowledge of God already implanted in the soul. As Godet suggests, the animal sees the world as man sees it, but the animal lacks the *nous* (from the verb *noeō*) by which the mind of man ascends to spiritual contemplation of God.[34] We cannot avoid the conclusion that specific truth content about God is mediated by natural revelation, or, as Murray puts it and Kant to the contrary notwithstanding, "Phenomena disclose the noumena of God's transcendent perfection and specific divinity."[35] Scripture thus upholds a natural theology, if we mean by the term that which can be known about God through His works in nature and conscience. A hymn writer expresses this conviction elegantly in the following lines:

All thy works with joy surround Thee,
Earth and heaven reflect Thy rays,
Stars and angels sing around Thee,
Center of unbroken praise.
Field and forest, vale and mountain,
Flowery meadow, flashing sea,
Chanting bird and flowing fountain,
Call us to rejoice in Thee.[36]

The third assertion that Paul makes in the Romans 1 text is that *man consistently suppresses all forms of general revelation* (vv. 21-32). We will consider in some detail the matter of man's response to the knowledge of God mediated by nature. But first, attention must be directed to a further modality of general revelation—God's providential government of human life and history.

Scripture teaches that further knowledge of God is gained by attending to the providential ordering of human affairs. The wise and gracious supply of basic human needs (notwithstanding problems posed by famine, wars, natural catastrophes, etc.) points to the existence of a supreme Being who lovingly cares for His creatures (Matt. 6:8). The daily rising of the sun, the provision of rain for the fructification of the soil, and the regular ordering of the seasons all suggest that, far from being subject to chance, life is ordered by a wise and good Mind. Unexpected answers to prayer (Acts 12:5-11), judgment meted out on wrongdoers (Gen. 19:12-28), and the turning of evil into good (Gen. 50:20) likewise point to a world guided by an intelligent Power. The rise and fall of nations (Dan. 4:17-25), the occurrence of blessings and judgments in the historical arena (Ps. 94:10), and the preservation and prosperity of the Jewish state suggest that God is actively at work in the affairs of the world.

Paul's address to the Athenians, examined above, touches on this final modality of general revelation. We recall that the apostle, in seeking to communicate the gospel to pagan Greeks, astutely singled out features his audience would readily agree with. One such matter on which both Paul and the Athenians agreed was the wise ordering of life in the historical arena; so the apostle taught, "From one man he [God] made every nation of men, that they should inhabit the whole earth; and he determined the times set for them and the exact places where they should live" (Acts 17:26). The Athenians readily knew by study of the human and historical situation that God wisely prepared the earth to be a fit habitation for man. Moreover, they knew that God orders the various seasons, whose regular sequence insures the maintenance of life. In addition, God established the times during which national and cultural groups should prosper, and He likewise fixed the boundaries of their habitation. The ordering of the historical process is not a random matter, but it flows out of the will of the wise providential Ruler of men and nations. Between the human will and the divine will a mysterious

241

interplay operates. Plainly, Paul believed that man can learn much about God by being an alert student of world history.

The thesis that truths about God are disclosed to people by the workings of providence is supported by the apostle in his speech to the largely Gentile audience in the Roman colony of Lystra (Acts 14:15-17). In his attempt to dissuade his hearers from paganism, Paul appealed not to the Jewish Scriptures but to God's works in Creation and providential history. Paul cited common knowledge when in the first place he spoke of "the living God, who made heaven and earth and sea and everything in them" (v. 15). But addressing predominantly agrarian people, the apostle made more of the second point, namely, that by providing rain from heaven and full harvests season by season God's power, beneficence, and wisdom were publicly attested (v. 17). Indeed, during the course of His redemptive program until the revelation of the Christ, God permitted the nations of earth to walk in their own ways (v. 16). But while biding time, God through the providential supply of basic human needs did not leave Himself "without testimony" (*amarturon*)—that is, unattested or unknown. God's witness to Himself in general revelation consisted of His doing good (*agathourgon*) by conferring daily benefits on His creatures. Numerous mercies—the seasonal rains, the year-by-year provision of the basic need for food—were sufficient to point people to the greatness and goodness of the God who governs the nations. Behind these providential workings, man should have detected the living God. Man's ignorance was his own fault, for God's self-disclosure in providential history was sufficiently clear to lead him to the intelligent Ruler of the world.

At this point we pause to summarize what can be known about God from the modalities of general revelation. Luther correctly described the matter as "general knowledge." The religious a priori—that which man effably intuits from the first moment of self-consciousness—endows the creature with an awareness of the existence of a supreme Power who created the universe, who commands obedience, who invites worship, and who punishes wrongdoing. Equipped with this elemental a priori knowledge of God and enabled by a general illumination of the Logos (John 1:4, 9), man rationally reflects on the vastness, regularity, and order of the universe. He contemplates not only the purposeful flow of history as guided by a higher Mind but also the generous provision of basic needs for the sustenance of life. Reflecting on the data supplied by Creation, history, and providence, the rational mind infers further conclusions about the qualities and perfections of the Creator-God whose reality is indelibly inscribed in his heart. This acquired knowledge is not untrue, although it is imperfect because of the darkening effects of sin. Although it is non-salvific, it is not insignificant.[37] Scripture suggests that all human beings know more or less the following about God from the light of universal general revelation:

XII. SCRIPTURE SPEAKS: THE BIBLICAL TEACHING AND CONCLUSIONS

God exists (Ps. 19:1; Rom. 1:19)

God is uncreated (Acts 17:24)

God is Creator (Acts 14:15)

God is Sustainer (Acts 14:16; 17:25)

God is universal Lord (Acts 17:24)

God is self-sufficient (Acts 17:25)

God is transcendent (Acts 17:24)

God is immanent (Acts 17:26-27)

God is eternal (Ps. 93:2)

God is great (Ps. 8:3-4)

God is majestic (Ps. 29:4)

God is powerful (Ps. 29:4; Rom. 1:20)

God is wise (Ps. 104:24)

God is good (Acts 14:17)

God is righteous (Rom. 1:32)

God has a sovereign will (Acts 17:26)

God has standards of right and wrong (Rom. 2:15)

God should be worshiped (Acts 14:15; 17:23)

Man should perform the good (Rom. 2:15)

God will judge evil (Rom. 2:15-16)

In sum: God's glory (Ps. 19:1), divine nature (Rom. 1:20), and moral demands (Rom. 2:14−15) are to some extent known through general revelation!

Anthropological research confirms the biblical conclusion that all people, however primitive, have a rudimentary concept of God that roughly agrees with the above delineation. Although this knowledge may be distorted and suppressed, it is nevertheless an actual possession of man as man. For example, the Yoruba people of Nigeria have a name for God, "Osanobwa," that means "he who blesses and sustains the world." The Taro people, also of Nigeria, after a time of barrenness often call a baby girl "Nyambien," meaning "God is good." The Ibo people of Nigeria denote God as "Eze-elu," or "the King above." And the Mende people of Liberia designate God as the Chief, the King of all Kings.[38] The Gogo people of West Africa believe that Mulungu governs "the destiny of man sending rain and storm, well-being and famine, health or disease, peace or war. He is the Healer."[39] ∘ The Yoruba people say that in the afterlife the person-soul, the Oli, will give account of itself before Olódùmarè, the supreme God. Since, as anthropologists testify, these convictions appear to have been arrived at apart from Christian or Muslim teaching, they must derive from God's universal general revelation in nature, providence, and the implanted moral law.

Critical studies of the world's religions also attest what Aldous Huxley called the "Perennial Philosophy," or "Highest Common Factor," which appears universally in all the religious systems of mankind.[40] Huston Smith, in his perceptive study *Forgotten Truth: The Primordial Religion,*[41] finds a similar agreement between the core beliefs of the world's religions, as does S. H. Kellog.[42] The four fundamental doctrines that Kellog finds embedded at the core of all religions are: (1) man acknowledges a superior Power (or powers) that governs his destiny; (2) certain things are obligatory on man and other things must be avoided; (3) the relationship between man and the supreme Power has been disrupted and needs to be reestablished; and (4) man possesses an existence that transcends death.

We conclude from our study of Scripture and religion that general revelation mediates a modest fund of knowledge concerning God's existence, perfections, providential purposes, and moral demands.[43] The evidence leads us to identify with that broad tradition in the history of theology that has acknowledged the validity and limited utility of general revelation in leading man to an elementary knowledge of God. Correspondingly, we must take issue with other authorities, many of whom are men of undisputed faith, who depreciate revelation in nature and providence as a source for knowledge of God.

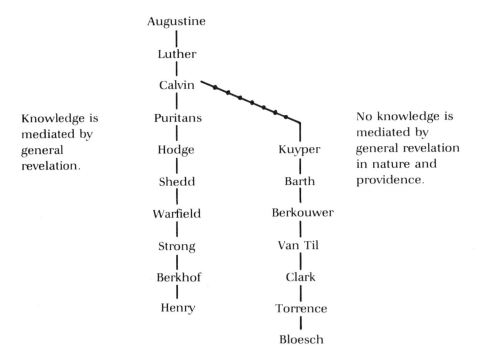

Augustine
|
Luther
|
Calvin
|
Puritans
|
Hodge
|
Shedd
|
Warfield
|
Strong
|
Berkhof
|
Henry

Kuyper
|
Barth
|
Berkouwer
|
Van Til
|
Clark
|
Torrence
|
Bloesch

Knowledge is mediated by general revelation.

No knowledge is mediated by general revelation in nature and providence.

General Knowledge of God Suppressed   We recall from our study of Romans 1 that four times in the text the apostle expressly declares that mankind possesses certain knowledge of God's existence and character (Rom. 1:19, 21, 28, 32). Indeed, general revelation was given that man might seek God and find Him (Acts 17:27). The overriding aim of the Creator in disclosing Himself in nature, providence, and conscience was that He might be known by His creatures. Yet Paul plainly teaches in Romans 1:21-32 that, in spite of the universal availability of knowledge of God, sinful man chooses to respond in a consistently negative way.

The creature's response to God's universal self-disclosure may be summed up in three main propositions. First, mankind uniformly repudiates the knowledge of God afforded by general revelation (Rom. 1:21-22, 28a). Man's response to God's loving self-disclosure should have been one of